# 携手同行　共创未来

## ——山东省与“友好省州领导人峰会”20年历程

赵玉霞　孙秀亭　编著

山东大学出版社
SHANDONG UNIVERSITY PRESS
·济南·

**图书在版编目(CIP)数据**

携手同行　共创未来：山东省与“友好省州领导人峰会”20年历程/赵玉霞，孙秀亭编著. —济南：山东大学出版社，2023.8

ISBN 978-7-5607-7904-1

Ⅰ. ①携…　Ⅱ. ①赵…　②孙…　Ⅲ. ①区域经济合作—国际合作—研究—山东　Ⅳ. ①F127.52

中国国家版本馆 CIP 数据核字(2023)第 165580 号

策划编辑　刘彤

责任编辑　刘彤　孙艳凤

封面设计　张荔

**携手同行　共创未来**

——山东省与“友好省州领导人峰会”20年历程

XIESHOU TONGXING GONGCHUANG WEILAI

出版发行　山东大学出版社

社　　址　山东省济南市山大南路20号

邮政编码　250100

发行热线　(0531)88363008

经　　销　新华书店

印　　刷　东港股份有限公司

规　　格　720毫米×1000毫米　1/16

　　　　　19.75印张　353千字

版　　次　2023年8月第1版

印　　次　2023年8月第1次印刷

定　　价　96.00元

# 目　录

## 第一篇　机制篇

## 第二篇　实践篇

## 第三篇　展望篇

# Contents

## Part Ⅰ Institutions

## Part Ⅱ Practices

# 第一篇　机制篇

## 第一章　友好省州领导人峰会概况

### 一、友好省州领导人峰会概述

#### (一)国际友好城市

国际友好城市(International Friendship Cities)是世界各国地方政府之间通过协议建立起来的一种国际联谊与合作关系,是“友好省州(大区、道、县)与友好城市”的简称,又称“姐妹城市”(Sister Cities)或“双胞城市”(Twin Cities)。建立国际友好城市的目的是促进城市间各领域、各行业的合作,增进双方的交流和友谊。

国际友好城市起源于第一次世界大战之后的欧洲。英国约克郡凯里市的官员在访问法国普瓦市时看到当地各方面工作因为战争而遭受巨大损失,主动提出希望两市建立友好关系,帮助普瓦市进行城市重建,由此诞生了世界上第一对国际友好城市。后来世界各地纷纷效仿,第二次世界大战后,国际友好城市开始大量涌现。很多国家开始采用“友好城市”这一形式进行国际交流,并由最初的文化逐步向社会、经济、科技等领域延伸。随着时代的发展,国际友好城市渐渐成为地方和民间对外交往的重要形式。

建立国际友好城市关系的主体是城市地方政府,国际友好城市间的交流合作需要政府层面进行规划和机制化运作实施。由于建立在协议和契约的基础上,国际友好城市间的相互交流一般呈现出稳定性、全面性的特点,通常涵盖政府、议会、企业和民间各个层面,包含经贸、文化、艺术、教育、司法和城市管理等各个领域。

实践证明，国际友好城市关系的建立对促进双方城市开放和发展有重要的推动作用。国际友好城市架起了城市间相互交流的桥梁，有助于各国不同发展体制、不同经济发展阶段的城市之间更好地理解沟通。更重要的是，国际友好城市是各国城市开展区域经济合作的重要平台和载体，不仅有助于官方合作，而且为企业在国际友好城市框架下的发展提供了稳定可靠的途径和保障。

### （二）友好省州领导人峰会的创建背景

友好省州领导人峰会又称“地方领导人峰会”（Regional Leaders’ Summit，RLS），这一地方政府多边国际合作机制是在国际合作，特别是国际友好城市蓬勃发展的历史背景和基础上创建的。

20世纪90年代以来，全球化趋势日益增强，国际交流与合作日益密切。山东省是中国东部沿海的重要开放地区，与世界各地开展了广泛的国际合作，发展了大量的国际友好城市。1987年，山东省与德国巴伐利亚州建立了友好省州关系。随着中国对外开放步伐的不断加快，山东省与巴伐利亚州的关系得到日益巩固与发展，各领域的交流合作空前活跃，实质性成果显著增加。1996年，山东省与奥地利上奥地利州（简称“上奥州”）建立了友好省州关系。1998年，山东省与南非西开普省正式缔结了友好省州关系。随着山东省国际行为能力的提升，进一步构建国际合作的长效机制成为拓展地方国际交往的必然走向，而友好省州领导人峰会国际合作机制就是这样的长效机制之一。

2000年，中共山东省委副书记、山东省省长李春亭访问德国慕尼黑，巴伐利亚州州长埃德蒙德·施托伊贝尔（Edmund Stoiber）提出“我的朋友也是你的朋友”，建议双方在巴伐利亚州开展友好省州间的多边交流与合作。山东省对此积极响应，友好省州领导人峰会正式提上了议事日程。巴伐利亚州按照在选择友好省州时长期坚持的“少而精”的原则，主要邀请了在本国综合实力最强或较强的省州参与该机制的创建。应邀参与友好省州领导人峰会的“发起人”最初仅限于德国巴伐利亚州、中国山东省、加拿大魁北克省、奥地利上奥州和南非西开普省，巴西圣保罗州及美国佐治亚州后来加入友好省州领导人峰会。

### (三)友好省州领导人峰会的成员构成

友好省州领导人峰会发端于国际友好城市事业，是一个国际友好城市政府间的多边国际合作机制。友好省州领导人峰会于 2002 年正式开始运行，由德国巴伐利亚州、中国山东省、奥地利上奥州、南非西开普省、加拿大魁北克省、巴西圣保罗州和美国佐治亚州七个成员省州构成。

七省州的综合实力都在本国名列前茅，且七省州在经贸、人文等方面都极具特色并有很强的代表性。七省州总人口约 1.9 亿，总面积 232 万平方公里，总体国内生产总值约 3.5 万亿美元。如果作为一个联合经济体，其国内生产总值可以在世界各国中排第五位，超过英、法等国，所以友好省州领导人峰会机制又被称为“世界强省(州)俱乐部”。[①] 如巴伐利亚州是欧洲最重要的科研基地之一，有三个世界一流的研究中心，上奥州的能源开发利用、圣保罗州的生物燃料、魁北克省的生物制药、佐治亚州的纤维素燃料研究都处于国际领先水平，山东省是中国经济实力最强、工业门类最齐全的省份之一，是中国农业第一大省，其制造业数字化水平居全国首位。

## 二、历次友好省州领导人峰会

友好省州领导人峰会由各省州轮流举办，每两年举办一次，2002 年以来已成功举办十次。

友好省州领导人峰会自成立之初就以推动不同地域、不同民族、不同制度、不同文化背景下的各国人民之间的相互理解及解决共同面对和关心的问题为基本目标。每次讨论一至两个与可持续发展有关的主题。

### (一)第一次友好省州领导人峰会

2002 年 1 月 30 日至 31 日，第一次友好省州领导人峰会在德国巴伐利亚州慕尼黑市举行，峰会的主题是“可持续发展战略”和“不同文化间的对话”(见图 1-1)。德国巴伐利亚州州长埃德蒙德·施托伊贝尔、奥地利上奥

---

① 参见满倩倩:《山东将于 2023 年举办第十一次友好省州领导人峰会》，2021 年 12 月 7 日，https://sd.dzwww.com/sdnews/202112/t20211207_9529234.htm。

州州长约瑟夫·普林格(Josef Pühringer)、加拿大魁北克省副省长保利尼·马洛伊斯(Pauline Marois)、中国山东省副省长林书香、南非西开普省省长彼得·马拉伊思(Peter Marais)出席峰会,并正式签署了关于“可持续发展政策”第一次会议的联合宣言。通过该宣言,五省州强调彼此间进一步加强对话和密切合作的意愿,积极推行对当代人和后代人负责的可持续发展政策。面对全球一体化的浪潮,五省州强调在保持文化多样性的同时,发达国家还要帮助发展中国家增强在国际市场上的竞争力,以缩小地区之间因贫困带来的经济差异,从而消除犯罪、环境污染、人为破坏等不利于人类可持续发展的因素。

图 1-1　第一次友好省州领导人峰会

图片来源:《走向世界》2002 年第 2 期,董礼智摄。

## (二)第二次友好省州领导人峰会

2004 年 12 月 8 日至 10 日,第二次友好省州领导人峰会在加拿大魁北克省魁北克市举行(见图 1-2)。山东省省长韩寓群、巴伐利亚州州长埃德蒙德·施托伊贝尔、上奥州州长约瑟夫·普林格、西开普省省长拉苏(Rasool)、魁北克省省长让·沙雷(Jean Charet)出席峰会。峰会的主题是“创新是经济发展的关键”“青年在社会发展中的作用”,来自五省州的科技、青年界代表围绕各自主题分别举办了科技和青年论坛,并向峰会提交了论坛报告,五省州领导人以此为基础展开了讨论。这次峰会高度评价了首次峰会以来各省州在推动可持续发展和文化对话方面取得的可喜进展，与会者一致认为面对经济全球化带来的机遇和挑战，省州间应本着优势互补、互惠互利的原则继续加强对话，深化在科技和青年等领域的交流与合作。会议商定于 2005 年在山东省举办五省州青年交流活动。五省州领导人共同签署了会议决议并发表了新闻公报。

图 1-2　第二次友好省州领导人峰会

图片来源：友好省州领导人峰会官方网站，https://www.regionalleaderssummit.org/summits/all-summits/。

### （三）第三次友好省州领导人峰会

2006 年 7 月 11 日至 12 日，第三次友好省州领导人峰会在奥地利上奥州林茨市举行，巴伐利亚州州长埃德蒙德·施托伊贝尔、魁北克省省长让·沙雷、圣保罗州环境部部长约瑟·戈登堡(José Goldemberg)、山东省省长韩寓群、西开普省省长拉苏和上奥州州长约瑟夫·普林格参加峰会(见图 1-3)。各省州领导人热烈欢迎圣保罗州的加入。本次峰会的主题为“世世代代的政治——创造可持续的未来是我们共同的责任”，峰会同意在“可再生能源及能源效率”和“教育和青年”两个领域进行集中讨论。在可再生能源及能源效率领域，各方一致认为能源利用方面的创新是提高竞争力和环保水平的关键，各地区要把清洁和对气候友善的技术应用作为可持续能源政策的基础方针。在教育和青年领域，各方认为社会若能通过国际接触和国际比较适时认识到发展并做出应对，在国际竞争中就能处于优势地位。各方领导人同意通过培训进一步促进各地区学生和青年之间的交流，通过友好省州间早期接触了解国际标准，积极参与国际竞争与合作，增强自信。

图 1-3　第三次友好省州领导人峰会

图片来源：友好省州领导人峰会官方网站，https://www.regionalleaderssummit.org/summits/all-summits/。

### (四)第四次友好省州领导人峰会

2008 年 8 月 6 日至 7 日，第四次友好省州领导人峰会(见图 1-4)在中国山东省济南市举行，中国山东省省长姜大明、加拿大魁北克省省长让·沙雷、奥地利上奥州州长约瑟夫·普林格、美国佐治亚州州长索尼·珀杜(Sonny Perdue)、德国巴伐利亚州联邦和欧洲事务部部长马库斯·索德尔(Markus Söder)、南非西开普省地方政府环境与发展规划部部长尤里斯(Yuris)以及各国专家、企业家等出席会议。峰会主题为“建设节约型社会”和“卫生与健康”，各方代表就共同推进可持续发展、加强国际合作与交流、加快建设节约型社会、推进世界和谐等问题达成一系列共识。峰会上，各省州代表一致同意美国佐治亚州正式加入友好省州领导人峰会；上奥州州长约瑟夫·普林格介绍了落实第三次峰会签署的共同宣言《林茨宣言》的情况。峰会还通过了西开普省承办第五次峰会的申请，并确认第五次峰会的主题为“保障食品安全”和“交通发展战略”。峰会期间，加拿大魁北克省与中国山东省正式签署了建立友好省州关系协议书。“卫生与健康”首次被确定为峰会的主题之一，同时也首次在峰会期间举办了卫生合作洽谈会。洽谈会期间，与会各方就相关医疗合作项目进行了深入洽谈，共同签署了合作意向书及合作协议书近 20 项。

图 1-4　第四次友好省州领导人峰会

图片来源：山东省人民政府外事办公室。

## （五）第五次友好省州领导人峰会

2010 年 9 月 27 日至 29 日，第五次友好省州领导人峰会在南非西开普省开普敦市举行（见图 1-5）。应南非西开普省省长海伦・兹勒（Helen Zille）邀请，中国山东省省长姜大明、德国巴伐利亚州州长霍斯特・泽霍夫（Horst Seehofer）、奥地利上奥州州长约瑟夫・普林格、美国佐治亚州政府行政执行官特雷・切尔杰斯（Trey Childress）、加拿大魁北克省国际关系部部长莫尼卡・加依-全布雷（Monique Gagnon-Tremblay）参加了本次峰会。本次峰会的主题是“粮食安全”和“一体化交通”。各省州领导人一致认为粮食是人类最基本的生存资源，任何时候各国政府都要高度重视粮食生产。各省州应互相学习保护耕地、促进粮食生产的经验，政府要对农业生产给予扶持，对青年农民加大技术培训力度，加强在农业科技研究、农业技术推广、农产品加工技术以及农产品贸易等方面的交流合作。各省州领导人认为一体化交通直接影响人们的生活方式,随着科学技术的不断发展,交通出行呈现出快速化、多样化的趋势。各省州要加强交通一体化的研究,制定有关规划,本着快捷节约的原则统筹考虑交通一体化体制机制问题。要加强交通基础设施建设,构建一体化交通格局,造福各省州人民。各省州商定了第二年将围绕粮食、交通方面举办一系列交流合作活动。山东省将先后举办国际港口发展与管理论坛、烟台国际葡萄酒节、国际农产品交易会等活动。第五次友好省州领导人峰会通过了联合宣言,就粮食安全、一体化交通等主题达成了共识。

图 1-5 第五次友好省州领导人峰会

图片来源:友好省州领导人峰会官方网站,https://www.regionalleaderssummit.org/summits/all-summits/。

### (六)第六次友好省州领导人峰会

2012 年 4 月 12 日,第六次友好省州领导人峰会在巴西圣保罗州圣保罗市举办,巴伐利亚州州长霍斯特·泽霍夫、魁北克省省长让·沙雷、佐治亚州副州长凯西·凯格尔(Casey Cagle)、山东省副省长才利民、上奥州州长约瑟夫·普林格、西开普省省长海伦·兹勒、圣保罗州州长热拉尔多·阿克敏(Geraldo Alckmin)出席峰会。峰会的主题为"可持续能源和提高能源效率"

(见图 1-6)。会议强调在努力实现可持续发展的过程中,应注重政策倡导活动、能源效率和节能举措、可再生能源技术的高级推广应用。能源效率和节能举措及可再生能源使用率的提高对创造一个可持续能源未来是非常必要的,而且能带来重大的经济机遇。与会代表一致同意支持联合国关于指定 2012 年为“人人享有可持续能源国际年”的第 65/151 号决议,并认为这是一次能够使人们进一步认识到在省州层面更多使用可持续能源、提高能源效率、可再生能源重要性的机会。各省州将采取一系列措施,努力促使可再生能源成为最具竞争力的能源形式之一。

图 1-6　第六次友好省州领导人峰会

图片来源:山东省人民政府外事办公室。

## (七)第七次友好省州领导人峰会

2014 年 6 月 2 日至 3 日,第七次友好省州领导人峰会在美国佐治亚州亚特兰大市举行(见图 1-7)。应美国佐治亚州州长纳森・迪尔(Nathan Deal)邀请,中国山东省省长郭树清、奥地利上奥州州长约瑟夫・普林格、加拿大魁北克省国际关系部部长克里斯蒂娜・圣皮埃尔(Christine St-Pierre)、德国巴伐利亚州欧洲和国际事务部部长贝亚特・默尔克(Beate Merk)、南非西开普省财政部部长梅耶・温格(Mireille Wenger)参加了峰会。本次峰会的主题是"全球物流供应链的发展"和"大型体育活动促进经济可持续发展",各省州领导人一致认为当今全球经济中物流供应链的重要性日益凸显。采购和贸易方式的改变要求必须调整当前的物流模式,以有效满足全球发展的需要。各省州将建立共享知识库,分享物流业的机遇。峰会各方认为各省州都曾举办过一次或多次大型体育活动,要积极鼓励各方交流体育基础设施管理方面的经验,促进地区经济发展和改善民生。各省州领导人围绕上述两个主题进行了深入讨论,通过了峰会联合宣言。各友好省州领导人进行了务实友好的双边会谈,为下一步扩大合作奠定了更加坚实的基础。

图 1-7 第七次友好省州领导人峰会

图片来源:友好省州领导人峰会官方网站,https://www.regionalleaderssummit.org/summits/all-summits/。

## (八)第八次友好省州领导人峰会

2016 年 7 月 14 日至 15 日,第八次友好省州领导人峰会在德国巴伐利亚州慕尼黑市举行,应巴伐利亚州州长霍斯特·泽霍夫邀请,佐治亚州州长纳森·迪尔、魁北克省省长菲利普·库亚尔(Philippe Couillard)、圣保罗州副州长玛西亚·弗兰萨(Márcio França)、山东省省长郭树清、上奥州州长约瑟夫·普林格和西开普省省长海伦·兹勒参加会议(见图 1-8)。会议围绕

“数字化和创新”的主题共同讨论了各地区人民关心的话题。巴伐利亚州的跨国公司领导人就一些关键议题参与了对话。各省州科学家介绍了共同参与的多边项目取得的进展，并确定了接下来的计划。各省州的学生参加了“未来领导人会议”，展示了他们对 2040 年使用数字技术的愿景。

图 1-8　第八次友好省州领导人峰会

图片来源：友好省州领导人峰会官方网站，https://www.regionalleaderssummit.org/summits/all-summits/。

### (九)第九次友好省州领导人峰会

2018 年 5 月 17 日至 18 日，第九次友好省州领导人峰会在加拿大魁北克省魁北克市举行，魁北克省省长菲利普·库亚尔、山东省副省长孙继业、巴伐利亚州数字媒体及欧洲事务国务部部长乔治·埃森海希(Georg Eisenreich)、佐治亚州经济发展署署长韦宏森(Pat Wilson)、圣保罗环境部部长毛利西奥·布鲁撒丁(Maurício Brusadin)、上奥州教育文化部部长克里斯蒂娜·哈博兰德(Christine Haberlander)出席峰会(见图 1-9)。本次峰会的主题为“推动能源转型，迈向低碳经济”。七省州代表一致同意为实现可持续技术发展和世界环境资源保护目标，各省州必须加快可再生能源转型，推进环境友好型生产和消费方式。各方重申在2030年努力走在能源转型的前列，大力发展可再生能源，提高能源利用率，构建新型、繁荣和低碳的经济。各方将加强峰会能源网络项目合作，深入交流能源转型，特别是可再生能源和能源效率等议题，并成立专门工作组研究能源转型的最佳实践。

图1-9 第九次友好省州领导人峰会

图片来源：友好省州领导人峰会官方网站，https://www.regionalleaderssummit.org/summits/all-summits/。

### （十）第十次友好省州领导人峰会

本次峰会原定于2020年9月在奥地利上奥州举行，受新冠肺炎疫情影响，会议于2021年11月11日在线上成功举办。此次峰会的主题为“智慧地区”（见图1-10）。德国巴伐利亚州、中国山东省、奥地利上奥州、加拿大魁北克省、南非西开普省、美国佐治亚州、巴西圣保罗州七个友好省州的领导人出席会议并分别发言，签署了共同宣言。同时，作为峰会配套项目，友好省州领导人峰会科学网络的负责人向大会报告了第九次峰会以来七省州科学家在可再生能源、航空航天、小卫星、数字化和数字健康等五个领域的合作成果。

图 1-10　第十次友好省州领导人峰会

图片来源：友好省州领导人峰会官方网站，https://www.regionalleaderssummit.org/summits/all-summits/。

## 三、友好省州领导人峰会的多元主题

历次友好省州领导人峰会始终发扬互利合作和多边交流精神，致力于增加各省州人民福祉。历次峰会的多元主题反映出各省州社会、政治和经济的多样性，推动了各省州的创新性发展，并不断为双边和多边合作注入新的动力（见表 1-1）。从前十次友好省州领导人峰会的举办情况来看，峰会的主要关注点集中在以下五个方面。

**表 1-1　历次友好省州领导人峰会举办的时间、地点及议题**

| | 年份 | 举办地 | 议题 |
|---|---|---|---|
| 第一次 | 2002 | 德国巴伐利亚州慕尼黑市 | 可持续发展战略<br>不同文化间的对话 |
| 第二次 | 2004 | 加拿大魁北克省魁北克市 | 创新是经济发展的关键<br>青年在社会发展中的作用 |
| 第三次 | 2006 | 奥地利上奥州林茨市 | 可再生能源及能源效率<br>教育和青年 |

续表

| | 年份 | 举办地 | 议题 |
|---|---|---|---|
| 第四次 | 2008 | 中国山东省济南市 | 建设节约型社会<br>卫生与健康 |
| 第五次 | 2010 | 南非西开普省开普敦市 | 粮食安全<br>一体化交通 |
| 第六次 | 2012 | 巴西圣保罗州圣保罗市 | 可持续能源和提高能源效率 |
| 第七次 | 2014 | 美国佐治亚州亚特兰大市 | 全球物流供应链的发展<br>大型体育活动促进经济可持续发展 |
| 第八次 | 2016 | 德国巴伐利亚州慕尼黑市 | 数字化和创新 |
| 第九次 | 2018 | 加拿大魁北克省魁北克市 | 推动能源转型,迈向低碳经济 |
| 第十次 | 2021 | 奥地利上奥州林茨市(线上) | 智慧地区 |
| 第十一次 | 2023 | 中国山东省济南市 | 绿色发展与低碳生活 |

### (一)经济贸易合作

加强各省州之间的优势互补,推动各省州之间在经济贸易方面的合作始终是峰会的重要内容之一。例如,第一次峰会“可持续发展战略”的主题,第二次峰会“创新是经济发展的关键”的主题,第三次峰会“可再生能源及能源效率”的主题,第四次峰会“建设节约型社会”的主题,第六次峰会“可持续能源和提高能源效率”的主题,第七次峰会“全球物流供应链的发展”“大型体育活动促进经济可持续发展”的主题,第九次峰会“推动能源转型,迈向低碳经济”的主题,以及即将在济南召开的第十一次峰会“绿色发展与低碳生活”的主题,历次峰会在本质上都是紧紧围绕经济贸易方面的合作交流进行的。另外,历次领导人峰会都要进行多边、双边交流,其内容也主要集中于经济贸易方面。尤其是每次峰会前后都伴随的经贸洽谈会,更是凸显了合作的基本目标。

### (二)人文交流

自创建之初,友好省州领导人峰会就把推动不同文化背景下的人们之间的对话与沟通、促进相互理解作为目标之一。例如，首次峰会就将“不同文化间的对话”作为主题之一，其后的历次峰会也都重申了文化之间交流合作的必要性并努力寻找文化交流合作的具体路径。各省州领导人强调有必要宣传各地区的文化特性，为国际对话与合作创造基础。青年人是21世纪的未来，青年人在国际合作中应发挥积极作用，促进社会变革与创新，促进不同文化间的相互了解以及世界的和平、稳定与发展。

### (三)绿色发展

此类合作议题占据了友好省州领导人峰会的重要地位。例如，第三次峰会将“可再生能源及能源效率”作为主题，各方一致认为能源利用方面的创新是提高竞争力和环保水平的关键，各地区要把清洁的和对气候友善的技术应用作为可持续能源政策的基础方针。从第四次峰会“建设节约型社会”的主题及其落实情况看，开发和应用可再生能源安全生产、运输、分配技术以及提高能源利用效率方面的交流，鼓励各省州相关部门在现有国际能源网络下的合作是主要目标。第六次峰会围绕“可持续能源和提升能源效率”的主题进一步明确了各省州在节约利用有限的自然资源并开发可再生的资源和能源、大力开展节能减排、提高资源和能源的利用效率、发展循环经济、推行清洁生产、创新资源回收利用技术、树立节约观念、培养节约习惯、反对过度消费、保护环境、改善生态等各个方面的合作目标。第九次峰会以“推动能源转型，迈向低碳经济”为主题，以可再生能源推动低碳经济发展，积极减少碳排放，着力发展绿色经济。2016年7月，实施了《友好省州可再生能源联盟路线图》，第一阶段对各省州可再生能源生产、技术和资源情况进行全面数字化调查，检验各方可再生能源潜力；第二阶段旨在通过跨洲合作示范项目，开发、测试并评估新技术。

### (四)科技创新

各省州将科学和创新视为实现经济社会现代化的主要途径，相信通过合作能够实现知识互通、创意联通、创新共享。例如，第二次峰会就以“创新是经济发展的关键”为讨论与合作的主题之一，强调科技进步与创新之间的合作对促进省州之间合作的基础性作用。峰会提出开展协商合作，尤其是在对经济发展起关键作用的科研与创新方面，以增强各地经济之间的协同效应，应对全球一体化的挑战。第五次峰会“一体化交通”的主题、第八次峰会“数字化和创新”的主题、第十次峰会“智慧地区”的主题都关注了技术创新、社会创新带来的社会公共福利优化及公民生活便利化，“智慧地区”最佳实践案例还重点关注了数字化和人工智能、智慧生产、智慧能源和医疗技术。

### （五）社会治理

第二次峰会讨论的“青年在社会发展中的作用”、第三次峰会讨论的“教育和青年”、第四次峰会讨论的“卫生与健康”，强调要关注环境和气候对健康的影响，建立并完善惠及全社会的医疗保障体制，加强疾病预防控制，提高健康水平，提倡养生与保健。第五次峰会讨论的“一体化交通”解决方案、第七次峰会讨论的“大型体育活动促进经济可持续发展”、第十次峰会讨论的“智慧地区”，这些社会性问题的良好解决是地方政府的重要职责，加强这些领域的合作对提高本地区的管理水平、提高居民幸福指数乃至推动长远发展都具有重要意义。

# Part Ⅰ Institutions

## Chapter 1
## Introduction to Regional Leaders' Summit

### 1.1 Overview of Regional Leaders' Summit

#### 1.1.1 International Friendship Cities

International Friendship Cities are a form of international friendship and cooperation established through agreements between local governments of various countries worldwide. They are commonly referred to as "sister provinces and states (regions, prefectures and counties) and sister cities", or alternatively, "Sister Cities" or "Twin Cities". The objective of establishing international sister cities is to promote cooperation between cities in various fields and industries, and to enhance their exchanges and friendship.

The concept of international sister cities originated in Europe after the World War I. Officials from the city of Carey in Yorkshire, the UK, visited the city of Poix-de-Picardie in France, where they witnessed the significant losses suffered in all aspects due to the war. They offered to establish friendly relations between the two cities and assist the city of Poix-de-Picardie in carrying out urban reconstruction, thus giving birth to the world's first pair of international sister cities. Subsequently, many countries adopted the form of sister cities for international exchanges, and after the World War II, international sister cities began to emerge in large numbers. Over time, the scope of sister cities extended from original cultural exchanges to social, economic, scientific, and technological fields. As the world continues to evolve, international sister cities have become an essential form of local and non-governmental foreign exchanges.

The establishment of international sister city relationships is primarily carried out by the local governments of the cities involved, and their exchanges and cooperation require planning and implementation at the government level. These relationships are typically based on agreements and covenants, and the exchanges between international sister cities are generally characterized by stability and comprehensiveness. They involve interactions at various levels, including government, parliament, business, and civil society, and encompass a wide range of fields such as economy, trade, culture, art, education, justice, and urban management.

It has been proven that the establishment of international sister city relationships plays a crucial role in promoting the openness and development of cities. International sister cities serve as a bridge for mutual exchanges between cities, facilitating better understanding and communication among cities with different development systems and at different stages of economic development. Moreover, sister cities are an essential platform and carrier for regional economic cooperation between cities of various countries, providing both opportunities for official cooperation and a stable and reliable pathway for corporate development within the framework of sister cities.

### 1.1.2 Background of the Establishment of Regional Leaders' Summit

The Regional Leaders' Summit (RLS) is a multilateral international cooperation mechanism established by local governments amidst the growing trend of international cooperation, particularly in sister cities.

Since the 1990s, globalization has been on the rise, leading to increasingly close international exchanges and cooperation. Shandong Province, located along the eastern coast of China, is an important open area that has engaged in extensive international cooperation with other regions of the world, leading to the development of numerous international sister cities. In July 1987, Shandong Province established a sister province and state relationship with Bavaria, Germany. As China's opening-up continues to expand, the Shandong-Bavaria relationship has been increasingly consolidated, leading to vigorous exchanges and cooperation in various fields and substantive achievements. Shandong Province established a sister province and state relationship with Upper Austria, Austria, in 1996, and formal friendly relations with the Western Cape Province of South Africa in 1998. As Shandong Province's international capabilities continued to improve, building a long-term mechanism of international cooperation became an inevitable trend to expand international exchanges. The international cooperation mechanism of the Regional Leaders' Summit is one such long-term mechanism.

In 2000, Li Chunting, Deputy Secretary of the CPC Shandong Provincial Committee and Governor of Shandong Province, visited Munich, where he was met by Edmund Stoiber, Minister-President of Bavaria. Stoiber proposed the idea of "Your partner is my partner" and suggested promoting multilateral exchanges and cooperation among sister provinces and states in Bavaria. Shandong Province responded positively to this proposal, and the Regional Leaders' Summit was officially put on the agenda. Following the principle of "selecting fewer but stronger" sister provinces and states, Bavaria invited the strongest or relatively strong provinces and states in their respective countries to participate in the creation of the mechanism. The initial "sponsors" invited to participate in the cooperation mechanism of the summit were limited to Bavaria (Germany), Shandong Province (China), Quebec (Canada), Upper Austria (Austria), and Western Cape (South Africa). Later, São Paulo (Brazil) and Georgia (USA) also joined the mechanism.

### 1.1.3 Members of Regional Leaders' Summit

The Regional Leaders' Summit originated from the international Sister City program and is a multilateral international cooperation mechanism between the governments of international sister cities. The summit officially started in 2002 and is composed of seven regions, including Bavaria (Germany), Shandong Province (China), Upper Austria (Austria), Western Cape (South Africa), Quebec (Canada), São Paulo (Brazil) and Georgia (USA).

The seven regions are among the strongest in their respective countries, with unique and highly representative characteristics in economy, trade, culture, and other aspects. The seven provinces and states have a total population of approximately 190 million, covering an area of 2.32 million square kilometers, with a combined GDP of about US \$3.5 trillion. If considered as a united economic entity, their GDP would rank fifth in the world, surpassing that of countries such as the UK and France. Therefore, the summit mechanism is also known as the "World's Strong Province (State) Club".① For instance, Bavaria is one of the most important scientific research bases in Europe, with three world-class research centers; the energy development and utilization in Upper Austria, biofuels in São Paulo, biopharmaceuticals in Quebec, and cellulosic fuel research in Georgia are all at the international leading level; and Shandong Province is one of the provinces with the strongest economic strength and the most complete industrial categories in China, its manufacturing industry ranks first in the country in terms of digitalization level, and it is the largest agricultural province in China.

## 1.2 Review of Previous Regional Leaders' Summits

The Regional Leaders' Summit is held every two years by the regions

① Man Qianqian, "Shandong is Going to Hold the 11th Regional Leaders' Summit in 2023", https://sd.dzwww.com/sdnews/202112/t20211207_9529234.htm, 7 December, 2021.

taking turns. To date, it has been successfully held ten times since 2002.

Since its establishment, the Regional Leaders' Summit has aimed to promote mutual understanding and address common concerns and issues faced by people from different regions, ethnic groups, systems, and cultural backgrounds. The summit focuses on discussing one or two topics related to sustainable development at a time.

### 1.2.1 The First Regional Leaders' Summit

Bavaria hosted the first Regional Leaders' Summit in Munich from 30 to 31 January 2002, with the themes of "Sustainable Development Strategies" and "Intercultural Dialogue" (see Figure 1-1). Edmund Stoiber, Minister-President of Bavaria, Germany, Josef Pühringer, Governor of Upper Austria, Austria, Pauline Marois, Deputy Premier of Quebec, Canada, Lin Shuxiang, Vice Governor of Shandong Province, China, and Peter Marais, Premier of the Western Cape, South Africa attended the summit and officially signed the joint declaration on the "Sustainable Development Policy" during the first meeting. Through this declaration, the five sister provinces and states emphasized their willingness to further strengthen dialogue and close cooperation, pursuing sustainable development policies that are responsible to present and future generations. In the face of globalization, the five states and provinces stressed the importance of preserving cultural diversity and the proposal that developed countries should support developing nations in improving their competitiveness in the global market for the purposes of reducing economic disparities caused by poverty, and eliminating factors such as crime, environmental pollution and human damage that hinder sustainable development.

Figure 1-1 The first Regional Leaders' Summit
Photo Credit: *Openings*, No.2(2002), photographed by Dong lizhi.

### 1.2.2 The Second Regional Leaders' Summit

Quebec City hosted the second Regional Leaders' Summit from 8 to 10 December 2004 (see Figure 1-2). Han Yuqun, Governor of Shandong Province, Stoiber, Minister-President of Bavaria, Josef Pühringer, Governor of Upper Austria, Rasool, Premier of the Western Cape, and Jean Charet, Premier of Quebec attended the summit. The themes of the summit were "Innovation Is Key to Economic Development" and "Role of Youth in Social Development". Representatives from the science and technology and youth sectors of the five provinces and states held forums on their respective themes and submitted reports to the summit. The leaders of the five provinces and states conducted discussions based on these reports. The summit commended the regions for their progress in promoting sustainable development and cultural dialogue since the first summit, and agreed that, in the face of opportunities and challenges brought about by economic globalization, the provinces and states should continue to strengthen dialogue and deepen exchanges and cooperation in science and technology, youth and other fields based on complementary advantages and mutual benefit. It was also agreed at the summit to hold youth exchange activities in Shandong in 2005. The leaders of the five provinces and states jointly signed the resolution of the summit and issued a press communique.

Figure 1-2 The second Regional Leaders' Summit

Photo Credit: Official Website of Regional Leaders' Summit (https://www.regionalleaderssummit.org/summits/all-summits/).

### 1.2.3 The Third Regional Leaders' Summit

From 11 to 12 July 2006, the third Regional Leaders' Summit was held in Linz, Upper Austria and attended by Stoiber, Minister-President of Bavaria, Jean Charet, Premier of Quebec, José Goldemberg, São Paulo's Secretary of State for the Environment, Han Yuqun, Governor of Shandong Province, Rasool, Premier of the Western Cape and Josef Pühringer, Governor of Upper Austria (see Figure 1-3). Regional leaders warmly welcomed the participation of São Paulo. Under the theme "Politics for Generations—A Sustainable Future Arising from a Shared Responsibility", the summit agreed to focus discussions on "Renewable Energy and Energy Efficiency" and "Education and Youth". In the area of renewable energy and energy efficiency, all parties agreed that innovation in energy utilization was key to improving competitiveness and environmental protection. They also recognized the importance of applying clean and climate-friendly technologies as the basis for sustainable energy policies in all regions. In the field of education and youth, it was agreed that societies that recognize and respond to development through international engagement and comparison would be in a better position to compete internationally. The leaders agreed to further promote exchanges between students and young people across the regions through training and hoped that early international contacts with sister provinces and states would enable them to understand international standards and participate in international competition and cooperation, thereby enhancing their confidence.

Figure 1-3 The third Regional Leaders' Summit

Photo Credit: Official Website of Regional Leaders' Summit, https://www.regionalleaderssummit.org/summits/all-summits/.

### 1.2.4 The Fourth Regional Leaders' Summit

The Fourth Regional Leaders' Summit was held in Jinan, Shandong Province, China from 6 to 7 August 2008 (see Figure 1-4), and attended by Jiang Daming, Governor of Shandong Province, Jean Charet, Premier of Quebec, Canada, Pühringer, Governor of Upper Austria, Austria, Sonny

Perdue, Governor of Georgia, USA, Markus Söder, Bavarian Minister for Federal and European Affairs, Germany, and Yuris, Minister of Local Government, Environmental Affairs and Development Planning of Western Cape, South Africa, as well as experts and entrepreneurs from various countries. The themes of the summit were "Building a Conservation-Oriented Society" and "Sanitation and Health". During the summit, representatives from all parties reached a series of agreements on jointly promoting sustainable development, strengthening international cooperation and exchanges, building a conservation-oriented society, and promoting global harmony. At the summit, representatives from the regions unanimously agreed to accept Georgia, the USA, as a formal member of the sister province and state cooperation mechanism. Pühringer, Governor of Upper Austria reported on the implementation of the *Linz Declaration* from the third summit, where a Joint Declaration was signed. The summit also approved the Western Cape's application for hosting the fifth summit, with confirmed themes of "Ensuring Food Security" and "Transport Development Strategy". During the summit, the Quebec Province of Canada and Shandong Province officially signed an agreement to establish a sister province and state relationship. Sanitation and health were identified as one of the themes of the summit for the first time, and the Health Cooperation Fair was also held for the first time at the Regional Leaders' Summit. During the fair, the participants held in-depth discussions on medical cooperation projects and signed nearly 20 letters of intent and cooperation agreements.

Figure 1-4 The fourth Regional Leaders' Summit

Photo Credit: Foreign Affairs Office of Shandong Provincial People's Government.

### 1.2.5 The Fifth Regional Leaders' Summit

Cape Town (Western Cape) hosted the fifth Regional Leaders' Summit from 27 to 29 September 2010 (see Figure 1-5). Jiang Daming, Governor of Shandong Province, China, Horst Seehofer, Minister-President of Bavaria, Germany, Pühringer, Governor of Upper Austria, Austria, Trey Childress, Chief Operating Officer, State of Georgia, USA, and Monique Gagnon-Tremblay, Minister of International Relations of Quebec, Canada attended the summit at the invitation of Helen Zille, Premier of the Western Cape, South Africa. The summit focused on the themes of "Food Security" and "Integrated Transport". The leaders of the regions unanimously agreed that food is the most fundamental means of human survival, and that governments should prioritize food production at all times. They also emphasized the importance of learning from each other's experiences in protecting arable land and promoting grain production, supporting agricultural production, increasing technical training for young farmers, and strengthening exchanges and cooperation in agricultural science and technology research, popularization of agricultural technology, processing technology of agricultural products, and trade of agricultural products. The leaders of the regions recognized that integrated transport has a direct impact on people's way of life. As science and technology continue to advance, transport has become increasingly fast-paced and diverse. The regions should enhance their research on transport integration, develop relevant plans, and consider the system and mechanism of transport integration in a coordinated manner, guided by the principles of efficiency and cost-effectiveness. It is essential to strengthen the transportation infrastructure and build an integrated traffic pattern to benefit the people of the regions. The regions agreed to hold a series of exchange and cooperation activities in the food and transportation fields in the next year. Shandong Province would host events such as the International Port Development and Management Forum, the Yantai International Wine Festival, and the International Agricultural Trade Fair. The fifth Regional Leaders' Summit adopted a joint declaration and reached consensus on topics such as food security and integrated transport.

Figure 1-5 The fifth Regional Leaders' Summit

Photo Credit: Official Website of Regional Leaders' Summit (https://www.regionalleaderssummit.org/summits/all-summits/).

### 1.2.6 The Sixth Regional Leaders' Summit

On 12 April 2012, the sixth Regional Leaders' Summit was held in São Paulo, Brazil, and attended by Horst Seehofer, Minister-President of Bavaria, Jean Charet, Premier of Quebec, Casey Cagle, Lieutenant Governor of Georgia, Cai Limin, Vice Governor of Shandong Province, Josef Pühringer, Governor of Upper Austria, Helen Zille, Premier of the Western Cape and Geraldo Alckmin, Governor of São Paulo. With the theme of “Sustainable Energy and Improving Energy Efficiency” (see Figure 1-6), the summit emphasized the need to prioritize policy advocacy, energy efficiency and conservation initiatives, and the advanced popularization and application of renewable energy technologies in the pursuit of sustainable development. The energy efficiency and conservation initiatives, as well as the improved utilization rate of renewable energy, are essential for creating a future of sustainable energy and can bring about significant economic opportunities. Representatives presented at the summit unanimously agreed to support the UN General Assembly resolution 65/151, which designated 2012 the “International Year of Sustainable Energy for All”. They believed that it is an important opportunity for people to raise their awareness of the importance of more use of sustainable energy, higher energy efficiency and renewable energy at the regional level. The regions will turn renewable energy into one of the most competitive forms of energy through a series of measures.

Figure 1-6 The sixth Regional Leaders' Summit

Photo Credit: Foreign Affairs Office of Shandong Provincial People's Government.

### 1.2.7 The Seventh Regional Leaders' Summit

The seventh Regional Leaders' Summit took place in Atlanta, Georgia, the USA from 2 to 3 June 2014 (see Figure 1-7). At the invitation of Nathan Deal, Governor of Georgia, Guo Shuqing, Governor of Shandong Province, China, Pühringer, Governor of Upper Austria, Austria, Christine St-Pierre, Minister of International Relations of Quebec, Canada, Beate Merk, Bavaria's State Minister for European and International Affairs, Germany, and Mireille Wenger, Minister of Finance and Economic Opportunities of Western Cape, South Africa, attended the summit. The summit was themed on "Global Changes in Logistics Supply Chains" and "The Use of Large-Scale Events to Promote Sustainable Economic Development". Leaders of the regions agreed that the importance of the logistics supply chain in the global economy is increasingly evident. They also recognized that changes in sourcing and trading modes require current logistics models to be adapted to effectively meet global development needs. The regions will create a shared knowledge base for challenges and opportunities in the logistics industry. The parties at the summit agreed that all regions have hosted one or more major sports events and should be actively encouraged to share their experiences in sports infrastructure management for the purpose of promoting regional economic development and improvement of people's livelihood. Leaders of the regions held in-depth discussions on the two themes and adopted a joint declaration at the summit. They also held pragmatic and friendly bilateral talks, laying a stronger foundation for the next step of expanding cooperation.

Figure 1-7 The seventh Regional Leaders' Summit

Photo Credit: Official Website of Regional Leaders' Summit (https://www.regionalleaderssummit.org/summits/all-summits/).

### 1.2.8 The Eighth Regional Leaders' Summit

The eighth Regional Leaders' Summit was held in Munich, Bavaria, Germany from 14 to 15 July 2016. At the invitation of Horst Seehofer, Minister-President of Bavaria, Nathan Deal, Governor of Georgia, Philippe Couillard, Premier of Quebec, Márcio França, Vice Governor of São Paulo, Guo Shuqing, Governor of Shandong Province, Josef Pühringer, Governor of Upper Austria, and Helen Zille, Premier of the Western Cape attended the summit (see Figure 1-8). Centering around “Digitalization and Innovation”, the participants discussed topics concerned by people in their respective regions. Executives of multinational companies in Bavaria joined in the dialogue about some key topics. Scientists from the regions presented the progress made in their joint multilateral projects and determined the next plans. Students from the regions participated in the "Future Leaders' Conference" and demonstrated their vision of applying digital technology in 2040.

Figure 1-8 The eighth Regional Leaders' Summit

Photo Credit: Official Website of Regional Leaders' Summit (https://www.regionalleaderssummit.org/summits/all-summits/).

### 1.2.9 The Ninth Regional Leaders' Summit

From 17 to 18 May 2018, Québec City hosted the ninth Regional Leaders' Summit, which was attended by Philippe Couillard, Premier of Quebec, Sun Jiye, Vice Governor of Shandong Province, Georg Eisenreich, Bavarian State Minister for Digital Agenda, Media and Europe, Pat Wilson, Commissioner of Georgia Department of Economic Development, Maurício Brusadin, Minister of Environment of the State of São Paulo, and Christine Haberlander, Minister of Education and Culture, Upper Austria (see Figure 1-9). The theme of the summit was "Energy Transition: Towards a Low-Carbon Economy". The representatives of the seven member regions agreed that the sister provinces and states must accelerate renewable energy transition and promote environment-friendly production and consumption modes for the purpose of achieving sustainable technological development and the world's environment and resource protection goals. All parties reiterated their efforts to reach the forefront of energy transition by 2030, devotedly develop renewable energy, improve energy efficiency and build a new, prosperous and low-carbon economy. The parties will strengthen cooperation on the RLS Energy Network project, have in-depth exchanges on energy transition, especially on topics such as renewable energy and energy efficiency, and set up task forces studying best practices in energy transition.

Figure 1-9 The ninth Regional Leaders' Summit

Photo Credit: Official Website of Regional Leaders' Summit (https://www.regionalleaderssummit.org/summits/all-summits/).

### 1.2.10 The Tenth Regional Leaders' Summit

The summit, originally scheduled to take place in September 2020 in Upper Austria, under the theme of “Smart Region”, was successfully held online on 11 November 2021 due to the impact of the COVID-19 pandemic under the original theme (see Figure 1-10). Leaders of the seven member regions, namely Bavaria (Germany), Shandong Province (China), Upper Austria (Austria), Quebec (Canada), Western Cape (South Africa),

Georgia (USA) and São Paulo (Brazil), attended the summit and delivered speeches respectively, and a joint declaration was signed. At the same time, the head of RLS-Sciences (a supporting program of the summit) reported to the conference on the results of the cooperation between scientists from the seven member regions in renewable energy, aerospace, small satellites, digitalization and digital health since the last summit.

Figure 1-10 The tenth Regional Leaders' Summit

Photo Credit: Official Website of Regional Leaders' Summit (https://www.regionalleaderssummit.org/summits/all-summits/).

## 1.3 Diverse Themes of Regional Leaders' Summits

All previous Regional Leaders' Summits have carried forward the spirit of mutually beneficial cooperation and multilateral exchanges, and have been committed to improving the well-being of the people in the member regions. The diverse summit themes demonstrate the social, political and economic diversity of the sister provinces and states, driving the innovative development in the regions and constantly giving new impetus to bilateral and multilateral cooperation (see Table 1-1). From the agenda of the previous ten sessions, the Regional Leaders' Summit has primary concerns in the following five areas.

**Table 1-1 Time, Venue and Topic of Previous Regional Leaders' Summits**

| | Year | Venue | Topics |
|---|---|---|---|
| First | 2002 | Munich, Bavaria, Germany | Sustainable Development Strategies; Intercultural Dialogue |
| Second | 2004 | Quebec City, Quebec, Canada | Innovation Is Key to Economic Development; Role of Youth in Social Development |
| Third | 2006 | Linz, Upper Austria, Austria | Renewable Energy and Energy Efficiency; Education and Youth |
| Fourth | 2008 | Jinan, Shandong Province, China | Building a Conservation-Oriented Society; Sanitation and Health |
| Fifth | 2010 | Cape Town, Western Cape, South Africa | Food Security; Integrated Transport |
| Sixth | 2012 | São Paulo City, São Paulo, Brazil | Sustainable Energy; Improving Energy Efficiency |
| Seventh | 2014 | Atlanta, Georgia, USA | Global Changes in Logistics Supply Chains; The Use of Large-Scale Events to Promote Sustainable Economic Development |
| Eighth | 2016 | Munich, Bavaria, Germany | Digitalization and Innovation |
| Ninth | 2018 | Quebec City, Quebec, Canada | Energy Transition: Towards a Low-Carbon Economy |
| Tenth | 2021 | Linz, Upper Austria, Austria (Online) | Smart Region |
| Eleventh | 2023 | Jinan, Shandong Province, China | Green Development and Low-Carbon Life |

### 1.3.1 Economic and Trade Cooperation

Strengthening the member regions' efforts to complement each other's advantages and promoting their economic and trade cooperation have always been topics of the summit. The themes of the summit are in essence closely related to economic cooperation and exchange. For example, the themes of the first through fourth, sixth, seventh and ninth summits, in order, were "Sustainable Development Strategies" "Innovation Is Key to Economic Development" "Renewable Energy and Energy Efficiency" "Building a Conservation-Oriented Society" "Sustainable Energy and Improving Energy Efficiency" "Global Changes in Logistics Supply Chains & The Use of Large-Scale Events to Promote Sustainable Economic Development", and "Energy Transition: Towards a Low-Carbon Economy", and the eleventh summit to be hosted by Jinan will be themed by "Green Development and Low-Carbon Life". Furthermore, multilateral and bilateral exchanges have been a necessary part of all previous summits, with their main content focused on economic and trade aspects. In particular, the economic and trade fairs that were held before and after each summit further underline the fundamental goal of cooperation.

### 1.3.2 People-to-People Exchange

Since its establishment, the summit mechanism has aimed, among other things, to promote dialogue, communication and mutual understanding among people of different cultural backgrounds. For example, the first summit had "intercultural dialogue" as one of its topics, and subsequent summits reiterated the need for intercultural exchange and cooperation and the efforts to seek concrete paths for intercultural cooperation and exchange. Leaders of the member regions have emphasized the need to strengthen the awareness of the cultural identities of their respective regions to build up a foundation for international dialogue and cooperation. Keenly aware that the youth is the future of the 21st century, the leaders of the member regions have also emphasized that the youth should play an active role in international cooperation to promote social change and innovation, mutual understanding between cultures, as well as world peace, stability and development.

### 1.3.3 Green Development

Such topics of cooperation occupy an important place at the Regional Leaders’ Summit. For example, at the third summit with “Renewable Energy and Energy Efficiency” as the topic, all parties agreed that innovation in energy utilization was key to improving competitiveness and environmental protection, and they also recognized the importance of applying clean and climate-friendly technologies as the basis for sustainable energy policies in all regions. Based on its discussions on the topic of “Building a Conservation-Oriented Society” and its subsequent implementation, the fourth summit set the main objectives to encourage exchanges in the development and application of technologies for the safe production, transport, distribution and efficient utilization of renewable energy, as well as to encourage cooperation among the member regions in the existing international energy network. Furthermore, centering again on the topic of “Sustainable Energy and Energy Efficiency”, the sixth summit further defined the objectives of cooperation among member regions in various aspects, including conserving limited natural resources, developing renewable resources and energy, vigorously carrying out energy conservation and emission reduction, improving the utilization efficiency of resources and energy, developing circular economy, promoting cleaner production, innovating resource recycling technology, establishing the concept of conservation, developing conservation habits, opposing overconsumption, protecting the environment, and improving the ecology. Under the theme of “Energy Transition: Towards a Low-Carbon Economy”, the ninth summit called for driving low-carbon economy with renewable energy, actively reducing carbon emissions and prioritizing the development of green economy. In July 2016, the *Roadmap for the Alliance of Sister Provinces and States for Renewable Energy* was implemented. In its first phase, a comprehensive digitalization survey of renewable energy production, technologies and resources in the member regions was conducted to test their respective renewable energy potential; and its second phase aimed to develop, test and evaluate new technologies through collaborative cross-continental demonstration projects.

### 1.3.4 Technological Innovation

The member regions suggest that science and innovation should act as vehicles for the modernization of the economy and society, and that they can share knowledge and support creativity and innovation through cooperation. For example, with "Innovation Is Key to Economic Development" as one of the topics for discussion and cooperation, the second summit emphasized the fundamental role of cooperation in scientific and technological progress and innovation in promoting cooperation between the regions. At the summit, consultative cooperation was also proposed, especially in the area of scientific research and innovation, which plays a key role in economic development, for the purposes of increasing synergies between local economies and addressing the challenges of globalization. The fifth summit under the theme of "Integrated Transport", the eighth summit under the theme of "Digitalization and Innovation", and the tenth summit under the theme of "Smart Region" all focused on the optimization of social welfare and the facilitation of citizens' life brought about by technological and social innovations. In addition, the best practices of "Smart Region" also focused on digitalization, AI, smart production, smart energy and medical technologies.

### 1.3.5 Social Governance

For example, the second summit addressed the topic of "Role of Youth in Social Development"; the third summit addressed the topic of "Education and Youth"; the fourth summit addressed the topic of "Sanitation and Health", emphasizing that we should pay attention to the impact of the environment and climate on health, establish a sound health care system that benefits the whole society, strengthen disease prevention and control, improve health conditions, and advocate health maintenance and care; the fifth summit addressed the solutions to "Integrated Transport"; the seventh summit addressed the topic of "The Use of Large-Scale Events to Promote Sustainable Economic Development"; and the tenth summit addressed the topic of "Smart Region". Seeking effective solutions to these social issues mentioned at these summits is an important responsibility of local governments, and strengthening cooperation on these issues is of great significance for improving the management level, the well-being of residents and even the long-term development of the member regions.

# 第二章　友好省州领导人峰会运行机制

友好省州领导人峰会是各友好省州政府领导人参加的会议，是友好省州交往的最高级别会议。为充分反映各方意见和诉求，取得务实成果，峰会探索形成了有效机制，确保持续关注共同关切的重大议题，达成共识，推动双边和多边合作走向深入。

## 一、友好省州领导人峰会举办机制

友好省州领导人峰会每两年举办一次，与会各省州轮流承办。在正式举办峰会之前，由东道主组织各省州高级官员预先召开一次事务级筹备会议，讨论峰会的议程、活动安排及峰会宣言等相关事宜。峰会期间，承办方会组织专题论坛、展览、文体比赛等线上线下相结合的交流活动，营造合作氛围。正式峰会上，省州领导人则围绕主题发表意见、交流观点、展开讨论并审查签署峰会宣言。宣言既是对与会各方达成共识的归纳，也是对各方阐述的主张、观点或原则立场的记载，同时又是对会后两年内围绕主题开展的一系列双边及多边交流与合作项目的认可和部署。

为更便于协调和实施多边合作项目，保证多边项目的延续性，确保合作项目取得务实成果，2016 年慕尼黑峰会期间上奥州提出的“三驾马车”式运行模式得到与会各方同意，即由本次峰会主办方、上次峰会主办方及下次峰会主办方三方共同组成工作小组，当前峰会主办方负责峰会前后一年的有关工作，之后下个主办方接手下次峰会前后一年的有关工作。各方通过该模式增进交流，深化多边合作，确保合作成效。峰会主办方应当做好峰会筹划工作和设计峰会有关活动。按照惯例，峰会预备会于峰会召开数月前举行，建议每年举办一次预备会(必要时可进行电话会议)以跟进各省州执行情况、多边项目进展情况并做好下次峰会的筹备工作。“三驾马车”式运行模式通过深入细致的前期准备工作和各方的协调配合有效提升了工作效率,能够统筹各方资源与力量、强化多边沟通,为峰会的顺利筹备与成功举办奠定了坚实的基础。

峰会注重媒体宣传工作,通过各类媒体的广泛报道,向全世界及时有效地传递了峰会的主题与交流合作的成果,极大地提升了峰会的国际影响力。

## 二、友好省州领导人峰会议题机制

友好省州领导人峰会从一开始就明确了“可持续发展”这一根本性主题,第三次友好省州领导人峰会明确提出“创造可持续的未来是我们共同的责任”,此后每次峰会都根据经济与社会发展趋势,选取一至两个重点议题展开讨论。从历次友好省州领导人峰会的主题来看,所涉及的议题较为广泛,涵盖经济贸易、人文交流、绿色发展、科技创新和社会治理等方面,主要集中在经济、文化、教育、科技、卫生、能源、青年等有关经济社会发展及与提高人民生活水平密切相关的非政治类领域。各方围绕可持续发展的主线和每次峰会确定的不同但延续或相关的主题,适时调整重点,不断挖掘潜力,既保持了连续性,又拓展了新的渠道,超越了时空的限制,为友好省州间的合作注入源源不断的活力。

## 三、友好省州领导人峰会协调机制

在慕尼黑召开的首次峰会上,与会省州决定建立两个机构,即指导委员会和工作组。指导委员会旨在协调各方合作事宜,主要负责促进议定目标的实现和执行措施的实施,并负责项目的推动以及对建议的项目的检查。指导委员会由各省州政府长官指定的最高级别公务人员组成,由即将举办首脑会议的省州轮流担任,每年召开一次会议。工作组由各省州负责可持续发展政策的部长组成,在环保领域制定共同目标,确定示范项目。

指导委员会和工作组的设立,为就各省州之间合作的必要性、主要目的、主要领域以及合作机制达成一致奠定了基础。这个机制确立了峰会的组织机构和运行规则,将过去相对松散的友好关系或合作伙伴转变为较为严格的制度化合作关系。按照这个机制，此后新成员必须与原有的一个或多个成员间有友好城市关系，并在一方提议的基础上征得各方同意后才能加入。至此，友好省州领导人峰会这一地方政府多边合作机制正式建立[①]，并顺利运转至今。

① 参见王立军：《全球化背景下的中国地方政府国际合作》，山东大学博士学位论文，2012年。

# Chapter 2 Operating Mechanism of Regional Leaders' Summit

The Regional Leaders' Summit is a conference of government leaders of sister provinces and states, and is the top-level meeting on the exchanges between sister provinces and states. To fully reflect the views and demands of all parties and achieve pragmatic results, effective summit mechanisms have been explored and formed, so that the summit continues to focus on major issues of common concern, reaches consensus, and facilitates in-depth bilateral and multilateral cooperation.

## 2.1 Organizing Mechanism of Regional Leaders' Summit

The Regional Leaders' Summit is held every two years by the member regions taking turns. Prior to the formal summit, the host will organize a transaction-level preparatory meeting in advance with senior officials from the member regions to discuss the summit agenda, schedule and the *Summit Declaration* and other related matters. During the summit, the organizers will organize online and offline exchange activities, such as thematic forums, exhibitions and cultural and sports competitions, to create an atmosphere for cooperation. At the formal summit, leaders of the regions will express their opinions, exchange views and conduct discussions on the topics, and will examine and sign the *Summit Declaration*, which serves as a summary of the consensus reached by the participants, a record of their proposals, views or principled stands, as well as an approval and arrangement for a series of bilateral and multilateral exchange and cooperation projects centering on the summit topics over the next two years.

In order to further facilitate the coordination and implementation of multilateral cooperation projects, and ensure the continuity of multilateral projects as well as practical results, the "troika" structure of the preparatory committee of the summit proposed by Upper Austria at the 2016 edition in Munich was agreed by the participants. Specifically, in such a structure, the hosts of the current, previous and next summits form a working group, in which the host of the current summit undertakes the related work in the year around the summit, and similarly the host of the next summit will undertake the related work in the year around the next summit. The parties have adopted this mode to enhance communication, deepen multilateral cooperation and ensure the effectiveness of cooperation. In its turn, the host province or state should carefully plan the summit and design the related activities. By convention, the preliminary meeting for the summit is held several months before the summit and once a year as recommended (teleconference is allowed when necessary) to follow up on the implementation by provinces and states and the progress of multilateral projects and to prepare for the next summit. The "troika" operating mode has proven to be a success in coordinating resources and efforts of all parties, strengthening multilateral communication, and facilitating the successful preparation and holding of the summits, for its implementation in subsequent summits has resulted in thorough preparatory work and coordination among all parties, effectively enhancing the work efficiency and laying a solid foundation for the success of the summits.

The summit, attaching importance to media publicity, has effectively delivered its topics and results of exchange and cooperation in time worldwide through extensive coverage by various media, which has greatly enhanced its international influence.

## 2.2 Topic Mechanism of Regional Leaders’ Summit

The RLS determined the fundamental topic of “Sustainable Development” from the very beginning. The third RLS clearly proposed “A Sustainable Future Arising from a Shared Responsibility”, and the summits thereafter always selected one or two key topics in accordance with economic and social trends. In view of the themes of previous sessions of the RLS, the topics are relatively wide-ranging, covering economic and trade, people-to-people exchanges, green development, technological innovation, and social governance, and largely focusing on non-political fields closely related to economic and social development and improving people’s living standards, such as economy, culture, education, science and technology, health, energy and youth. The parties, centering on the main line of sustainable development and different but continuing or related themes determined at each summit, have realigned their priorities in due time and continuously tapped their potentials. As a result, the summits not only maintain continuity, but also expand new channels, continuously revitalizing the cooperation between the member regions beyond the limits of time and space.

## 2.3 Coordination Mechanism of Regional Leaders’ Summit

At the first RLS held in Munich, the participating member regions decided to establish two institutions, namely a coordination committee and a working group. The Coordination Committee aims to coordinate matters concerning the cooperation of all parties and is primarily responsible for facilitating the achievement of agreed objectives, the implementation of executive measures, project promotion, and the examination of proposed projects. It is composed of the persons of the highest civil servant rank designated by the heads of the government of the member region that will host the summit and serves on a rotating basis. It convenes one meeting every year. The Working Group is composed of ministers responsible for sustainable development policies in the member regions, and is responsible for setting common goals and determining demonstration projects in the field of environmental protection.

The establishment of the Coordination Committee and the Working Group laid the foundation for the agreement on the necessity, primary purposes, key areas, and mechanisms of cooperation among member regions. This mechanism established the organizational structure and operating rules of the summit and guided the relatively loose amicable relations or partnerships in the past to a relatively rigorous and institutionalized channel of cooperation. Under this mechanism, a new member joining the summit thereafter must be one with whom one or more of the original members already have established the sister city relationship and who has obtained the consent of such original members on the basis of a proposal by one of such parties. At this point, the RLS, a multilateral cooperation mechanism for local governments, was established and[①] has been evolving well since then.

① Wang Lijun, "International Cooperation between Local Governments in China under the Background of Globalization," Dissertation, Shandong University (2012).

# 第三章　友好省州领导人峰会成效

友好省州领导人峰会成员是各国经济、科技实力较为雄厚的地方政府，相互之间的合作可谓"强强联合"。峰会成员中有四个属于发达国家，三个属于发展中国家，它们之间的合作具有典型性和示范性。这种合作机制对提升本省州的国际化水平，通过互利共赢增强自身实力发挥了十分重要的作用。

## 一、深化友好省州间的交流合作

2002 年以来，友好省州领导人峰会已成功举办十次。各省州领导人率领政府代表团出席会议，围绕可持续发展主题进行讨论，通过并联合发表了十项联合宣言。各省州企业领导人、科教文卫等领域专家以及青少年代表参加了峰会，开展了广泛深入的交流合作活动。在友好省州领导人峰会机制下，各省州努力践行联合宣言的承诺，把握科技革命带来的新挑战、新机遇，加快推动创新发展，促进各省州的合作迈向更高水平。

友好省州领导人峰会秉承和发扬在经济、社会、环境等领域的全面、协调、可持续发展的理念，以相互借鉴、取长补短、平等互利、增进友谊、促进合作为宗旨，围绕节约资源、降低消耗、减少排放、适度消费、保护环境、关注气候、改善生态、促进医疗、保障卫生、提高健康等共同关心的问题进一步推动各省州之间开展全方位、深层次、多渠道的务实合作与交流，提高各省州在经济全球化和区域竞争中的综合实力，强力推动各省州之间合作共赢。

友好省州领导人峰会机制启动以来，各省州紧扣主题，切实履行峰会达成的共识，各省州间的友好交往日益密切，合作领域不断拓宽，合作成效日渐显现。据统计，自 2002 年第一次友好省州领导人峰会以来，在峰会机制下各省州达成的双边和多边合作项目超过300个，通过双边、多边项目不断扩大交流，在多个领域取得了务实成果。

此外，各省州领导人还会利用参加峰会的时机出访峰会举办地所在国的友好城市以及途经的其他友好城市，开展全面深入的沟通与交流，增进彼此的了解，加强双边合作，全面深入促进与友好城市关系的发展，拓展和扩大国际"朋友圈"。

## 二、促进共同关注问题的解决

友好省州领导人峰会是一个新型的多边国际合作机制，是有关国家的地方政府为寻求加强相互之间的理解和尊重、探讨共同关心的国际热点难点问题并寻求解决问题的合理渠道而建立的。

友好省州领导人峰会成员既有发达国家的地方政府也有发展中国家的地方政府，所讨论的国际热点难点问题是这些地方政府共同面临而又需要合作解决的问题。友好省州领导人峰会紧密结合可持续发展的主题和各省州的实际，将共同面临的热点难点问题作为讨论与开展合作的主题，这对在世界经济一体化进程中推动各省州取长补短、合作共赢发挥了十分重要的作用，促进了有关国际问题的有效解决。[①]

## 三、推动有关国际议题的设定

友好省州领导人峰会作为各省州间的合作平台，在加强有关国际问题的沟通交流、协调各省州间的立场、推动本国中央政府之间的合作及有关国际议题的设定、国际问题的解决方面发挥了重要作用。如第一次峰会中，各省州接受了上奥州提出的"可持续发展国际(行动)十年(2003—2012)"的决议，并请上奥州州长向联合国秘书长递交申请，要求各省州提请本国中央政府支持这一申请。[②] 再如，在各省州的共同努力下，联合国教科文组织于2005年10月20日通过了加拿大魁北克省倡议的关于保护和促进文化多样

① 参见王立军:《全球化背景下的中国地方政府国际合作》，山东大学博士学位论文，2012年。

② 参见《第一次友好省州领导人峰会联合宣言》，德国巴伐利亚州，2002年12月31日。

性的协议。[①] 又如，在各省州的积极推动下，联合国将全球环境奖项授予了山东省科学院。[②] 这也说明在友好省州领导人峰会机制的推动下，地方政府已经逐渐成为国际关系中一支十分重要的力量，尤其在可持续发展领域，对一些重要的国际事件能够产生实质性影响。

① 参见《第三次友好省州领导人峰会联合宣言》，奥地利上奥州，2006 年 7 月 12 日。

② 参见《第四次友好省州领导人峰会联合宣言》，山东省济南市，2008 年 8 月 7 日。

# Chapter 3
# Results of Regional Leaders' Summit

The members of the RLS are all local governments with strong economic, scientific and technological capabilities, and their cooperation with each other is bound to produce good results. Among the seven members of the RLS, four are in developed countries and the other three in developing countries, so the cooperation among them is typical and demonstrative. The cooperation mechanism has played an important role in enhancing the internationalization of the member regions and increasing their respective strength through mutual benefit.

## 3.1 Deepening Exchanges and Cooperation between Sister Provinces and States

To date, the RLS has been successfully held ten times since 2002. Leaders of the member regions have led government delegations to the summits to conduct discussions centering on the topic of sustainable development and have adopted and jointly issued ten joint declarations. Business leaders, experts in the fields of science, education, culture, and health, as well as youth representatives also attended the summits and participated in extensive and in-depth exchange and cooperation activities. Under the summit mechanism, the member regions strive to fulfill the commitments made in the joint declaration, respond to the new challenges and seize the new opportunities brought about by the technological revolution, accelerate innovation and development, and facilitate a higher level of cooperation among them.

The RLS upholds and promotes the concept of comprehensive, coordinated and sustainable economic, social and environmental development, and aims to achieve mutual learning, complementary strengths, equality and mutual benefits, closer friendship and further cooperation among the member regions. Centering on issues of common concern such as resource conservation, consumption reduction, emission reduction, moderate consumption, environment protection, climate, ecological and medical improvement, and health protection and enhancement, the summit has further promoted all-round, in-depth and multi-channel practical cooperation and exchanges among the member regions, improved their respective comprehensive strength in economic globalization and regional competition, and boosted the cooperation and mutual benefits among them.

Since the launch of the summit mechanism, by sticking to the topics and effectively implementing the consensus reached at the summit, the members have been carrying out increasingly close friendly exchanges and constantly broadening the areas of cooperation, achieving increasingly significant effectiveness of cooperation. According to statistics, since the first RLS in 2002, the member regions have finalized more than 300 bilateral and multilateral cooperation projects under the summit mechanism and constantly expanded their exchanges through such projects, achieving practical results in various fields.

In addition, on the occasion of the summit, leaders of the regions can also visit the sister cities of the host country and other sister cities they pass through and conduct comprehensive and in-depth communication and exchange with them to enhance mutual understanding, strengthen bilateral cooperation, develop comprehensive and in-depth relations with them, and expand their respective international “circle of friends”.

## 3.2 Facilitating the Resolution of Issues of Common Concern

The RLS is a new type of multilateral international cooperation mechanism established by the local governments of the relevant countries for the purposes of strengthening mutual understanding and respect, discussing international hot and difficult issues of common concern, and seeking reasonable channels to solve problems.

Its members are local governments in both developed and developing countries, and the international hot and difficult issues discussed are those that are of common concern and need to be addressed through cooperation. The RLS always takes into account the theme of sustainable development and the realities of the member regions, and takes the hot and difficult issues of common concern as the topics for discussion and cooperation, which has played a key role in promoting the complementation and win-win cooperation among the member regions in the process of global economic integration, and contributed to the effective resolution of relevant international issues.①

## 3.3 Promoting the Setting of Relevant International Topics

The RLS is a platform for cooperation between sister provinces and states to strengthen mutual communication and exchange on international issues, coordinate their positions, and promote cooperation between the central governments of their respective countries, playing an important role in setting international topics and addressing international problems. For example, at the first summit, the member regions accepted the resolution "International (Action) Decade (2003—2012) for Sustainable Development"

① Wang Lijun, "International Cooperation between Local Governments in China under the Background of Globalization," Dissertation, Shandong University (2012).

proposed by Upper Austria, and requested Governor of Upper Austria to submit an application to the Secretary General of the United Nations and to request the sister provinces and states to ask their respective central governments to support the application. ①With joint hands of provinces and states, the UNESCO approved the protocol of Quebec, Canada on 20 October 2005, protecting and facilitating cultural diversity. ②Under the common efforts of sister provinces and states, the United Nations granted Shandong Academy of Sciences the Global Environment Award. ③ Therefore, under the summit mechanism, local governments are becoming significant contributors to international relations, and have a profound effect on some key international events, especially in the sustainable development.

---

① Joint Declaration of the First Regional Leaders' Summit. Bavaria, Germany. 31 December, 2002.

② Joint Declaration of the Third Regional Leaders' Summit. Upper Austria, Austria. 12 July, 2006.

③ Joint Declaration of the Forth Regional Leaders' Summit. Jinan, Shandong. 7 August, 2008.

# 第二篇　实践篇

## 第四章　地方政府交流合作

山东省是经济大省、文化大省、资源大省，当前正在按照国家战略部署要求加快新旧动能转换、推动黄河流域生态保护和高质量发展，建设绿色低碳高质量发展先行区，实现经济转型发展，建设现代化强省。七个友好省州均是经济强省州、科研技术高地，在友好省州领导人峰会框架下的合作具有很大潜力和广阔空间。回顾近20年，山东省与各省州在多个领域进行了密切的交流合作，取得了丰硕的成果。

### 一、山东省与巴伐利亚州的交流合作

1983年，山东省开始与德国巴伐利亚州进行正式的交流和互访。1984年，双方领导人签署经济技术合作意向书。1985年，签署合作备忘录。1987年7月9日，正式缔结友好省州关系，此后山东省与巴伐利亚州高层互访频繁，人员交流活跃，合作项目众多，合作成果斐然，逐步构建起了全方位、宽领域、多层次的友好关系。在双方多年成功合作的基础上，2010年，中共山东省委书记、山东省人大常委会主任姜异康在慕尼黑市与巴伐利亚州州长霍斯特·泽霍夫共同签署了《关于鲁巴建立战略伙伴关系的协议》，将双方关系推向了更高层次。2017年5月，巴伐利亚州州长霍斯特·泽霍夫率团访鲁，中共山东省委书记刘家义会见了霍斯特·泽霍夫一行（见图4-1），中共山东省委副书记、山东省省长龚正与霍斯特·泽霍夫在山东省济南市签署了《关于进一步加强友好合作与深化战略伙伴关系的共同声明》，为山东省与巴伐利亚州的友好合作注入了新的动力。巴伐利亚州邓肯多夫乐团随巴伐利亚

州州长霍斯特·泽霍夫访鲁，山东省省长龚正观看乐团演出并与乐团合影（见图 4-2）。2017 年 11 月，山东省常务副省长李群和巴伐利亚州欧盟与国际事务部部长贝亚特·默尔克、巴伐利亚州第一副议长博克莱特（Bocklet）、汉斯·赛德尔基金会主席孟勒（Männl）、山东省驻慕尼黑总领事毛静秋共同出席山东省与巴伐利亚州结好 30 周年活动（见图 4-3、图 4-4、图 4-5）。

图 4-1　2017 年，巴伐利亚州州长霍斯特·泽霍夫访鲁与中共山东省委书记刘家义会晤

图片来源：山东省人民政府外事办公室。

图 4-2　2017 年 5 月，巴伐利亚州邓肯多夫乐团与山东省省长龚正合影

图片来源：山东省人民政府外事办公室。

图 4-3　2017 年 11 月，热烈庆祝山东省与巴伐利亚州结好 30 周年活动

图片来源：巴伐利亚州中国代表处网站，http://www.bavaria-china.com/article.aspx?id=5。

图 4-4　2017 年 11 月，山东省与巴伐利亚州结好 30 周年活动孔府乐舞演出

图片来源：山东省人民政府外事办公室。

图 4-5　2017 年，山东省常务副省长李群和巴伐利亚州欧盟与国际事务部部长贝亚特·默尔克出席庆祝山东省与巴伐利亚州结好 30 周年活动

图片来源：山东省人民政府外事办公室。

在友好省州关系的基础上，山东省与巴伐利亚州之间的城市也开展了积极的交流合作，目前山东省已与巴伐利亚州建立了四对市级/县级友好关系（济南—奥格斯堡，潍坊—弗赖辛，泰安—施瓦本，莱州—施万多夫），五对市级友好合作关系（青岛—雷根斯堡，东营—巴特基辛根，济宁—上弗兰肯，潍坊—阿莎芬堡，曲阜—班贝格）。

双方领导人的互访日趋频繁。山东省领导人梁步庭（1985）、赵志浩（1991）、姜春云（1994）、李春亭（1996、2000）、韩寓群（2003）、姜异康（2010）、郭树清（2016）、龚正（2018）等曾多次率团访问巴伐利亚州。巴伐利亚州州长施特劳斯（Strauss，1985）、埃德蒙德·施托伊贝尔（1995、2003）、霍斯特·泽霍夫（2010、2017）也曾率团访问山东省。巴伐利亚州议长波姆（Böhm，2000）、格吕克（Glück，2008）、施塔姆（Stamm，2011、2012、2017）也曾先后访问山东省。2021 年 9 月 2 日，中共山东省委副书记、山东省省长李干杰以视频形式与巴伐利亚州州长马库斯·索德尔举行高层对话。

2023 年 1 月 26 日，山东省商务厅在德国巴伐利亚州慕尼黑市成功举办“山东-巴伐利亚产业合作交流会”。在交流会的园区推介环节，来自中国和德国的企业及园区参会人员就市场潜力、产业政策、投资成本、配套措施等领域进行了深入交流以增进相互了解、探讨合作机遇。

2023 年 3 月 1 日，中国（山东）与德国巴伐利亚合作对话会在线上成功举办，山东省副省长邓云锋、德国巴伐利亚州州长马库斯·索德尔出席活动。

随着山东省与巴伐利亚州友好省州关系的不断深入发展，双方政府部门和机构之间建立了对口合作机制，保证和推动了重点合作领域的发展。

在经济和贸易领域，山东重工潍柴动力集团先后投资 23 亿欧元参与德国凯傲集团的上市重组，投资 4.5 亿欧元完成林德液压重组，为当地提供了大量优质就业岗位，推动了山东省潍坊市与巴伐利亚州阿莎芬堡市缔结友好城市关系，并实现了返程投资，取得了突出的经济效益和社会效益。中国重汽集团与德国曼公司进行的长期战略合作大大提高了中国重汽集团的自主研发能力。空客直升机德国公司在青岛设立了欧洲以外的第一条 H135 直升机总装生产线，2018 年 9 月，首架 H135 直升机在青岛交付。西门子在青岛成立的创新中心成为西门子在中国唯一一家以“智能制造”为核心课题的研发创新中心。中国潍坊歌尔公司与德国英飞凌公司历经十年合作，涉及硅麦克风项目、传感器项目等。

1993 年 11 月，山东省与巴伐利亚州共同成立了“鲁巴教育项目合作委员会”，每两年在巴伐利亚州或山东省轮流召开一次会议，以协调双方在教育领域的合作。2007 年，山东省与巴伐利亚州在此基础上分别成立了协调双方高校合作的“山东省中德高校合作中心”和“巴伐利亚州对华高教中心”。1996 年，双方成立鲁巴城建顾问委员会，定期举行会议，举办研讨会和培训班。1999 年，山东省广播电视台与巴伐利亚州广播电视台签署了合作协议，定期开展交流并每两年续签一次合作协议。2018 年 3 月，鲁巴战略协调小组第一次会议在山东省济南市召开，山东省与巴伐利亚州有关部门共同制订了 2018—2019 年度合作计划，计划涉及经济科技、教育培训、农村发展和城镇规划、健康环保、文化体育五大领域。

在山东省与巴伐利亚州的众多合作领域中，包括中小学教育、职业教育和高等教育在内的教育领域的全方位合作是双方合作的亮点。在巴伐利亚州办公厅、教育部、农业部及慕尼黑工业大学、迪林根教师进修学院的支持和参与下，汉斯·赛德尔基金会与山东省不断开展合作，1989 年在潍坊建立了鲁巴潍柴职业培训中心，1990 年在青岛平度建立了双元制农业职业教育培训中心，1998 年在潍坊青州建立了鲁巴职教师资培训中心，2012 年在青岛经济技术开发区与中德生态园管理委员会、西海岸职业教育有限公司和职业中专合作建立了培训基地。巴伐利亚州为上述项目投入的资金超过 3000 万欧元，派遣长期和短期专家 300 余人次。

山东省与巴伐利亚州在高等教育领域的合作成果也十分显著。山东大学、山东师范大学、中国海洋大学、山东科技大学、青岛大学、山东农业大学等高校与巴伐利亚州的高校缔结了友好校际交流关系，开展了各种形式的合作。山东行政学院与巴伐利亚行政学院之间的友好关系由来已久，双方往来与合作频繁高效。

图 4-6　2020 年 4 月，山东省人民政府为巴伐利亚州捐赠口罩

图片来源：山东省人民政府外事办公室政府网站。

巴伐利亚州政府资助山东省在铁路、航空、财政、金融、电信、通信、计量、啤酒、企业管理、公安、行政管理、农村发展等领域培训了 1000 多名专业技术人才。在齐鲁工业大学建立了啤酒技术中心，在山东省邮电学校建立了电信技术中心。

2020 年 4 月，作为巴伐利亚州的友好省州，山东省人民政府为巴伐利亚州捐赠了口罩，助力友好省州抗击新冠肺炎疫情（见图 4-6）。

## 二、山东省与上奥州的交流合作

1996 年 9 月，山东省省长李春亭率山东省政府代表团访问了奥地利上奥州，与上奥州州长约瑟夫·普林格共同签署了缔结友好省州关系协议。自结好以来，两省州往来频繁，在经贸、人文、教育、能源领域交往密切。

山东省领导人韩寓群(2006)、姜异康(2010)、王随莲(2012)、夏耕(2015)、于建成(2016)、于晓明(2017)、孙立成(2018)、白玉刚(2023)曾访问上奥州。上奥州副州长西格尔(Sigl,2007)、州长约瑟夫·普林格(2008)、副州长鲁道夫·安绍伯(Rudolf Anschober,2010)、常务副州长黑泽尔(Hiesl,2010)、常务副州长克里斯蒂娜·哈博兰德(2019)曾访问山东省。

2016 年 10 月,为庆祝山东省与上奥州结好 20 周年,山东省文化馆赴上奥州林茨市举办“来自孔子家乡的文化展”,促进了两地传统文化的交流。2016 年 11 月,奥地利上奥州州长麦格·托马斯·施泰尔泽(Mag. Thomas Stelzer)与山东省金融工作办公室代表团进行会晤(见图 4-7)。2017 年 7 月,青岛市市南区政府邀请来自奥地利等国的艺术家参加“2017 青岛·市南管乐艺术周”。2017 年 12 月,青岛举办“无界·德国奥地利瑞士当代雕塑艺术展”,展览展出作品 49 件。2018 年 5 月,山东省副省长孙继业在加拿大魁北克省参加第九次友好省州领导人峰会期间与奥地利上奥州常务副州长克里斯蒂娜·哈博兰德女士会晤(见图 4-8)。

图 4-7 2016 年 11 月,奥地利上奥州州长麦格·托马斯·施泰尔泽与山东省金融工作办公室代表团会晤

图片来源:山东省人民政府外事办公室。

图 4-8　2018 年 5 月，山东省副省长孙继业在第九次友好省州领导人峰会期间与奥地利上奥州常务副州长克里斯蒂娜·哈博兰德女士会晤

图片来源：山东省人民政府外事办公室。

山东财经大学与上奥应用科技大学有着良好的合作关系。2019 年 9 月，双方共同主办了“2019 北京洪堡论坛-齐鲁论坛”，并邀请了 14 位上奥州企业家与山东省企业家进行深入交流。2019 年 10 月，奥地利上奥州常务副州长克里斯蒂娜·哈博兰德率团访问山东省，参加山东国际友城合作发展大会。其间，克里斯蒂娜·哈博兰德访问了山东财经大学，与山东省教育厅签署了教育合作领域伙伴关系备忘录。

2013 年，山东省体育局与奥地利上奥州体育部签署了双边体育友好交流协议，此后双方交流频繁，定期举行体育高层互访，在击剑、马术、乒乓球、羽毛球等项目中开展竞赛信息共享、教练员互访任教、运动员互访比赛训练等交流活动。双方在乒乓球和羽毛球项目上的交流尤为频繁，自 2014 年起采取对等接待的方式，每年由奥地利上奥州乒乓球羽毛球代表队和中国山东省乒乓球羽毛球运动管理中心互派管理人员、教练员和运动员约 15 人进行访问，进行为期三至四周的训练比赛活动。此项交流活动已经成为双边机制性体育交流活动。

2023 年 5 月，中共山东省委常委、宣传部部长白玉刚访问上奥州。其间，山东代表团进行了“(奥地利)上奥州体育部(中国)山东省体育局——青少年运动员高水平训练基地”揭牌仪式。该基地是山东省体育局在海外建立的第一个高水平青少年体育训练基地(见图 4-9)。

图 4-9　2023 年 5 月 2 日,中共山东省委常委、宣传部部长白玉刚与上奥州州长麦格·托马斯·施泰尔泽为"(奥地利)上奥州体育部(中国)山东省体育局——青少年运动员高水平训练基地"揭牌

图片来源:山东省体育局。

## 三、山东省与西开普省的交流合作

1998 年 11 月 26 日,南非西开普省与中国山东省正式缔结友好省州关系,这是中国与南非建交后缔结的第一对省级友好关系,也是山东省在非洲大陆缔结的第一对友好省份关系。

1998 年 11 月,山东省常务副省长宋法棠率团访问南非,与西开普省省长杰拉尔德·莫克尔(Gerald Morkel)签署了《中华人民共和国山东省与南非共和国西开普省关于建立友好省州关系的协议书》。

结好以来,双方高层互访频繁。西开普省来访的主要有省长杰拉尔德·莫克尔(2000)、议长多曼(Doman,2001)、社会安全部部长拉马特拉坎(Ramatlakane,2004)、社会服务与扶贫部部长穆库娃娜(Mqulwana,2004)、议长拜奈乌德特(Byneveldt,2006)、省长拉苏(2007)、地方政府环境与发展规划部部长尤里斯(2008)、农业部部长范·雷斯伯格(Van Rensburg,2011、

2012、2013)、财政部部长阿兰·温德(Alan Winde,2013)。

山东省出访的主要有蔡秋芳(2002)、王修智和林书香(2004)、林廷生(2005)、韩寓群(2006)、时立军(2008)、贾万志(2009)、王军民(2009)、姜大明(2010)、焉荣竹(2011)、张建国(2013)、孙伟(2016)、才利民(2016)。

山东省访问团在访问南非西开普省期间,多次在当地举行经贸洽谈会等推介活动,推动两省间的经贸往来。2013 年 3 月,中非发展基金与海信集团签署了投资合作协议,在亚特兰蒂斯经济特区投资建设了海信南非工业园。2016 年 5 月,中共山东省委常委、山东省常务副省长孙伟在率领山东省政府代表团访问南非期间,实地考察了海信南非工业园(见图 4-10)、非洲(中国)生产资料展销中心、济南域潇集团莫桑比克公司、威高医疗内罗毕展销中心等山东省在南非的投资企业。2016 年 9 月,山东省人大常委会副主任才利民在率领代表团访问南非期间,出席了山东省在南非投资合作企业座谈会(见图 4-11)。截至 2023 年 1 月,海信南非家电产业园年产能为冰箱 50 万台、电视机 100 万台,不仅促进了当地制造业的可持续发展,而且为当地带来了大量的就业机会。

图 4-10　2016 年 5 月,山东省副省长孙伟一行视察海信南非工业园

图片来源:山东省人民政府外事办公室。

图 4-11 2016 年 9 月，山东省人大常委会副主任才利民出席山东省在南非投资合作企业座谈会

图片来源：山东省人民政府外事办公室。

西开普省是南非受教育程度最高的省份，有开普敦大学等知名院校。2004 年 6 月，山东省与西开普省签署了《关于进一步加强友好关系和文化教育合作的联合声明》。2007 年 1 月，山东省教育厅与南非西开普省教育厅签署了关于加强教育合作的备忘录。2007 年 10 月，南非西开普省省长拉苏尔带领教育代表团访问山东省，对山东省实验小学、山东省泰山中学和泰山外国语学校、山东省泰安市实验学校、山东省泰安第一中学、泰山职业技术学院等进行了考察。西开普省省长拉苏尔还向山东省实验小学捐赠了价值 4 万元人民币的英语图书。在西开普省省长拉苏尔访问期间举行的“山东-西开普省对口部门洽谈会”上，青岛农业大学和西开普省博兰德学院签署了《青岛农业大学和博兰德学院关于继续教育与培训交流项目的合作声明》，确立了两校的姊妹学校关系及开展海洋生物与水产养殖等多方面合作的意向。2008 年 3 月，青岛农业大学派出一个由 5 人组成的专业小组赴西开普省进行鲍鱼养殖研究和培训，双方的教育合作逐步深化。

2007 年 10 月，山东省体育局与西开普省文化和体育部签署了合作备忘录，建立了今后对口交流的合作机制。2014 年 7 月，双方签署了体育交流合作协议，就加强教练员、运动员、科研人员互访及高水平运动员训练、青少年培养、训练设施建设和体育产业等进行了广泛的交流合作。

2015 年，山东省青岛市副市长栾新率代表团拜会西开普省文化事务和体育部及帆船协会并签署了帆船交流合作协议。2016 年 9 月，青岛市与西开普省商定继续履行已经签署的合作协议，继续加强体育高层互访交流，双方多次互派帆船、自行车、马拉松、风筝等项目运动员赴友好省州参加相关赛事。2017 年 8 月，青岛国际帆船周·青岛国际海洋节期间，青岛市帆船运动管理中心与南非西开普省帆船协会签署了《2017—2018 青岛市和南非西开普省帆船协会青少年帆船互访交流协议》。2019 年 3 月，双方续签《2019—2020 青岛市和南非西开普省帆船协会青少年帆船互访交流协议》。2015—2019 年，南非西开普省举行帆船锦标赛，山东省青岛市每年均派代表团参赛并进行青少年帆船运动交流。2016—2019 年，南非西开普省派青少年代表团参加了青岛国际 OP 帆船营暨帆船赛（见图 4-12）。2022 年 8 月，南非西开普省帆船协会前主席贝夫·勒·叙厄尔（Bev Le Sueur）通过发送祝福视频的方式参与了第十四届青岛国际帆船周·青岛国际海洋节。

2023 年 3 月，山东省人民政府外事办公室副主任李荣率工作组访问南非西开普省，拜会西开普省政府，与西开普省政府办公厅主任哈利·马里拉（Harry Malila）进行了工作会谈，双方就进一步加强友好省州交往、职业教育、新能源等领域的合作达成了共识。

图 4-12　2016 年 8 月，青岛国际 OP 帆船营暨帆船赛闭营式合照

图片来源：山东省人民政府外事办公室。

## 四、山东省与魁北克省的交流合作

1991 年 10 月山东省与加拿大魁北克省建立友好合作关系，2008 年 8 月双方正式缔结友好省州关系，建立了山东省-魁北克省联合工作组，形成了定期交流的工作组机制，建立了各层级和各领域的友好关系。在友好省州框架下，双方人员互访频繁，经贸、科技、文化、旅游等领域合作进展顺利。

魁北克省来访的主要有省长让・沙雷(2005、2008、2011)，国际关系部部长莫尼卡・加依-全布雷(2005、2006、2008)，国际关系部部长皮埃尔・阿尔康(Pierre Arcand，2009)，国际关系、法语地区事务及国际贸易部部长让-弗朗索瓦・利泽(Jean-François Lisée，2013)，省长菲利普・库亚尔(2014)，国民议会议长雅克・夏农(Jacques Chagnon，2016)，国际关系及法语国家事务部部长克里斯蒂娜・圣皮埃尔(2016)，卫生部部长盖伊丹・巴莱特(Gaetan Barrette，2017)，能源与自然资源部部长皮埃尔・阿尔康(2017)。

山东省出访的领导人主要有姜春云(1991)、朱正昌(2003)、韩寓群(2004)、王军民(2005)、尹忠显(2005)、才利民(2012)、夏耕(2012)、孙伟(2015)、贾万志(2015)、龚正(2016)、孙继业(2018)。

2008 年，山东省和魁北克省签署了建立友好省州关系协议书。2009 年 6 月山东省与魁北克省在魁北克市成立友好省州联合工作组，并召开第一次工作组会议，共同筛选了第一批合作项目，建立了定期交流工作组机制，每两年筛选一批合作项目。此后，分别于 2011 年 8 月、2013 年 10 月、2015 年 9 月、2018 年 1 月、2019 年 7 月召开了会议，筛选确定了六批 39 个合作项目，涉及航空、文化、教育、环保、旅游、新材料、医疗卫生等领域。

山东省与魁北克省同为友好省州领导人峰会机制的倡议方与创始成员，友好省州领导人峰会成为两省领导定期会见、交流经验、推动合作的重要平台，促进了两省友好省州关系的正式建立和各领域交流活动的开展。在历次峰会期间，山东省领导人都与魁北克省领导人进行了会见。2008 年 1 月，山东省副省长才利民会见了来访的魁北克省国际关系部部长莫尼卡・加依-全布雷(见图 4-13)。2008 年 8 月，在第四次友好省州领导人峰会期间，山东省与魁北克省正式建立了友好省州关系。2011 年 8 月，中共山东省委书记姜异康会见来访的魁北克省省长让·沙雷(见图 4-14)。2014 年 10 月,山东省省长郭树清会见来访的魁北克省省长菲利普·库亚尔(见图 4-15)。2015 年 9 月,山东省人大常委会副主任贾万志率团访问了魁北克省,会见了魁北克省国民议会议长雅克·夏农。2016 年 1 月,魁北克省国民议会议长雅克·夏农率团访问了济南和济宁,中共山东省委书记、山东省人大常委会主任姜异康在济南会见了魁北克省国民议会议长雅克·夏农,山东省人大常委会副主任柏继民与魁北克省国民议会议长雅克·夏农共同签署了《山东省人民代表大会与魁北克省国民议会合作谅解备忘录》。2016 年 3 月,山东省副省长夏耕会见来访的魁北克省国际关系部部长克里斯蒂娜·圣皮埃尔(见图 4-16)。2020 年 9 月,奥地利上奥州主办友好省州领导人峰会科学网络新冠肺炎疫情专题线上会议,山东省副省长任爱荣出席并致辞,魁北克省双边关系部副部长纳丁·吉罗(Nadine Girault)出席会议。

图 4-13　2008 年 1 月,山东省副省长才利民会见来访的魁北克省国际关系部部长莫尼卡·加依-全布雷

图片来源:山东省人民政府外事办公室。

图 4-14　2011 年 8 月，中共山东省委书记姜异康会见来访的魁北克省省长让·沙雷

图片来源：山东省人民政府外事办公室。

图 4-15　2014 年 10 月，山东省省长郭树清会见来访的魁北克省省长菲利普·库亚尔

图片来源：山东省人民政府外事办公室。

图 4-16　2016 年 3 月，山东省副省长夏耕会见来访的魁北克省国际关系部部长克里斯蒂娜·圣皮埃尔

图片来源：山东省人民政府外事办公室。

2009 年，山东省教育厅与魁北克国际教育署签署协议，支持山东省与魁北克省开展学生、教师互换交流项目。2011 年，曲阜师范大学与凡尼尔学院开展第二语言教学合作，并纳入第二次联合工作组会议重点支持项目。2013 年，山东大学法学院与希尔布鲁克大学就环境领域争端问题的和平解决与预防开展合作，并纳入第三次联合工作组会议重点支持项目；山东省教育厅与魁北克省普通及职业教育厅签署协议，开展职业教育领域合作。2015 年，山东省教育厅与魁北克省大专院校联盟(CEGEP)签署协议，深化魁北克省大专院校与山东省大专院校间的交流合作。2014 年，在山东省省长郭树清与魁北克省省长菲利普·库亚尔的见证下，山东师范大学附属小学与蒙特利尔玛格丽特·布尔瓦教育局签署了合作协议。2014 年，山东师范大学附属小学派出 30 名小学生前往魁北克圣乔治学校、圣玛丽学校进行为期一年的留学生活。

此外，山东省与魁北克省还开展了一系列人员交流培训合作。2008—2009 年，山东省人民政府外事办公室与魁北克省国际关系部签署了青年公务员交流协议，互派工作人员前往对方部门进行交流访问，加深了双方的相互了解。2015 年，由中共山东省委组织部、山东省民政厅及山东省人民政府外事办公室共同组织的“山东省养老服务产业精准交流团”一行 14 人访问了魁北克省蒙特利尔市，与魁北克省开启了养老服务领域的交流与合作。

2011 年，山东大学齐鲁医院与希尔布鲁克医院合作开展放射肿瘤学领域综合研究合作。2016 年，青岛大学与蒙特利尔大学签署了《青岛大学、蒙特利尔大学、蒙特利尔大学中心医院、圣贾斯汀医院医疗与大学合作项目框架协议》。2017 年，魁北克省卫生部部长盖伊丹・巴莱特率团访问山东省，与山东省卫生健康委员会开展了座谈。2017 年，山东省疾病预防控制中心与麦吉尔大学皇家进修学院签署了合作备忘录。2018 年，山东大学齐鲁医院放射肿瘤科与希尔布鲁克大学开展放射肿瘤学领域的合作。2021 年，加拿大驻华大使馆参赞、魁北克省政府驻华办事处主任雷平江（Jean-François Lépine）一行访问山东省，双方共同举办了“魁北克绿色建筑与生命科学企业 2021 山东省路演”。

2009 年，山东省旅游局与魁北克省旅游部在济南签署了《中国山东省旅游局和加拿大魁北克省旅游部合作备忘录》。2009 年，山东省向魁北克省赠送《孔子像》（见图 4-17）。山东省副省长王随莲、魁北克省省长让・沙雷、中国驻加拿大大使兰立俊及魁北克省当地政要和华侨华人约 70 人参加了落成典礼。《孔子像》被安置在魁北克市议会大厦旁，成为两省友好合作的见证。2011 年，魁北克省向山东省回赠大型铝制镂空雕塑艺术品《曲柳和北欧松》（见图 4-18）。雕塑坐落于济南市泉城公园，山东省省长姜大明与魁北克省省长让・沙雷为雕塑揭幕。2013 年，山东省文物局与魁北克省文明博物馆达成协议，深化博物馆领域的交流合作。2014 年，魁北克省参加在山东省青岛市举办的世界园艺博览会并设立展园，获得世园会室外展园竞赛银奖。2018 年，魁北克省驻北京和青岛办事处公共政治处主管何文涛（Tommie Hamel）一行赴山东大学参加了“三月香颂饕餮”音乐巡演活动。

图 4-17　2009 年，山东省向魁北克省赠送《孔子像》

图片来源：山东省人民政府外事办公室。

图 4-18　2011 年，魁北克省向山东省回赠大型铝制镂空雕塑艺术品《曲柳和北欧松》

图片来源：山东省人民政府外事办公室。

## 五、山东省与佐治亚州的交流合作

佐治亚州位于美国东南部，是山东省与美国东南地区交往合作的重要支点。2004 年，佐治亚州参议员泽尔·米勒(Zell Miller)访问山东省，开启了两省州的正式交往。2008 年，佐治亚州加入友好省州领导人峰会。2011 年，山东省和佐治亚州建立友好合作关系。

佐治亚州来访的领导主要有参议员泽尔·米勒(2004)、州长索尼·珀杜(2008)、州长纳森·迪尔(2011、2013)。山东省访问佐治亚州的领导主要有副省长王随莲(2009)、省长郭树清(2014)。

2008 年，佐治亚州在第四次友好省州领导人峰会期间正式加入了友好省州领导人峰会；佐治亚州州长索尼·珀杜参加了峰会并访问了山东省青岛市；中共山东省委书记姜异康会见了佐治亚州代表团一行，山东省省长姜大明与佐治亚州州长索尼·珀杜举行了工作会谈，达成了在医疗卫生、生物制药、体育管理等方面开展合作交流的意向。2010 年，在第五次友好省州领导人峰会期间，山东省省长姜大明与佐治亚州政府行政执行官特雷·切尔杰斯进行了双边会谈。2012 年，在第六次友好省州领导人峰会期间，山东省副省长才利民与佐治亚州副州长凯西·凯格尔进行了双边会谈。2014 年，在第七次友好省州领导人峰会期间，山东省省长郭树清与佐治亚州州长纳森·迪尔进行了双边会谈。2016 年，在第八次友好省州领导人峰会期间，山东省省长郭树清与佐治亚州州长纳森·迪尔进行了双边会谈。2018 年，在第九次友好省州领导人峰会期间，山东省副省长孙继业与佐治亚州经济发展署署长韦宏森进行了双边会谈。

2011 年 1 月，中美省州长论坛成立，由中国人民对外友好协会与美国全国州长协会联合建立，是山东省与美国地方政府间交往的重要平台。2011 年 10 月，在北京首届中美省州长论坛第二轮对话期间，山东省省长姜大明与佐治亚州州长纳森·迪尔进行了双边会谈，双方签署了《山东省与佐治亚州建立友好合作关系协议》，正式建立友好合作关系。

2008 年，山东省体育局派代表团访问了亚特兰大市的奥运体育场馆。2009 年，山东省副省长王随莲率山东省政府代表团访问了佐治亚州，会见了佐治亚州众议院执行议长贝赫特(Burkhalter)，访问了埃默里大学整形和脊柱中心针灸诊所、美国联邦疾病控制中心。2013 年 8 月 26 日，山东省-佐治亚州经贸洽谈会在济南开幕，山东省省长郭树清、佐治亚州州长纳森·迪尔出席开幕式并致辞(见图 4-19)。2014 年，佐治亚州在青岛世界园艺博览会设立展园，并获得室外展园竞赛特等奖。2014 年 6 月，山东省在佐治亚州立大学里阿托艺术中心举办了孔子圣迹图片展，山东省省长郭树清在第七次友好省州领导人峰会期间与佐治亚州总检察长及亚特兰大市市长代表等出席了图片展开幕式(见图 4-20)。

图 4-19　2013 年 8 月，山东省省长郭树清出席山东省-佐治亚州经贸洽谈会开幕式

图片来源：山东省人民政府外事办公室。

图 4-20　2014 年 6 月，山东省省长郭树清出席第七次友好省州领导人峰会

图片来源：山东省人民政府外事办公室。

2015年,美中文化教育基金会组织佐治亚童声合唱团赴中国巡演。2017年,山东省旅游发展委员会派团访问亚特兰大市,参加“2017中美旅游高层对话”会议。2019年春节期间,山东省组派艺术团赴亚特兰大市举办“欢乐春节”演出活动,参加了当地举行的第二十六届春节文艺晚会。2021年6月15日,山东省人民政府外事办公室和佐治亚州经济发展署共同举办“共商疫后合作:中国山东-美国佐治亚线上交流会”(见图4-21)。

图4-21　2021年6月,中国山东-美国佐治亚线上交流会成功举办

图片来源:山东省人民政府外事办公室。

## 六、山东省与圣保罗州的交流合作

圣保罗州是山东省在巴西开展合作的重点州之一。近年来,双方在体育、教育、警务、抗疫等领域开展了交流合作。

山东省出访的领导主要有莫振奎(2004)、韩寓群(2006)、高新亭和王随莲(2010)、才利民(2012)、柏继民(2014)等。

2006年,圣保罗州加入友好省州领导人峰会。在第三次友好省州领导人峰会期间,山东省省长韩寓群与圣保罗州副州长古登伯格(Guttenberg)进行了交流。2010年,山东省副省长王随莲访问巴西,并会见圣保罗州秘书长墨雷(Murray)(见图4-22)。2012年,山东省副省长才利民出席了第六次友好省州领导人峰会(见图4-23),与圣保罗州州长阿尔克明(Alckmin)进行了会谈。2016年,在第八次友好省州领导人峰会期间,山东省省长郭树清与圣保罗州副州长玛西亚·弗兰萨进行了会谈。2018 年，山东省副省长孙继业出席了第九次友好省州领导人峰会，与圣保罗州环境部部长毛利西奥·布鲁撒丁进行了会谈。2020 年，圣保罗州国际关系厅厅长出席了友好省州领导人峰会科学网络新冠肺炎疫情专题线上会议并发言。

图 4-22　2010 年，山东省副省长王随莲会见圣保罗州秘书长墨雷

图片来源：山东省人民政府外事办公室。

图 4-23　2012 年，山东省副省长才利民出席第六次友好省州领导人峰会

图片来源：山东省人民政府外事办公室。

在教育和文化领域，山东省高校与巴西建立了六对友好合作关系，其中与巴西圣保罗州建立了两对友好合作关系。2013 年，山东省政协副主席张传林一行拜会了巴西圣保罗市文化中心（见图 4-24）。2018 年，山东省向圣保罗州提供友城奖学金，圣保罗州国际关系厅派代表来山东省高校交流学习。2019 年，潍坊医学院与巴西大学开展校际互访并签署合作协议，双方主要开展师生交流、医疗相关领域的学术交流和科研合作等。

图 4-24　2013 年，山东省政协副主席张传林一行拜会巴西圣保罗市文化中心

图片来源：山东省人民政府外事办公室。

在体育领域，2013 年，山东省体育局率团访问圣保罗州，就足球教练员引进、球员培养等进行了洽谈。2015 年，山东省体育局再次率团访问圣保罗州，与圣保罗州体育、娱乐及青年厅就推动两省州体育机构、教练和运动员交流与举办友谊赛事等签署了意向书。2017 年，圣保罗州国际关系厅派代表访问山东省，与山东省体育局就加强体育合作、落实意向书相关内容进行了交流。

2021 年，山东省人民对外友好协会授予圣保罗州投资促进局国际事务经理佩德罗·巴雷托·朗西亚罗（Pedro Barreto Ranciaro）“友好使者”称号。

# Part Ⅱ　Practices

## Chapter 4　Exchanges and Cooperation between Local Governments

Shandong is a leading province in economy, culture and resources. Following the national strategic plan, Shandong is accelerating transformation of growth drivers, promoting ecological conservation and high-quality development of the Yellow River Basin and establishing remarkable low-carbon pilot zones to achieve economic transformation and build itself into a great modern province. The seven sister provinces and states are among the strongest both in economy and technology in their respective countries, providing great possibilities to the cooperation within the framework of the summit. Over the last two decades, Shandong Province has forged close partnerships with other sister provinces and states with great achievements.

### 4.1　Exchanges and Cooperation between Shandong Province and Bavaria

The official reciprocal visits between Shandong Province and Bavaria, Germany started from 1983. The two sides signed the Letter of Intent for Economic and Technical Cooperation in 1984 and the Memorandum of Understanding in 1985. On 9 July 1987, they formally established a sister province/state relationship. Frequent high-level reciprocal visits and multiple cooperation projects have bred incredible achievements and resulted in an all-dimensional, multi-tiered and wide-ranging connection between Shandong and Bavaria. Based on years of cooperation, Jiang Yikang, then Secretary of the CPC Shandong Provincial Committee and Chairman of the Standing Committee of the Shandong Provincial People's Congress, and Seehofer, then Minister-President of Bavaria, signed the *Agreement on Strategic Partnership between Shandong and Bavaria* in Munich of Germany in 2010, bringing their relationship of sister cities to a higher level. In May 2017, Horst Seehofer, Minister-President of Bavaria, led a delegation to visit Shandong and met with Liu Jiayi, Secretary of the CPC Shandong Provincial Committee (see Figure 4-1). Gong Zheng, then Deputy Secretary of the CPC Shandong Provincial Committee and Governor of Shandong Province, and Seehofer, signed the *Joint Statement on Furthering Cooperation and Strategic Partnership*, fostering the cooperation between the two sides. The Denkendorfer Blasmusik of Bavaria came to Shandong with Minister-President Seehofer. Gong Zheng, the then Governor of Shandong Province, appreciated its performance and took a group photo with the Denkendorfer Blasmusik (see Figure 4-2). In November 2017, Executive Vice Governor Li Qun, along with Ms. Beate Merk, Bavaria's State Minister for European and International Affairs, Mr. Bocklet, First Vice President of the Bavarian State Parliament, Ms. Männl, Chairman of the Hanns Seidel Stiftung, and Ms. Mao Jingqiu, Consul General of Shandong Province in Munich, jointly attended the reception for the 30-year Partnership betwen Shandong Province and Bavaria, Germany (see Figure 4-3, 4-4, 4-5).

Figure 4-1 Horst Seehofer, Minister-President of Bavaria, meeting with Liu Jiayi, Secretary of the CPC Shandong Provincial Committee, during his visit to Shandong (November 2017)

Photo Credit: Foreign Affairs Office of Shandong Provincial People's Government.

Figure 4-2 Photo of Denkendorfer Blasmusik of Bavaria and Gong Zheng, Governor of Shandong Province (November 2017)

Photo Credit: Foreign Affairs Office of Shandong Provincial People's Government.

Figure 4-3  Shandong and Bavaria mark 30 years of relations (November 2017)

Photo Credit: Website of the State of Bavaria China Office (http://www.bavaria-china.com/article.aspx? id=5).

Figure 4-4  *Confucius Ceremony Musical Dance* in the reception
for the 30-year Partnership betwen Shandong Province and Bavaria, Germany

Photo Credit: Foreign Affairs Office of Shandong Provincial People's Government.

Figure 4-5  Executive Vice Governor Li Qun and Ms. Beate Merk, Bavaria's State Minister for European and International Affairs attending the reception for the 30-year Partnership betwen Shandong Province and Bavaria, Germany (2017)

Photo Credit: Foreign Affairs Office of Shandong Provincial People's Government.

On the basis of the sister province/state partnership, Shandong and Bavaria have conducted extensive exchanges and cooperation, and established 4 pairs of prefecture/county-level partnerships (Jinan-Augsburg, Weifang-Freising, Tai'an-Swabia, and Laizhou-Schwandorf), and 5 pairs of prefecture-level partnerships (Qingdao-Regensburg, Dongying-Bad Kissingen, Jining-Upper Franconia, Weifang-Aschaffenburg, and Qufu-Bamberg).

Both sides are seeing increasingly frequent high-level reciprocal visits. Previous leaders of Shandong Province, such as Liang Buting (1985), Zhao Zhihao (1991), Jiang Chunyun (1994), Li Chunting (1996, 2000), Han Yuqun (2003), Jiang Yikang (2010), Guo Shuqing (2016), and Gong Zheng (2018) have led delegations to visit Bavaria many times. The previous Minister-Presidents of Bavaria, Strauss (1985), Edmund Stoiber (1995, 2003) and Horst Seehofer (2010 and 2017), also led delegations to visit Shandong. The Presidents of the Landtag of Bavaria, Böhm (2000), Glück (2008), and Stamm (2011, 2012, 2017), also visited Shandong

Province successively. On 2 September 2021, Li Ganjie, then Deputy Secretary of the CPC Shandong Provincial Committee and Governor of Shandong Province, held a high-level virtual dialogue with Markus Söder, Minister-President of Bavaria.

On 26 January 2023, "Shandong-Bavaria Industry Cooperation Seminar" was successfully held by the Department of Commerce of Shandong Province in Munich, Bavaria, Germany. During the campaign for the park promotion, participants from Chinese and German enterprises and the park had in-depth discussions on market potential, industrial policies, investment costs, supporting measures and other fields to enhance mutual understanding and seek cooperation opportunities.

On 1 March 2023, the dialogue between China (Shandong) and Bavaria, Germany was successfully held online, the participants of which include Deng Yunfeng, Vice Governor of Shandong Province, and Söder, Minister-President of Bavaria, Germany.

With the ever-deepening sister province/state relationship between Shandong and Bavaria, paired cooperation mechanisms between branches of government and institutions were established, guaranteeing and amplifying the growth of key cooperation fields.

In the field of economy and trade, Weichai Power has successively invested EUR 2.3 billion to participate in the listing and restructuring of German KION Group, and EUR 450 million to complete the restructuring of Linde Hydraulics. As a result, a large number of high-quality jobs have been created for the local people, and sister city relationships have been established between Weifang and Aschaffenburg, Bavaria. All of these have yielded remarkable economic and social benefits through round-trip investment. The long-term strategic cooperation between China National Heavy Duty Truck Group Co., Ltd. (CNHTC) and MAN in Germany has greatly improved CNHTC's independent research and development capabilities. In September 2018, the first H135 helicopter was delivered in

Qingdao, where Airbus Helicopter Germany established the first H135 helicopter final assembly line outside Europe. Siemens established an innovation center in Qingdao, the only Siemens R&D and Innovation Center in China focusing on "smart manufacturing". Weifang Goertek has been cooperating with Germany Infineon for ten years, and the areas of cooperation involve silicon microphone and sensor projects.

Shandong and Bavaria jointly established the "Shandong-Bavaria Educational Cooperation Programme Commission" in November 1993, and take turns to hold meetings every two years to coordinate their cooperation on education. Against this background, Sino-German University Cooperation Center and Bavaria-China Higher Education Cooperation Center were established by the two sides separately in 2007. In 1996, the two sides created the Shandong-Bavaria Urban Construction Advisory Committee to hold meetings, seminars and training courses periodically. Shandong Radio & TV Station and Bavarian Radio (Bayerischer Rundfunk) signed an agreement in 1999 for regular exchanges and renew the cooperation agreement every two years. In March 2018, the first meeting of the Shandong-Bavaria Strategic Coordination Group was held in Jinan, Shandong Province, at which the relevant departments of both sides jointly made the 2018-2019 annual cooperation plan, covering economy and technology, education and training, rural development and urban planning, health and environmental protection, culture and sports.

One of the highlights of the extensive cooperation between Shandong Province and Bavaria is the comprehensive education cooperation, from primary and secondary education, vocational education, to higher education. Supported and joined by the State Office and the Ministries of Education and Agriculture of Bavaria, Technical University of Munich, and Academy for Teacher Training and Personnel Development in Dillingen, Hanns Seidel Foundation headquartered in Munich has cooperated with Shandong Province in related aspects. They established the Weichai

Vocational Training Center in Weifang in 1989, the Center of Dual-System of Vocational Education and Training in Agriculture in Pingdu, Qingdao in 1990, the Center of Teachers' Training of Vocational Education in Qingzhou, Weifang in 1998, and training bases with Qingdao Economic and Technological Development Zone, Management Committee of the Sino-German Ecopark, Qingdao West Coast Vocational Education Construction Development Co., Ltd. and vocational schools in 2012. Bavaria has poured more than EUR 30 million into the above projects and sent over 300 short and long-term experts for them.

The collaboration between Shandong Province and Bavaria in higher education also yielded impressive results. Shandong University, Shandong Normal University, Ocean University of China, Shandong University of Science and Technology (SDUST), Qingdao University, Shandong Agricultural University (SDAU) and other universities have built friendly inter-university relations with Bavaria for various forms of cooperation. Shandong Academy of Governance and the Bavarian Administrative School (Bayerische Verwaltungsschule or "BVS") share a long history of close relations, and maintain frequent and efficient exchanges and cooperation.

Bavaria has funded Shandong to cultivate more than 1,000 professional and technical personnel in railways, aviation, finance, telecommunications, communications, measurement, beer, enterprise management, public security, administrative management, and rural development. It has created Beer Technology Center at Qilu University of Technology, and Telecommunication Technology Center at Shandong Telecommunication School.

In April 2020, Shandong Provincial People's Government, a sister province of Bavaria, donated masks to Bavaria to fight against the COVID-19 pandemic (see Figure 4-6).

Figure 4-6 Shandong Provincial People’s Government donating masks to Bavaria (April 2020)
Photo Credit: Foreign Affairs Office of Shandong Provincial People’s Government.

## 4.2 Exchanges and Cooperation between Shandong Province and Upper Austria

In September 1996, Li Chunting, Governor of Shandong Province, and his delegation visited Upper Austria, and signed an agreement to establish a sister province/state partnership with Upper Austria with Pühringer, Governor of Upper Austria. Since then, both sides have witnessed frequent high-level exchanges, and worked together closely on economy and trade, humanity, education and energy.

Leaders of Shandong Province that have visited Upper Austria include Han Yuqun (2006), Jiang Yikang (2010), Wang Suilian (2012), Xia Geng (2015), Yu Jiancheng (2016), Yu Xiaoming (2017), Sun Licheng (2018), and Bai Yugang (2023).

Leaders of Upper Austria that have visited Shandong Province include Deputy Governor Sigl (2007), Governor Pühringer (2008), Deputy

Governor Rudolf Anschober (2010), Deputy Governor Hiesl (2010), and Deputy Governor Haberlander (2019).

In October 2016, the members of Shandong Provincial Cultural Centre went to Linz, Upper Austria and held the"Cultural Exhibition from the Hometown of Confucius" to celebrate the 20th anniversary of the partnership between the two provinces, bolstering the exchange of traditional culture between the two sides. In November 2016, Mag. Thomas Stelzer, Governor of Upper Austria, met with a delegation of the Finance Office of Shandong Provincial People's Government (see Figure 4-7). In July 2017, the Government of Shinan District, Qingdao, invited artists from Austria and other countries to join the 2017 Shinan Wind Music Week. In December 2017, the exhibition"Europe in China • Contemporary Sculpture Exhibition from Germany, Austria and Switzerland", which encompassed 49 works, was held in Qingdao. In May 2018, Vice Governor Sun Jiye met with Ms. Haberlander, Deputy Governor of Upper Austria, Austria, during the Regional Leaders' Summit in Quebec, Canada (see Figure 4-8).

Figure 4-7　Mag. Thomas Stelzer, Governor of Upper Austria, meeting with a delegation of the Finance Office of Shandong Provincial People's Government (November 2016)

Photo Credit: Foreign Affairs Office of Shandong Provincial People's Government.

Figure 4-8 Vice Governor Sun Jiye meeting with Ms. Haberlander, Deputy Governor of Upper Austria, Austria, during the Leader's Summit in Quebec, Canada (May 2018)

Photo Credit: Foreign Affairs Office of Shandong Provincial People's Government.

Shandong University of Finance and Economics has a close partnership with University of Applied Sciences Upper Austria. In September 2019, the two universities co-hosted the “Beijing Humboldt Forum-Qilu Forum 2019”, and invited 14 upper Austrian entrepreneurs to have in-depth discussions with Shandong's entrepreneurs. In October 2019, Haberlander, Deputy Governor of Upper Austria, Austria, led a delegation to visit Shandong Province and attended the Shandong International Friendship Cities Conference for Cooperation and Development. During the conference, Haberlander visited Shandong University of Finance and Economics, where she signed a memorandum of partnership on education with the Shandong Provincial Education Department.

In 2013, the Shandong Administration of Sports and the Upper Austria Administration of Sports, Austria, signed a bilateral sports friendly exchange agreement. Since then, both sides have maintained frequent exchanges, high-level sports reciprocal visits and held exchange activities in fencing, equestrian, table tennis, badminton and other sports—from competition information sharing, reciprocal visits and coaching, to sports contests.

This is especially true in table tennis and badminton. Since the adoption of peer reception in 2014, the table tennis team and the badminton team of Upper Austria, Austria and the Shandong Province Table Tennis Badminton Sports Management Center would send each other a group of about 15 people for reciprocal visits each year, including executives, coaches and athletes for training and competition that last 3 to 4 weeks. This is called the bilateral sports exchange activity.

In May 2023, Bai Yugang, member of the Standing Committee of the CPC Shandong Provincial Committee and head of the Publicity Department visited Upper Austria. During the visit, the Shandong delegation held the unveiling ceremony for the "Upper Austria Administration of Sports (Austria)-Shandong Administration of Sports (China)—High-Level Training Base for Young Athletes". This is the first overseas high-level youth training base established by the Shandong Administration of Sports (see Figure 4-9).

Figure 4-9 Bai Yugang, member of the Standing Committee of the CPC Shandong Provincial Committee and head of the Publicity Department, and Mag. Thomas Stelzer, Governor of Upper Austria, inaugurating the "Upper Austria Administration of Sports (Austria)-Shandong Administration of Sports (China)—High-Level Training Base for Young Athletes" (2 May 2023)

Photo Credit: Shandong Administration of Sports.

## 4.3 Exchanges and Cooperation between Shandong Province and Western Cape

The Western Cape of South Africa established a formal partnership with Shandong Province on 26 November 1998, which marked the first pair of province-level relations established after China and South Africa established diplomatic relations and the first pair of provincial relations between Shandong and Africa.

In November 1998, Song Fatang, Executive Vice Governor of Shandong Province led a delegation to visit South Africa and signed the *Agreement on Establishing Friendly Inter-Provincial Relations between Shandong Province of the People's Republic of China and the Western Cape of the Republic of South Africa* with Morkel, Premier of the Western Cape Province.

Since then, both sides have maintained frequent high-level reciprocal visits. Visitors from Western Cape mainly include: Premier Gerald Morkel (2000), Speaker Doman (2001), Minister of Community Safety Ramatlakane (2004), Minister for Social Services and Poverty Alleviation Mqulwana (2004), Speaker Byneveldt (2006), Premier Rasool (2007), Minister of Local Government Environment and Development Planning Yuris (2008), Minister of Agriculture and Rural Development Van Rensburg (2011, 2012), and Minister for Finance Alan Winde and Minister of Agriculture and Rural Development Van Rensburg (2013). Visitors from Shandong mainly include: Cai Qiufang (2002), Wang Xiuzhi, Lin Shuxiang (2004), Lin Tingsheng (2005), Han Yuqun (2006), Shi Lijun (2008), Jia Wanzhi (2009), Wang Junmin (2009), Jiang Daming (2010), Yan Rongzhu (2011), Zhang Jianguo (2013), Sun Wei (2016), and Cai Limin (2016).

During our provincial leaders' visit to Western Cape, South Africa, many promotional activities such as economic and trade talks were held there to promote economic and trade exchanges between the two provinces. In March 2013, China-Africa Development Fund signed an investment cooperation agreement with Hisense Group Co., Ltd. to jointly invest in the construction of Hisense South Africa Industrial Park in the Atlantis Special Economic Zone. In May 2016, Sun Wei, member of the Standing Committee of the CPC Shandong Provincial Committee and Executive Vice Governor of Shandong Province, led a delegation to visit South Africa and investigated the Hisense South Africa Home Appliance Industrial Park (see Figure 4-10), the Africa (China) Production Means Exhibition and Sales Center, Mozambique Subsidiary of Jinan Yuxiao Group, Nairobi Exhibition and Sales Center of Weigao Medical, etc. invested by Shandong Province in the country. In September 2016, Cai Limin, the then Vice Chairman of the Standing Committee of the Shandong Provincial People's Congress, led his delegation to visit South Africa and attended the Symposium on "Shandong Invests in South Africa" (see Figure 4-11). As of January 2023, Hisense South Africa Appliance Industrial Park is capable of producing 500,000 refrigerators and 1 million TV sets annually, which not only promotes the sustainable development of local manufacturing industry, but also brings a lot of job opportunities to the local area.

Figure 4-10 The delegation led by Sun Wei, Vice Governor of Shandong Province, visiting Hisense South Africa Industrial Park (May 2016)

Photo Credit: Foreign Affairs Office of Shandong Provincial People's Government.

Figure 4-11 Cai Limin, then Vice Chairman of the Standing Committee of the Shandong Provincial People's Congress, attending the Symposium on “Shandong Invests in South Africa” (September 2016)

Photo Credit: Foreign Affairs Office of Shandong Provincial People's Government.

The Western Cape is the most educated province in South Africa and is home to renowned universities such as the University of Cape Town. In June 2004, Shandong Province and the Western Cape signed a joint statement on *Further Strengthening Friendly Relations and Cooperation in Culture and Education*. In January 2007, the Shandong Provincial Education Department and the Western Cape Education Department of South Africa signed a memorandum of understanding on enhancing educational cooperation. In October 2007, an education delegation of the Western Cape, South Africa led by Premier Rasool visited Shandong. They inspected Shandong Experimental Primary School, Taishan High School and Taishan Foreign Language School, Taian Experimental School of Shandong Province, Shandong Taian No. 1 Senior High School, and Taishan Polytechnic. Premier Rasool donated English books worth more than RMB 40,000 to the Shandong Experimental Primary School. At the “Shandong-Western Cape Counterpart Departments Meeting” held during the premier's visit, Qingdao Agricultural University and Boland College of the Western Cape signed a *Declaration of Qingdao Agricultural University and Boland College on Collaboration in Continuing Education and Training Exchange Programs*, to establish a sister school partnership and their intention to collaborate in various aspects such as marine biology and aquaculture. In March 2008, Qingdao Agricultural University sent a professional team of 5 to the Western Cape for abalone cultivation research and training, enhancing cooperation in education.

In October 2007, the Shandong Administration of Sports signed the *Memorandum of Cooperation* with the Department of Cultural Affairs & Sport of the Western Cape, establishing a mechanism for future exchanges and cooperation. In July 2014, both sides signed the *Sports Exchange and Cooperation Agreement*. They exchanged views on strengthening reciprocal visits of coaches, athletes and researchers, training of high-level athletes, youth cultivation, training facility construction, sports industry, etc.

In 2015, Luan Xin, then Vice Mayor of Qingdao, led a delegation to visit the Department of Cultural Affairs and Sport (DCAS) of Western Cape and the South African Sailing (SAS) and signed a sailing exchange and cooperation agreement. In September 2016, both sides agreed to continue performing their cooperation agreement and increase high-level reciprocal visits and exchanges in sports. Both sides have sent athletes of such events as sailing, cycling, marathon, and kiting to participate in relevant competitions in the sister province. During the Qingdao International Sailing Week • Qingdao International Marine Festival in August 2017, the Qingdao Administration Center of Sailing Sport and the South African Sailing signed the *Agreement on Youth Sailing Exchange between Qingdao and the South African Sailing from 2017 to 2018*. In March 2019, the two sides renewed the agreement for the period of 2019-2020. From 2015 to 2019, Western Cape of South Africa held the Sailing Champs, during which Qingdao sent a delegation to participate in the event and carried out youth sailing exchanges every year. From 2016 to 2019, Western Cape of South Africa sent delegations of teenagers to Qingdao to participate in the Qingdao International

Optimist Sailing Camp & Regatta (see Figure 4-12). In August 2022, Bev Le Sueur, former Chairman of South African Sailing (SAS), participated in the fourth Qingdao International Sailing Week • Qingdao International Marine Festival by means of sending a blessing video to Qingdao.

In March 2023, Li Rong, Deputy Director-General of Foreign Affairs Office of Shandong Provincial People's Government, led a working group to visit the Western Cape Government. A work talk was held between the working group and Harry Malila, Director-General (Administrative Head) of the Western Cape Government, during which the two sides have reached a consensus on further strengthening cooperation in sister city exchanges, vocational education, new energy and other fields.

Figure 4-12 Group photo on the Cosing Ceremony of Qingdao International Optimist Sailing Camp & Regatta (August 2016)

Photo Credit: Foreign Affairs Office of Shandong Provincial People's Government.

## 4.4 Exchanges and Cooperation between Shandong Province and Quebec

Shandong Province established partnerships with Quebec, Canada in October 1991. In August 2008, they established friendly inter-provincial relations and built the Shandong-Quebec Joint Working Group, creating the working mechanism of regular exchanges and building close relations of different levels and fields. In this framework, both sides remain frequent reciprocal visits and cooperation in economy and trade, science and technology, culture, and tourism.

Visitors from Quebec mainly include: Premier Jean Charet (2005, 2008, 2011), Minister of International Relations Tremblay (2005, 2006, 2008), Minister of International Relations Pierre Arcand (2009), Minister of International Relations, La Francophonie and External Trade Jean-François Lisée (2013), Premier Couillard (2014), President of the National Assembly of Quebec Jacques Chagnon (2016), Minister of International Affairs and La Francophone (MRIF) Québec Christine St-Pierre (2016), Quebec Health Minister Gaetan Barrette (2017), Minister of Energy and Natural Resources Pierre Arcand (2017).

Leaders from Shandong that have visited Quebec mainly include: Jiang Chunyun (1991), Zhu Zhengchang (2003), Han Yuqun (2004), Wang Junmin (2005), Yin Zhongxian (2005), Cai Limin (2012), Xia Geng (2012), Sun Wei (2015), Jia Wanzhi (2015), Gong Zheng (2016), and Sun Jiye (2018).

In 2008, Shandong Province and Quebec signed the *Agreement on Establishing Friendly Inter-provincial Relations*. In June 2009, Shandong Province and Quebec Province established a sister cities joint working group in Quebec City, and held the first working group meeting. During the meeting, they selected the first cooperation projects, and established a mechanism of regular exchanges and selecting projects every two years. Following this, they held meetings in August 2011, October 2013, September 2015, January 2018, and July 2019, identifying 6 batches of 39 cooperation projects, which cover the fields like the aviation, culture, education, environmental protection, tourism, new materials, medical and health care.

Shandong Province and Quebec are one of the initiators and creators of the summit. This summit facilitated the formal establishment of their friendly inter-provincial relations, and promoted both sides to meet regularly, exchange experience in a range of fields, and reinforce cooperation. During the previous summits, the leaders of Shandong Province met with the leaders of Quebec Province. In January 2008, Vice Governor Cai Limin met with a delegation led by Monique Gagnon-Tremblay, Minister of International Relations of Quebec, Canada (see Figure 4-13). In August 2008, during the fourth Regional Leaders' Summit held in Jinan, Shandong Province, the two provinces officially established a friendly inter-provincial relationship. In August 2011, Jiang Yikang, Secretary of the CPC Shandong Provincial Committee met with Jean Charet, Premier of Quebec, and his delegation (see Figure 4-14). In October 2014, Guo Shuqing, Governor of Shandong Province, met with Philippe Couillard, Premier of Quebec, and his delegation (see Figure 4-15). In September 2015, Jia Wanzhi, Vice Chairman of the Standing Committee of the Shandong Provincial People's Congress, led a delegation of the Shandong People's Congress to visit the President of the National Assembly of Quebec Jacques Chagnon. In January 2016, President of the National Assembly of Quebec Jacques Chagnon, and his delegation visited Jinan and Jining. Jiang Yikang, Secretary of the CPC Shandong Provincial Committee and Chairman of the Standing Committee of the Shandong Provincial People's Congress, met with President Chagnon and his delegation in Jinan. Bai Jimin, Vice Chairman of the Standing Committee of the Shandong Provincial People's Congress and President Chagnon signed the *Memorandum of Understanding on Cooperation between the Shandong Provincial People's Congress and the National Assembly of Quebec*. In March 2016, Vice Governor Xia Geng met with Christine, the then Minister of International Relations of Quebec, Canada (see Figure 4-16). In September 2020, Upper Austria, Austria, hosted the RLS-Sciences Virtual Symposium on COVID-19 pandemic during the Regional Leaders' Summit, which was attended by Nadine Girault, Deputy Minister for Bilateral Relations for the Québec Department of International Relations and Vice Governor of Shandong Province Ren Airong who delivered a speech.

Figure 4-13 Vice Governor Cai Limin meeting with a delegation led by Monique Gagnon-Tremblay, Minister of International Relations of Quebec, Canada (January 2008)

Photo Credit: Foreign Affairs Office of Shandong Provincial People's Government.

Figure 4-14 Jiang Yikang, Secretary of the CPC Shandong Provincial Committee meeting with Jean Charet, Premier of Quebec, and his delegation (August 2011)

Photo Credit: Foreign Affairs Office of Shandong Provincial People's Government.

Figure 4-15 Guo Shuqing, Governor of Shandong Province, meeting with Philippe Couillard, Premier of Quebec, and his delegation (October 2014)

Photo Credit: Foreign Affairs Office of Shandong Provincial People's Government.

Figure 4-16 Vice Governor Xia Geng meeting with Christine, the then Minister of International Relations of Quebec, Canada (March 2016)

Photo Credit: Foreign Affairs Office of Shandong Provincial People's Government.

In 2009, the Shandong Provincial Education Department signed an agreement with the Quebec International Education Department to support exchange programs of students and teachers between Shandong Province and Quebec Province. In 2011, Qufu Normal University worked with the Vanier College in second language teaching, and selected it as one of the key projects of the second joint working group meeting. In 2013, University of Sherbrooke and the Shandong University School of Law collaborated on the peaceful resolution and prevention of environmental disputes, and selected them as one of the key projects of the third joint working group meeting. Shandong Provincial Education Department signed an agreement with the Quebec Provincial Department of General and Vocational Education to cooperate in vocational education. In 2015, the Shandong Provincial Education Department signed an agreement with the CEGEP to deepen exchanges and cooperation between colleges and universities of Quebec and Shandong Province. In 2014, the Primary School Attached to Shandong Normal University signed a cooperation agreement with the Marguerite-Bourgeoys School Board, Montreal, witnessed by Guo Shuqing, Governor of Shandong Province, and Couillard, Premier of Quebec Province. In 2014, the Primary School Attached to Shandong Normal University sent 30 students to St. George's School and St. Mary's School in Quebec for one-year study.

Both provinces also worked together on personnel exchanges and training. From 2008 to 2009, the Foreign Affairs Office of Shandong Provincial People's Government and the Ministry of International Relations of Quebec signed an agreement for exchanges between young civil servants, and sent members to each other, enhancing mutual understanding. In 2015, the "Precise Exchanges Group of Shandong's Elderly Care Service Industry" of 14 people, organized by the Organization Department of the Shandong Provincial Committee, the Department of Civil Affairs of Shandong Province and the Foreign Affairs Office of Shandong Provincial People's Government visited Montreal, and started exchanges and cooperation in elderly care services with Quebec.

In 2011, Qilu Hospital of Shandong University and Sherbrooke Hospital cooperated in comprehensive research of radiation oncology. In 2016, Qingdao University and the University of Montreal signed the *Framework Agreement on*

*Cooperation Projects between Qingdao University, University of Montreal, and Central Hospital University of Montreal, CHU Sainte-Justine*. In 2017, Quebec Health Minister Gaetan Barrette led a delegation to visit Shandong Province and had a discussion with Health Commission of Shandong Province. In 2017, Shandong Center for Disease Control and Prevention signed a memorandum of cooperation with the Royal Institution for the Advancement of Learning (RIAL) of McGill University. In 2018, the Radiation Oncology Department of Qilu Hospital of Shandong University and the University of Sherbrooke cooperated in the radiation oncology. In 2021, Jean-François Lépine, Counselor of the Embassy of Canada to China and Director of the Quebec Government Office in China, visited Shandong Province. Both sides held the "2021 Shandong Roadshow of Quebec Green Buildings and Life Science Enterprises".

In 2009, the Shandong Provincial Tourism Administration and the Ministry of Tourism of Quebec signed the *Memorandum of Cooperation between the Shandong Provincial Tourism Administration of China and the Ministry of Tourism of Quebec of Canada* in Jinan. In 2009, Shandong presented a statue of Confucius to Quebec as a gift (see Figure 4-17). At the inauguration ceremony, about 70 guests attended, including Wang Suilian, Vice Governor of Shandong Province, Charet, Premier of Quebec, Lan Lijun, Chinese Ambassador to Canada, other Quebec politicians and overseas Chinese people. The statue of Confucius, a token of the close cooperation between the two provinces, is placed next to the Parliament Building of Quebec. In 2011, Quebec reciprocated with a large hollowed aluminum sculpture "Manchurian Ash and Nordic Pine" (see Figure 4-18). Jiang Daming, Governor of Shandong Province, and Charet, Premier of Quebec, inaugurated the sculpture, which is located in Quancheng Park, Jinan City. In 2013, Shandong Province Cultural Relics Bureau and Museum of Civilization of Quebec entered into an agreement, deepening exchanges and cooperation in the field of museum. In 2014, Quebec participated in the World Horticultural Exposition held in Qingdao, and won the silver award with its exhibition house in the outdoor exhibition houses competition of the exposition. In 2018, Tommie Hamel, head of the Public Political Affairs of the Quebec Offices in Shanghai and Qingdao, and his delegation went to Shandong University in Jinan for the Concert Mars en Folie.

Figure 4-17 Shandong presenting a statue of Confucius to Quebec as a gift (2009)

Photo Credit: Foreign Affairs Office of Shandong Provincial People's Government.

Figure 4-18 Quebec reciprocating with a hollowed aluminum sculpture' Manchurian Ash (2011)

Photo Credit: Foreign Affairs Office of Shandong Provincial People's Government.

## 4.5 Exchanges and Cooperation between Shandong Province and Georgia

As an important state in the southeastern United States, Georgia is key for exchanges and cooperation between Shandong Province and the southeastern United States. In 2004, Georgia Senator Zell Miller visited Shandong Province, starting the official exchanges between the two sides. In 2008, Georgia joined the Regional Leaders' Summit. In 2011, Georgia and Shandong built a close cooperative tie, leading the cooperation into a new era.

Leaders from Georgia that have visited Shandong mainly include Senator Zell Miller (2004), Governor Sonny Perdue (2008), and Governor Nathan Deal (2011 and 2013). Leaders from Shandong that have visited Georgia mainly include Vice Governor Wang Suilian (2009) and Governor Guo Shuqing (2014).

In 2008, Georgia officially joined the summit during the fourth Regional Leaders' Summit hosted by Shandong Province. Sonny Perdue, Governor of Georgia, participated in the summit and visited Qingdao City. Jiang Yikang, Secretary of the CPC Shandong Provincial Committee met with the delegation. Governor Jiang Daming held a working meeting with Governor Perdue, intending to implement cooperation and exchanges in medical care, biopharmaceuticals, and sports management. In 2010, during the fifth Regional Leaders' Summit in Western Cape, South Africa, Governor Jiang Daming held a bilateral meeting with Childress, Chief Operating Officer, State of Georgia. In 2012, during the sixth Regional Leaders' Summit in São Paulo, Brazil, Vice Governor Cai Limin held a bilateral meeting with Casey Cagle, Lieutenant Governor of Georgia. In 2014, during the seventh Regional Leaders' Summit in Georgia, Governor Guo Shuqing held a bilateral meeting with Nathan Deal, Governor of Georgia. In 2016, during the eighth Regional Leaders' Summit in Bavaria, Governor Guo Shuqing held a bilateral meeting with Nathan Deal,

Governor of Georgia. In 2018, during the ninth Regional Leaders' Summit in Quebec, Vice Governor Sun Jiye held a bilateral meeting with Pat Wilson, Minister of the Georgia Department of Economic Development.

The China-U.S. Governors Forum, founded in January 2011 by the Chinese People's Association for Friendship with Foreign Countries and the National Governors Association of the United States, is a key platform for exchanges between Shandong Province and the local governments of the United States. In October 2011, during the second round of dialogue at the first China-U.S. Governors Forum in Beijing, Governor Jiang Daming held bilateral talks with Governor of Georgia Nathan Deal, and the two sides signed the *Agreement on the Establishment of Friendly and Cooperative Relations between Shandong Province and Georgia*, marking the formal establishment of friendly cooperative relationships between the two sides.

In 2008, Shandong Administration of Sports sent a delegation to visit the Centennial Olympic Stadium in Atlanta. In 2009, Vice Governor Wang Suilian led a delegation of Shandong Province to visit Georgia. During the trip, she met with the Speaker Pro Tempore of the Georgia House of Representatives Burkhalter, and visited the Acupuncture Clinic at the Emory Orthopaedics & Spine Center of Emory University, and the Centers for Disease Control and Prevention of the Federal Government of the United States. On 26 August 2013, Shandong-Georgia Economic & Trade Fair opened in Jinan. Guo Shuqing, Governor of Shandong Province, and Nathan Deal, Governor of Georgia, attended the opening ceremony and delivered speeches (see Figure 4-19). During the 2014 World Horticultural Exposition in Qingdao, Georgia won the special award with its exhibition house in the outdoor exhibition houses competition. In June 2014, Shandong Province held a photography exhibition of Confucius' sacred sites at the Rialto Center for the Arts of Georgia State University. During the seventh RLS, Governor Guo Shuqing, Georgia Attorney General, representatives of the Mayor of Atlanta and other people attended the opening ceremony (see Figure 4-20).

Figure 4-19 Guo Shuqing, Governor of Shandong Province, meeting with the delegation led by Nathan Deal, Governor of Georgia, and attending the Opening Ceremony of Shandong-Georgia Economic & Trade Fair (August 2013)

Photo Credit: Foreign Affairs Office of Shandong Provincial People's Government.

Figure 4-20 Guo Shuqing, Governor of Shandong Province, attending the seventh Regional Leaders' Summit in Georgia, (June 2014)

Photo Credit: Foreign Affairs Office of Shandong Provincial People's Government.

In 2015, the Atlanta-based US-China Cultural & Educational Foundation organized the Georgia Children's Chorus to tour in China. In 2017, the Shandong Provincial Tourism Development Committee visited Atlanta and attended the conference of "USA-China Tourism Leadership Summit (2017)". During the Spring Festival of 2019, Shandong Province organized an art troupe to perform in Atlanta with the theme of "Happy Spring Festival" and participated in the 26th Spring Festival Gala held there. On 15 June 2021, the Foreign Affairs Office of Shandong Provincial People's Government and the Georgia Department of Economic Development, USA co-hosted the "Seeking Cooperation in the Post-Pandemic Era: Georgia, USA-Shandong, China Online Conference" (see Figure 4-21).

Figure 4-21 Shandong, China-Georgia, USA Online Conference successfully held (June 2021)

Photo Credit: Foreign Affairs Office of Shandong Provincial People's Government.

## 4.6 Exchanges and Cooperation between Shandong Province and São Paulo

São Paulo is one of the key partners of Shandong Province in Brazil. In recent years, the two sides have carried out exchanges and cooperation in sports, education, police services, and the fight against the COVID-19 pandemic.

Leaders from Shandong that have visited São Paulo mainly include Mo

Zhenkui (2004), Han Yuqun (2006), Gao Xinting, Wang Suilian (2010), Cai Limin (2012), and Bai Jimin (2014).

In 2006, São Paulo joined the Regional Leaders’ Summit. During the third Regional Leaders’ Summit in Upper Austria, Han Yuqun, Governor of Shandong Province, exchanged views with Guttenberg, Vice Governor of São Paulo. In 2010, Vice Governor Wang Suilian met with Murray, Secretary-General of São Paulo, during her visit to Brazil (see Figure 4-22). In 2012, Vice Governor Cai Limin attended the sixth Regional Leaders’ Summit held in São Paulo (see Figure 4-23) and held talks with Governor Geraldo Alckmin. In 2016, Governor Guo Shuqing held talks with Márcio França, Vice Governor of São Paulo at the eighth Regional Leaders’ Summit held in Bavaria, Germany. In 2018, Vice Governor Sun Jiye attended the ninth Regional Leaders’ Summit held in Quebec City, Canada, and held talks with Maurício Brusadin, São Paulo’s Secretary of State for the Environment. In 2020, Secretary of International Relations of the State of São Paulo attended the RLS-Sciences Virtual Symposium on COVID-19 held during the Regional Leaders’ Summit and delivered a speech.

Figure 4-22　Vice Governor Wang Suilian meeting with Murray, Secretary-General of São Paulo, during her visit to Brazil (2010)

Photo Credit: Foreign Affairs Office of Shandong Provincial People’s Government.

Figure 4-23 Vice Governor Cai Limin attending the sixth Regional Leaders' Summit (2012)

Photo Credit: Foreign Affairs Office of Shandong Provincial People's Government.

In the education and culture sector, universities in Shandong Province have established six partnerships with those in Brazil, including two with those in São Paulo. In 2013, Zhang Chuanlin, Vice Chairman of the Shandong Provincial Committee of the CPPCC, and his delegation visited the Centro Cultural São Paulo, Brazil (see Figure 4-24). In 2018, Shandong Province provided a sister city scholarship to São Paulo, and the Department of International Relations of the State of São Paulo sent representatives to universities in Shandong Province for exchanges and study. In 2019, Weifang Medical University conducted intercollegiate visits and signed a cooperation agreement with University of São Paulo. The two sides mainly carry out teacher and student communication, academic exchanges and scientific research cooperation in medicine-related fields.

Figure 4-24 Zhang Chuanlin, Vice Chairman of the Shandong Provincial Committee of the CPPCC, and his delegation visiting the Centro Cultural São Paulo, Brazil (2013)

Photo Credit: Foreign Affairs Office of Shandong Provincial People's Government.

In the sports sector, the Shandong Administration of Sports led a delegation to visit São Paulo in 2013 for talks over the introduction of football coaches and training of players. In 2015, the Shandong Administration of Sports led another delegation to visit São Paulo and signed a letter of intent with the Department of Sports, Leisure and Youth of São Paulo (SELJ) on promoting exchanges between sports institutions, coaches, and athletes of the Province and the State, and holding friendly competitions. In 2017, the Department of International Relations of the State of São Paulo sent representatives to visit Shandong Province for exchanges with the Shandong Administration of Sports on strengthening cooperation in the sports sector and implementing the relevant content of the letter of intent.

In 2021, the Shandong People's Association for Friendship with Foreign Countries awarded the title of “Envoy of Friendship” to Pedro Barreto Ranciaro, Foreign Affairs Manager of São Paulo's Agency for the Promotion of Investments and Competitiveness.

# 第五章　绿色发展交流合作

为应对全球气候变化，探索安全、清洁、可持续的绿色发展模式，友好省州在开发和应用可再生能源生产、运输和分配技术以及提高能源效率方面加强交流，并鼓励各地区相关部门充分发挥在市场、资本、技术、机制等方面的优势，深挖合作潜力，共享发展机遇，携手打造绿色发展交流合作新亮点。

## 一、绿色建筑领域

2022 年 12 月 7 日，山东省举办了第十一次友好省州领导人峰会绿色建筑交流合作研讨会，这是第十一次友好省州领导人峰会会前系列活动之一（见图 5-1）。山东国舜建设集团有限公司和奥地利上奥州、德国巴伐利亚州、南非西开普省绿色建筑行业主管部门代表及绿色建筑领域项目专家线上出席了活动并进行了推介交流发言。会上，各省州共同倡议并启动了“绿色建筑灯塔行动计划”，进一步促进了各省州在绿色建筑、节能减排领域的交流合作。

图 5-1　2022 年 12 月 7 日，第十一次友好省州领导人峰会绿色建筑交流合作研讨会举行

图片来源：山东省人民政府外事办公室网站，http://wb.shandong.gov.cn。

### (一)山东省与巴伐利亚州的交流合作

1995 年，山东省住房和城乡建设厅与巴伐利亚州最高建设管理局签署了《山东省与巴伐利亚州关于开展城建合作与交流的协议》，为双方开展长期、稳定的对口交流与合作奠定了基础。在此基础上，近 30 年来，双方在互访交流、专业技术人员培训、项目示范、企业合作等方面均开展了广泛合作并取得了丰硕成果。

1.搭建合作平台

1996 年，山东省住房和城乡建设厅与巴伐利亚州最高建设管理局成立了山东-巴伐利亚州城建混合委员会，每两年召开一次会议。自 2006 年开始，改为每年轮流在济南或慕尼黑召开一次混合委员会会议。每次会议都要总结交流过去一段时间的合作成果，根据实际情况和需要协商确定未来的合作领域与重点，这对双方的合作起到了积极的促进作用。至今共签署过八次会谈备忘录，四次在山东，四次在巴伐利亚州，最近一次于 2015 年签署。

2.开展交流培训

山东省住房和城乡建设厅选派住建系统专业技术人员赴巴伐利亚州进

行了两批次为期三个月的培训、一批次为期一个月的培训、七批次21天以下的短期培训，邀请了巴伐利亚州共四名专家、教授来访并分别在山东举办讲座六次。2007年，山东省在巴伐利亚州举办了“山东城建成就展”“山东风情图片展”，巴伐利亚州在山东省举办了“德国节能建筑的设计与施工”展览、“中德建筑节能技术论坛”各一次。

3.示范项目合作

选定青岛石老人旧村改造项目作为双方第一个城建示范项目，巴伐利亚州选派一名设计师在山东省工作一个月，专门参与该小区的规划设计。该示范项目获得了中国优秀绿色生态社区、中国优秀旅游住宅项目等多个荣誉称号。2008年，双方确定了淄博桓台县马桥镇、泰安肥城市石横镇、滨州邹平市魏桥镇三个规划设计示范项目，设计方案等都已顺利完成并通过了评审。

4.推动双方建筑企业开展合作

一是以山东-巴伐利亚建筑师合作平台为依托，发挥山东省勘察设计协会的作用，鼓励更多的建筑设计企业参与平台合作。2007年，山东省建筑设计研究院与巴伐利亚州17家规划与建筑设计师事务所签署合作协议，成立巴伐利亚州建筑师山东合作办公室。在山东省住房和城乡建设厅与巴伐利亚州最高建设管理局的大力推荐支持下，两省州建筑设计与规划企业之间进行了广泛的合作。二是推动双方企业在低碳、绿色建筑等节能环保领域的合作。山东省大力推进建筑节能，既促进了节能环保产业的发展，也带动了德国先进技术产品的引进和推广。三是推动双方在建筑科研方面的合作。自2014年起，山东省启动省级被动式超低能耗绿色建筑试点示范项目建设。2014年，共筛选、确定了11个项目，全部列入住房和城乡建设部中德合作试点示范工程，由住房和城乡建设部科技发展促进中心和德国能源署给予全程技术指导。对其中的8个公益性项目，山东省财政列支6000万元补贴项目增量成本。2015年，又确定省级被动式超低能耗绿色建筑试点示范项目11个，给予财政奖补5400万元。

5.鲁巴共建特色小镇示范镇

2017—2019年，山东省住房和城乡建设厅与巴伐利亚州最高建设管理局共同推进鲁巴合作共建3个特色小镇示范镇。2018年11月，山东省住房和城乡建设厅厅长王玉志率团赴德国与巴伐利亚州最高建设管理局负责人、巴伐利亚州建筑师协会的规划设计师代表，就鲁巴共建德州禹城市房寺镇、临沂市费县上冶镇、莱芜市莱城区口镇等3个特色小镇项目进行了正式磋商，在项目规划设计重点、资料清单、合同进度、费用标准等方面达成了一致意见，推动3个特色小镇的工作取得重大进展。经过规划设计方案、根据专家意见修改完善设计方案等一系列工作，3个小镇的规划设计于2019年年底通过了专家论证。规划设计在特色镇区规划、循环产业园区规划、生态景观设计方面引入了德国的理念和技术，为打造乡村振兴齐鲁样板提供了借鉴。

6.举办中德建筑节能对接交流会

2021年10月29日，山东省住房和城乡建设厅会同中国国际贸易促进委员会山东省委员会与德国巴伐利亚州经济、统筹发展和能源部共同举办了线上线下的中德建筑节能对接交流会。中德9家企业(机构)进行推介交流；46家企业(机构)开展“一对一”洽谈，12家达成合作意向；中德8家企业在现场签订4项、3家企业在线上签订2项战略合作协议，参会企业满意度超过95%。

### (二)山东省与圣保罗州的交流合作

2017年、2019年，山东省住房和城乡建设厅两次应邀出访巴西，拜访了圣保罗州住房厅厅长弗拉维奥·阿玛丽(Flavio Amary)、投资促进局商务处处长雷纳托(Renato)，并进行了座谈交流，同时在圣保罗州进行了有关建筑政策对接、市场调研、企业推介、项目考察等。全面了解了圣保罗的建筑市场现状和发展前景，切身体会了中资企业承包国际工程面临的风险和困难，主要风险是标准体系不同、投资周期较长以及中方员工在语言、饮食、生活等方面存在障碍和困难等。巴西圣保罗州专门开辟了一个区用于外国企业注册公司，投资促进局专职负责协调当地政府部门及保障水电等供应，帮助企业落地开办。圣保罗州投资促进局还在上海设立了办公室，方便中资企业洽谈合作。

### (三)山东省与上奥州的交流合作

2016年，山东省住房和城乡建设厅应邀出访奥地利，拜访了上奥州政府办公厅，听取了关于上奥州城镇规划与乡镇能源供给的报告，交流了奥地利村镇规划编制、村镇规划建设管理法律法规政策、乡村居民点现状及历史变化情况、小城镇基础设施建设经验。借鉴奥地利小城镇规划建设管理经验，山东省编制印发了《山东省城镇化地区设施向农村延伸导则》，科学引导全省镇村之间扩大基础设施、公共服务设施实际连接范围，促进更多村庄享受城镇基础设施和公共服务。

## 二、绿色交通领域

2010 年 9 月，第五次友好省州领导人峰会以“粮食安全”和“交通一体化”为主题在南非西开普省举办。各省州领导人认为交通一体化直接影响人们的生活方式。伴随着科学技术的日益发达，交通出行呈现出快速化、多样化的趋势。各省州要加强交通一体化的研究，制定有关规划，本着快捷节约的原则统筹考虑交通一体化体制和机制问题；要加强交通基础设施建设，构建一体化交通格局，造福各省州人民。各省州一致同意在以往合作基础上深化交通一体化领域的合作，为峰会成员间的合作指明了方向。

2023 年 3 月 28 日，山东省以线上线下相结合的方式成功举办了第十一次友好省州领导人峰会会前系列活动之绿色交通合作研讨会（见图 5-2）。山东省人民政府外事办公室主任、山东省人民对外友好协会会长蔡先金出席活动并致辞，山东省交通运输厅、山东交通学院、山东高速集团、山东港口集团、浪潮智慧科技有限公司、海信网络科技有限公司等部门有关负责人，德国巴伐利亚州、奥地利上奥州、南非西开普省、加拿大魁北克省、美国佐治亚州、巴西圣保罗州交通部门代表以及绿色交通领域专家和企业负责人出席活动。

各友好省州通过此次研讨会开展绿色交通领域交流对接，倡导共同应对当前交通领域面临的挑战，坚持走绿色低碳高质量发展之路。山东省交通运输厅介绍了山东交通运输绿色低碳发展规划，表示欢迎各友好省州同行来山东省考察，开展交流合作，共同为世界可持续交通运输发展做出贡献。德国巴伐利亚州、奥地利上奥州、南非西开普省、加拿大魁北克省、美国佐治亚州、巴西圣保罗州交通部门代表分别介绍了绿色交通领域的政策规划，各省州企业代表及业界专家分别介绍了在绿色交通领域的经验做法，并表示愿在友好省州领导人峰会机制下积极开展绿色交通领域的交流合作。会上发布了“绿色交通合作发展济南倡议”，为友好省州绿色交通领域的交流合作奠定了良好基础。

图 5-2　2023 年 3 月 28 日，第十一次友好省州领导人峰会绿色交通合作研讨会举行

图片来源：山东省人民政府外事办公室网站，http://wb.shandong.gov.cn。

## 三、绿色能源领域

### （一）友好省州领导人峰会期间的交流合作

2006 年 7 月，在第三次友好省州领导人峰会上，各省州政府领导人强调了安全、可持续和可承担的能源供应对未来地区经济发展的重要性，指出为更好地利用能源而不断创新对增强竞争力和建设健康环境至关重要，要努力为所有国家提供洁净环保的能源技术。各省州政府领导人还讨论了世界市场当前的发展状况以及能源政策在国际关系方面与日俱增的战略重要性，认为地区经济发展的责任要求各与会政府实行积极的能源政策，并开展国内和国际合作。各方一致认为，能源利用方面的创新是提高竞争力和环保水平的关键，必须通过各种方式开发新能源。各地区要把清洁的和对气候友善的技术应用作为可持续能源政策的基本方针，目的是在促进经济增长的同时不给气候带来额外负担。

2008 年 8 月，在第四次友好省州领导人峰会期间，各省州领导人举行了双边和多边会谈，举办了“建设节约型社会”专题论坛和合作项目洽谈会。峰会确定了此后两年举办能源大会、世界太阳城大会等 16 项联合行动，山东省关于成立山东-巴伐利亚-上奥州三方能源环保合作协调委员会的倡议得到了积极响应，山东省与其他各省州将采取措施推动节能环保、现代农业、现代服务业等相关领域的合作，峰会达成节能减排合作协议 4 个、合作意向 12 个。

2012 年 4 月，在第六次友好省州领导人峰会期间，各省州代表团进行了多场双边会晤。山东省重点介绍了在推动可持续能源发展、倡导绿色经济方面取得的主要成果，并倡议峰会各省州政府通过倡导绿色发展理念、构建政策扶持体系、加强技术教育合作、完善沟通协调机制等共同致力于壮大可持续能源产业、推动可持续发展。

2014 年 6 月，第七次友好省州领导人峰会期间，山东省与佐治亚州针对能源、物流、金融、节能环保、机械制造等领域的合作提出了一系列建议。

2016 年 7 月，第八次友好省州领导人峰会通过了《第八次友好省州领导人峰会联合宣言》，对可再生能源网络等领域的交流合作做出了规划。

2018 年 5 月，第九次友好省州领导人峰会围绕气候变化、环境与健康、地方政府在能源转型方面的作为，以及人工智能与能源转型等议题进行了深入交流(见图 5-3)。峰会通过了《魁北克峰会能源转型联合宣言》和《友好省州领导人峰会路线图(2018—2020)》，总结了 2016 年第八次友好省州领导人峰会以来的合作成果，对推动能源转型、加强能源合作、提高能源转型能力建设、开展技术产业合作、加强企业指导、促进人工智能发展、改善环境健康等方面做出了规划。

图 5-3　2018 年 5 月，第九次友好省州领导人峰会能源领域专家庄庆发与魁北克省省长菲利普・库亚尔会谈

图片来源：山东省科技厅。

## (二)友好省州领导人峰会机制下的交流合作

1.能源大会

2010 年 4 月 29 日，中国・青岛国际新能源论坛暨中德企业合作发展峰会在青岛举行。论坛以“新能源与可持续发展”为主题，组织开展了“新能源开发与利用”“节能减排与环境保护”“建筑节能”三个专题的讨论，并举行了企业间合作洽谈。中共山东省委书记、山东省人大常委会主任姜异康出席，中共山东省委副书记、山东省省长姜大明，德国前总理格哈德・施罗德(Gerhard Schröder)出席并致辞。会议指出，加快推进以绿色和低碳技术为标志的能源革命、大力发展可再生能源、加快新能源推广应用已成为各国各地区培育新的经济增长点和建设资源节约型、环境友好型社会的必然选择。论坛的举办有利于推动与会各方了解掌握世界新能源产业发展新趋势，学习借鉴新能源发展的新技术、新理念，进一步扩大新能源领域的国际合作，共同促进新能源产业发展和节能减排工作，为实现全人类可持续发展做出新的更大贡献。

2.世界太阳城大会

世界太阳城大会是由世界太阳城协会发起的国际性会议。大会目的是通过国际太阳能城市之间的积极合作交流，改进能源效率政策，打造可再生能源城市。

2010年9月16日至18日，第四届世界太阳城大会在山东德州举办。大会围绕“太阳能改变生活”这一主题举办了一系列会议、论坛、展览等丰富多彩的活动，充分展示了以太阳能为代表的新能源产业的最新发展成果。与会代表进行了广泛深入的交流，就太阳城发展、可再生能源开发利用及互利合作等问题进行了深入研讨，在智慧碰撞、思想交融中达成了共识，绿色、环保、低碳、可持续发展的理念更加深入人心。大会汇聚了大量信息、技术和智力资本，促进了政府、企业、科研机构之间的合作，对加快新能源产业发展、推动新能源综合利用、改变市民生活方式产生了深远影响。

大会发表了《德州宣言》。《德州宣言》认为以太阳能为代表的可再生能源的开发利用是应对全球气候变化、实施传统能源替代战略、实现可持续发展的重要途径。太阳城是追求人与自然和谐共处，最大限度开发利用以太阳能为代表的可再生能源，实现低碳、集约、循环、生态发展，环境优美、宜居宜业的人类聚居地。太阳城的建设需要多方共同努力。《德州宣言》呼吁各国更多城市加入太阳城行列，共同致力于提高能源效率，发展可再生能源，实现低碳发展，建立长期交流合作机制，为实现绿色发展、可持续发展做出应有贡献。①

3.绿色与可持续能源合作研究项目

2018年，济南大学化学化工学院与魁北克省的国立科学研究院开展了绿色与可持续能源合作研究项目。2019年，双方合作开展了用于环境改善与清洁能源生产的纳米复合物项目、有效光催化剂项目。

4.可再生能源领域相关活动

2019年，山东省科技厅组织中国科学院青岛生物能源与过程研究所两名代表参加了在巴西圣保罗州举行的技术协调人会议和可再生能源领域相关活动，齐鲁工业大学（山东省科学院）的三名青年科技人员参加了数字化

① 参见张宇鸿、王亚楠、朱殿封：《第四届世界太阳城大会通过〈德州宣言〉》，2010年9月19日，http://paper.dzwww.com/dzrb/data/20100919/html/2/content_10.html。

和可再生能源领域活动。

5.中德友城论坛

2022年6月15日，为庆祝中德建交50周年，中国人民对外友好协会在线上成功举办中德友城论坛。论坛以“绿色和数字化——中德友城互利合作新动能”为主题，设“绿色合作”和“数字化合作”两个平行分论坛，山东省承办“绿色合作”分论坛。“绿色合作”分论坛聚焦绿色低碳和可持续发展，围绕城市在应对气候变化中的作用、友城在绿色发展领域的合作新机遇等进行研讨。山东省介绍了本省绿色领域的发展情况。福建省、湖北省、广东省、辽宁省、上海市、武汉市、青岛市及德国友城代表，山东重工集团、华晨宝马公司、大众汽车（安徽）有限公司、中德生态园管理委员会及拜尔斯道夫集团等有关代表介绍了在绿色领域的发展经验和有效做法。各方表示，将继续深挖绿色合作潜力，共享绿色发展机遇，携手打造中德友好省州、市间合作共赢新亮点。

# Chapter 5 Exchanges and Cooperation in Green Development

In order to tackle global climate change and explore green development models that are safe, clean and sustainable, the regions are strengthening exchanges in the development and application of technologies for the production, transportation and distribution of renewable energy, and improving energy efficiency. Relevant departments in all sister provinces and states are encouraged to fully leverage their superiorities in such aspects as markets, capital, technology, and mechanisms to further tap into the potential for cooperation, share development opportunities, and work together to create new highlights for exchanges and cooperation in green development.

## 5.1 Green Building

On 7 December 2022, Shandong Province held the Green Building Seminar of the eleventh Regional Leaders' Summit, which was one of a series of events leading up to the eleventh Regional Leaders' Summit (see Figure 5-1). Shandong Guoshun Construction Group Co., Ltd., and representatives of departments responsible for the green building industry and project experts in the green building sector in Upper Austria (Austria), Bavaria (Germany), and Western Cape (South Africa) attended the seminar online and delivered promotional speeches. At the seminar, all sister provinces and states jointly initiated and launched the "Beacon Action Plan for Green Building" to further enhance their exchanges and cooperation in such sectors as green building, energy conservation and emission reduction.

Figure 5-1 Green Building Seminar of the eleventh Regional Leaders' Summit (7 December 2022)

Photo Credit: Website of the Foreign Affairs Office of Shandong Provincial People's Government (http://wb.shandong.gov.cn).

### 5.1.1 Exchanges and Cooperation between Shandong Province and Bavaria

In 1995, the Housing and Urban-Rural Development Department of Shandong Province and the Supreme Construction Authority of Bavaria signed the *Agreement between Shandong Province and Bavaria on Cooperation and Exchanges in Urban Construction*, which laid the foundation for long-term and stable counterpart exchanges and cooperation between the two sides. On this basis, the past 30 years have witnessed cooperation between the two sides in areas such as reciprocal visits and exchanges, training of professional technicians, project demonstration, and enterprise cooperation, and fruitful results.

#### 5.1.1.1 Building Platforms for Cooperation

The Housing and Urban-Rural Development Department of Shandong Province and the Supreme Construction Authority of Bavaria set up the Shandong-Bavaria Consultative Committee on Urban Construction in 1996, which was to meet every two years. Since 2006, the Consultative Committee has been meeting annually in Jinan and Munich alternatively. At each meeting, the fruits of cooperation in the past period would be summarized and communicated, and areas and priorities of cooperation in the future would be discussed and determined based on the actual situation to actively facilitate cooperation between the two sides. So far, eight *Memorandums of Understanding* have been signed, four in Shandong and four in Bavaria, the latest edition of which was signed in 2015.

#### 5.1.1.2 Carrying out Exchanges and Training Programs

The Housing and Urban-Rural Development Department of Shandong Province has selected and sent two batches of professional technicians in the housing and construction system for a three-month training program in Bavaria, one batch for a one-month training program, and seven batches for short-term training programs under 21 days. It has invited four experts and professors from Bavaria to visit and give six lectures in Shandong respectively. In 2007, Shandong Province held the "Shandong Urban Construction Achievements Exhibition" and "Shandong Style Photo Exhibition" in Bavaria; and Bavaria held an exhibition on the "Design and Construction of Energy Efficient Buildings in Germany" and the "China-Germany Energy-efficient Building Technology Forum" in Shandong once respectively.

#### 5.1.1.3 Promoting Cooperation in Demonstration Projects

The Shilaoren Old Village Renovation Project in Qingdao was selected as the first urban construction demonstration project for the two sides, where Bavaria sent a designer to work in Shandong for one month for exclusive participation in the planning and design of the community. This demonstration project has been awarded multiple honorary titles such as

Excellent Green Ecological Community in China and Excellent Tourist Housing Project in China. In 2008, the two sides specified three planning and design demonstration projects, namely Maqiao Town in Huantai, Zibo, Shiheng Town in Feicheng, Tai'an, and Weiqiao Town in Zouping, Binzhou. The design proposals have been successfully completed and passed the review.

#### 5.1.1.4 Promoting Cooperation between Construction Enterprises of Both Sides

First, more architectural design enterprises are encouraged to participate in cooperation based on the Shandong-Bavaria architect cooperation platform and with the Shandong Exploration and Design Association playing its role. In 2007, the Shandong Provincial Architectural Design Institute signed cooperation agreements with 17 planning and architectural design firms in Bavaria. The Office of Bavaria Architects for Cooperation in Shandong was established. With the strong recommendation and support of the Housing and Urban-Rural Development Department of Shandong Province and the Supreme Construction Authority of Bavaria, great cooperations have been made between architectural design and planning enterprises of the two regions. Second, efforts have been made to push for enterprises of both sides to partner up in energy conservation and environmental protection sectors such as low-carbon and green buildings. Shandong Province's vigorous promotion of energy-efficient buildings has boosted the development of energy-saving and environmental protection sectors, and facilitated the introduction and popularization of advanced German technologies and products. Third, work has been done to promote cooperation between the two sides in building research. In 2014, Shandong Province initiated the construction of provincial passive, ultra-low energy consumption and green building pilot demonstration projects. 11 projects were selected in 2014, all of which were included in the China-Germany cooperative pilot demonstration projects of the Ministry of Housing and Urban-Rural Development of the People's Republic of China (MOHURD), with the Science and Technology Development Promotion Center of the

MOHURD and the German Energy Agency providing technical guidance throughout the process. Shandong Province allocated RMB 60 million to subsidize the incremental costs of eight public welfare projects. In 2015, another 11 passive, ultra-low energy consumption and green building pilot demonstration projects were specified, which were given fiscal rewards and subsidies amounting to RMB 54 million.

#### 5.1.1.5 Co-building Characteristic Demonstration Towns between Shandong and Bavaria

From 2017 to 2019, the Housing and Urban-Rural Development Department of Shandong Province and the Supreme Construction Authority of Bavaria jointly promoted the building of three small characteristic demonstration towns through cooperation between Shandong and Bavaria. In November 2018, Wang Yuzhi, Director General of the Housing and Urban-Rural Development Department of Shandong Province, led a delegation to visit Germany for formal talks with the head of the Supreme Construction Authority of Bavaria and the planning designer representative of the Bavarian Chamber of Architects on Shandong and Bavaria jointly building the three characteristic towns, namely, Fangsi Town in Yucheng City, Dezhou, Shangye Town in Feixian County, Linyi City, and Kouzhen in Laicheng District, Laiwu City, and reached consensus on such aspects as the planning and design priorities, list of materials, contract schedule, cost standards of the projects, significantly advancing the work of the three characteristic towns. After a number of processes, including planning and design proposal demonstration, and design proposal modification and improvement based on expert opinions, the planning and design of the three small towns successfully passed expert evaluations at the end of 2019. German philosophy and technologies were introduced in the planning and design with respect to the planning of characteristic towns, the planning of circular industry parks, and the design of ecological landscapes to provide reference for creating a Shandong model of rural revitalization.

#### 5.1.1.6 Holding the Sino-German Symposium on Energy Efficiency in Buildings

On 29 October 2021, the Housing and Urban-Rural Development Department of Shandong Province, China Council for the Promotion of International Trade Shandong Sub-council, and Bavarian Ministry of Economic Affairs, Regional Development and Energy jointly held the online and offline Sino-German Symposium on Energy Efficiency in Buildings, at which nine Chinese and German enterprises (institutions) conducted promotional exchange; 46 enterprises (institutions) carried out “one-on-one” business talks and reached 12 cooperation intentions; and eight Chinese and German enterprises signed four strategic cooperation agreements on site, and three enterprises signed two strategic cooperation agreements online, with the satisfaction rate of participating enterprises exceeding 95%.

### 5.1.2 Exchanges and Cooperation between Shandong Province and São Paulo

In 2017 and 2019, the Housing and Urban-Rural Development Department of Shandong Province was invited to visit Brazil twice and met with Flavio Amary, Housing Secretary of São Paulo, and Renato, Business Director of São Paulo's Agency for the Promotion of Investments and Competitiveness, for discussions and exchanges. The Department conducted relevant construction policy synergy, market research, enterprise promotion, and project investigation in São Paulo. In addition to gaining a comprehensive understanding of the status quo and development prospects of the construction market in São Paulo, the Department also experienced first-hand risks and difficulties faced by Chinese enterprises in contracting international projects. The main risks include different standard systems, long investment cycles, and obstacles and difficulties faced by Chinese employees in language, diet, and life. São Paulo has established a special zone for the registration of companies by foreign enterprises, with the Agency for the Promotion of Investments and Competitiveness in charge of coordinating with local government departments and water and electricity supply to facilitate the operation of enterprises there. The Agency has also set up an office in Shanghai to facilitate negotiations and cooperation between Chinese enterprises.

### 5.1.3 Exchanges and Cooperation between Shandong Province and Upper Austria

In 2016, the Housing and Urban-Rural Development Department of Shandong Province was invited to lead a delegation to visit Austria. They visited the Office of the State Government of Upper Austria, heard reports on urban planning and township energy supply in Upper Austria, and carried out discussions and exchanges on Austria's village and town planning, laws, regulations, policies on the planning, construction and management of villages and towns, status quo and historical changes of rural settlements, and experience in infrastructure construction in small towns. Drawing on Austria's experience in the planning, construction and management of small towns, Shandong Province has formulated and issued the *Guidelines of Shandong Province for the Extension of Facilities in Urbanized Areas to Rural Areas* to scientifically guide towns and villages throughout the province to expand the actual connection ranges for infrastructure and public service facilities between them, and make urban infrastructure and public services accessible in more villages.

## 5.2 Green Transportation

In September 2010, the fifth Regional Leaders' Summit on the themes of "Food Security" and "Integrated Transport" was held in Western Cape, South Africa. The leaders of the regions recognized that integrated transport has a direct impact on people's way of life. As science and technology continue to advance, transport has become increasingly fast-paced and diverse. The regions should enhance their research on transport integration, develop relevant plans, and consider the system and mechanism of transport integration in a coordinated manner, guided by the principles of efficiency and cost-effectiveness. It is essential to strengthen the transportation infrastructure and build an integrated traffic pattern to benefit the people of the regions. On the basis of existing partnerships, all member regions of the summit have unanimously agreed to deepen cooperation in integrated transport, clarifying the direction for cooperation among the summit members.

On 28 March 2023, the Seminar on Green Transportation Cooperation of the eleventh Regional Leaders' Summit was held online and offline in Shandong (see Figure 5-2). Cai Xianjin, Director-General of the Foreign Affairs Office of Shandong Provincial People's Government, and President of Shandong People's Association for Friendship with Foreign Countries, attended the seminar and delivered a speech. Among the participants were heads of departments of the Shandong Provincial Department of Transportation, Shandong Jiaotong University, Shandong Hi-Speed Group Co., Ltd., Shandong Port Group Co., Ltd., Inspur Intelligent Technology Co., Ltd., and Hisense TransTech Co., Ltd., representatives of transportation authorities from Bavaria (Germany), Upper Austria (Austria), Western Cape (South Africa), Quebec (Canada), Georgia (USA), and São Paulo (Brazil), as well as experts and business leaders in the green transportation sector.

Through this seminar, all sister provinces and states exchanged ideas and aligned principles on green transportation, called for joint response to challenges faced in the transportation sector at the moment, and reaffirmed the path of green, low-carbon, and high-quality development. The Shandong Provincial Department of Transportation gave an account of Shandong's green and low-carbon development plan for transportation and welcomed peers from sister provinces and states to come to Shandong for inspection, exchanges and cooperation so as to jointly contribute to the sustainable development of transportation around the globe. Representatives from transportation authorities of Bavaria (Germany), Upper Austria (Austria), Western Cape (South Africa), Quebec (Canada), Georgia (USA), and São Paulo (Brazil) presented their policy plans in the green transportation sector respectively. Enterprise representatives and industry experts from the regions introduced their experience and practices in the sector of green transportation, and expressed their willingness to actively carry out exchanges and cooperation in the green transportation sector under the mechanism of the Regional Leaders' Summit. The "Jinan Initiative on Green Transportation Cooperation and Development" was released at the seminar, laying a solid foundation for exchanges and cooperation in the sector of green transportation among the sister provinces and states.

Figure 5-2　Seminar on Green Transportation Cooperation of the eleventh Regional Leaders' Summit (28 March 2023)

Photo Credit: Website of the Foreign Affairs Office of Shandong Provincial People's Government (http://wb.shandong.gov.cn).

## 5.3　Green Energy

### 5.3.1　Exchanges and Cooperation during the Regional Leaders' Summit

In July 2006, at the third Regional Leaders' Summit, government leaders of the regions emphasized the importance of safe, sustainable, and affordable energy supply for future economic development in the regions.

They pointed out that continuous innovation for better utilization of energy is crucial for enhancing competitiveness and building a healthy environment, and efforts should be made to provide clean and environment-friendly energy technologies to all countries. The regional leaders also discussed the development status quo of the global market and the increasing strategic importance of energy policies in international relations. They believed that the responsibility for regional economic development requires all participating governments to implement active energy policies and engage in domestic and international cooperation. All parties agree that innovation in energy utilization is the key to improving competitiveness and environmental friendliness. New energy must be developed through various means. All regions should make the application of clean and climate-friendly technologies a fundamental principle of their sustainable energy policies so as not to further burden the climate while pursuing economic growth.

In August 2008, during the fourth Regional Leaders' Summit, leaders of the regions were invited to attend bilateral and multilateral meetings, and a thematic forum on “Building a Conservation-Oriented Society” and discussions on cooperative projects were held. 16 joint actions were decided at the summit, including holding energy congress and the ISCI World Congress in the following two years. Shandong Province's initiative to establish the Shandong-Bavaria-Upper Austria Tripartite Coordination Committee for Cooperation in Energy and Environmental Protection received positive responses. Shandong Province and its sister provinces and states would take measures to promote cooperation in energy conservation and environmental protection, modern agriculture, modern services and related sectors. Four cooperation agreements and 12 cooperation intentions on energy conservation and emission reduction were reached.

In April 2012, during the sixth Regional Leaders' Summit, multiple bilateral meetings between delegations of the regions were held. Shandong Province gave an emphatic introduction of its main achievements in promoting the development of sustainable energy advocating green economy, and called on governments of the participating regions to work together to strengthen the sustainable energy sector and promote sustainable development by advocating the concept of green development, building supporting policy systems, enhancing cooperation in technology and education, and improving mechanisms for communication and coordination.

In June 2014, during the seventh Regional Leaders' Summit, Shandong Province and Georgia proposed a range of suggestions for cooperation in such sectors as energy, logistics, finance, energy conservation and environmental protection, and mechanical manufacturing.

In July 2016, at the eighth Regional Leaders' Summit, the *Joint Declaration of the Eighth Regional Leaders' Summit* was adopted and plans for exchanges and cooperation in such sectors as renewable energy networks were made.

In May 2018, during the ninth Regional Leaders' Summit, in-depth exchanges on topics such as climate change, environment and health, the role of local governments in energy transition, and AI and energy transition were conducted (see Figure 5-3). The summit featured the adoption of the *Quebec Summit Joint Declaration on Energy Transition* and the *Roadmap of the Regional Leaders' Summit (2018-2020)*, a summation of the cooperation achievements since the eighth Regional Leaders' Summit in Bavaria, Germany in 2016, and the plans for advancing energy transition, strengthening cooperation in energy, boosting the energy transition capacity, conducting technology-industry cooperation, enhancing enterprise guidance, promoting the development of AI, and improving environmental health.

Figure 5-3 Energy expert and academician Zhuang Qingfa meeting with Quebec Premier Philippe Couillard at the ninth Regional Leaders' Summit (May 2018)

Photo Credit: Science and Technology Cooperation Office, Department of Science & Technology of Shandong Province.

### 5.3.2 Exchanges and Cooperation under the Mechanism of the Regional Leaders' Summit

#### 5.3.2.1 Energy Congress

On 29 April 2010, the China Qingdao International Forum on New Energy & Sino-German Cooperation Qingdao Summit was held in Qingdao. Themed "New Energy and Sustainable Development", the forum featured discussions on three topics, namely, "New Energy Development and Utilization", "Energy Conservation, Emission Reduction and Environmental Protection", and "Energy Efficiency in Buildings", and talks between enterprises for cooperation. Jiang Yikang, Secretary of the CPC Shandong Provincial Committee and Chairman of the Standing Committee of the Shandong Provincial People's Congress, Jiang Daming, Deputy Secretary of the CPC Shandong Provincial Committee and Governor of Shandong Province, and former German Chancellor Gerhard Schröder attended the forum, and the latter two gave speeches as well. It was pointed at the congress that advancing energy revolution marked by green and low-carbon technologies, vigorously developing renewable energy, and accelerating the promotion and application of new energy have become an inevitable choice for countries and regions in tapping new sources of economic growth and building a resource-conserving, environment-friendly society. The forum was conducive to motivating all participants to understand and grasp new development tendencies in the world's new energy sector, learn from each other new technologies and concepts for new energy development, further expand international cooperation in the new energy sector, and jointly advance the development of the sector and energy conservation and emission reduction work to make new and greater contributions to the sustainable development of all mankind.

#### 5.3.2.2 ISCI World Congress

The ISCI World Congress is an international congress initiated by the International Solar Cities Initiative (ISCI). Its purpose is to improve energy efficiency policies and build renewable energy cities through active cooperation and exchanges among international solar cities.

From 16 to 18 September 2010, the Fourth ISCI World Congress was held in Dezhou, Shandong. With the theme of "Solar Energy Changes Life", the Fourth ISCI World Congress featured a variety of events including conferences, forums, and exhibitions to fully showcase the latest developments in the new energy sector represented by solar energy. Participants of the congress carried out extensive interactions with one another, including in-depth discussions on issues such as the development of solar cities, the development and utilization of renewable energy, and mutually beneficial cooperation. Consensus was reached in insightful exchanges and the integration of ideas, and concepts of green, environment-friendly, low-carbon, and sustainable development found their way deeper into the hearts of the people. The congress pooled great amounts of information, technologies and intellectual capital, and promoted cooperation between governments, enterprises, and scientific research institutions, which had a profound impact on accelerating the development of the new energy sector, pushing forward the comprehensive utilization of new energy, and changing the lifestyles of citizens.

The *Dezhou Declaration* was issued at the congress, which holds that the development and utilization of renewable energy represented by solar energy is an important way to tackle global climate change, implement traditional energy substitution strategies and achieve sustainable development. Solar cities are human settlements featuring the pursuit of harmonious coexistence between human and nature, and the development and utilization of renewable energy represented by solar energy to the greatest extent possible to realize low-carbon, intensive, circular and ecological development, the construction of which requires joint efforts from all sides. The *Declaration* calls on cities from all countries to join in the ranks of solar cities to work together to improve energy efficiency, develop renewable energy, realize low-carbon development, establish long-term mechanisms for exchanges and cooperation, and make due contributions to the realization of green and sustainable development. ①

#### 5.3.2.3 Cooperative Research Project on Green and Sustainable Energy

In 2018, the School of Chemistry and Chemical Engineering, University of Jinan and the National Institute of Scientific Research (INRS) of Quebec carried out a cooperative research project on green and sustainable energy. In 2019, the two parties jointly developed a nanocomposite project and an effective photocatalyst project for environmental improvement and clean energy production.

#### 5.3.2.4 Related Activities in the Renewable Energy Sector

In 2019, the Department of Science & Technology of Shandong

① Zhang Yuhong, Wang Yanan, Zhu Dianfeng, "The fourth ISCI Congress Passes the Dezhou Declaration", http://paper.dzwww.com/dzrb/data/20100919/html/2/content_10.html, 19 September, 2010.

Province sent two representatives from Qingdao Institute of Bioenergy and Bioprocess Technology (QIBEBT) of the Chinese Academy of Sciences (CAS) to attend the technical coordinators' meeting and related activities in the renewable energy sector held in São Paulo, Brazil. Three young scientists and technicians from Qilu University of Technology (Shandong Academy of Sciences) participated in events in the digitalization and renewable energy sectors.

#### 5.3.2.5 German-Chinese Forum on City and Provincial Partnerships

On 15 June 2022, the Chinese People's Association for Friendship with Foreign Countries held the online German-Chinese Forum on City and Provincial Partnerships (Das deutsch-chinesische Forum zu Städte-und Provinzenpartnerschaften) to celebrate the 50th anniversary of the establishment of diplomatic relations between China and Germany. Themed "Green Development and Digitalization—New Dynamics of Cooperation" (Grüne Entwicklung und Digitalisierung—Neue Dynamik der Zusammenarbeit), the forum included two sub-forums on the themes of "Cooperation on Green Development" and "Cooperation on Digitalization". Organized by Shandong Province, the sub-forum themed "Cooperation on Green Development" focused on green, low-carbon, and sustainable development, and featured discussions on the role of cities in addressing climate change and new cooperation opportunities for sister cities in the green development sector. Shandong Province presented the developments of its green sector. Representatives from Fujian Province, Hubei Province, Guangdong Province, Liaoning Province, Shanghai Municipality, Wuhan, Qingdao and its German sister cities, Shandong Heavy Industry Group, BMW Brilliance Automotive Ltd., Volkswagen (Anhui) Automotive Company Limited, Management Committee of the Sino-German Ecopark and Beiersdorf AG presented their development experience and effective practices in green-related sectors. The participants all said that they would continue to tap the potential for cooperation in the green sector, share opportunities in the development of the sector, and work together to create new highlights in win-win cooperation between sister provinces, states and cities in China and Germany.

# 第六章　文教体育交流合作

## 一、山东省文化和旅游厅与友好省州的交流合作

### (一)庆祝山东省与巴伐利亚州结好30周年文化活动

2017年11月20日,山东省与巴伐利亚州结好30周年庆祝活动在德国慕尼黑举行。山东省常务副省长李群与巴伐利亚州政府及议会各界人士300余人出席庆祝活动(见图6-1)。作为庆祝活动的重头戏,山东歌舞剧院表演的《孔府乐舞》让德国观众领略到了中华优秀传统文化的独特韵律。活动期间还举办了"'交流的目光'——山东省与巴伐利亚州缔结友好关系30周年摄影交流展"和"日照农民画展"。

图6-1　2017年11月20日,山东省常务副省长李群参加山东省与巴伐利亚州结好30周年活动

图片来源:山东省文化和旅游厅对外交流合作处。

### （二）国际友城合作发展大会文化和旅游合作论坛

2019年10月16日，山东国际友城合作发展大会文化和旅游合作论坛在济南南郊宾馆举办。山东省副省长于杰、奥地利上奥州常务副州长克里斯蒂娜·哈博兰德参加大会并致辞，山东省文化和旅游厅厅长王磊主持论坛。论坛以“民心相通——文化和旅游的融合”为主题，将山东文化旅游资源推介、国际友城代表演讲和展演洽谈相结合，突出展示山东和各国际友城的独特文化旅游资源与人文风情。国际友城代表团、国外驻华驻鲁机构及旅游从业者代表以及16市的文旅部门和企业代表出席论坛。

## 二、山东省体育局与友好省州的交流合作

自友好省州领导人峰会建立以来，各省州在体育领域交流频繁。目前，山东省体育局与奥地利上奥州、德国巴伐利亚州、加拿大魁北克省、南非西开普省、巴西圣保罗州以及美国佐治亚州体育政府部门或体育社团组织、俱乐部均建立了联系。其中，与奥地利上奥州体育部、巴西圣保罗州体育娱乐事务部签署了体育友好合作备忘录，与巴伐利亚州足球协会、田径协会签署了体育友好合作协议书，与加拿大魁北克省、南非西开普省、美国佐治亚州进行了体育高层互访活动。

### （一）与奥地利上奥州的交流合作

自2006年起，山东省体育局与奥地利上奥州在足球、乒乓球、羽毛球等领域开展了多次互访交流活动。随着体育交流的不断深入，双方于2014年、2019年、2023年三次签署体育交流谅解备忘录。2006年7月，山东省青年足球代表团赴奥地利上奥州参加第二十一届上奥杯国际青年足球赛，拉开了双方体育交流合作的序幕。2015年4月，山东省乒乓球队应上奥州乒乓球协会邀请访问上奥州并进行训练交流活动，上奥州体育部副部长、奥地利国家乒乓球协会主席及上奥州乒乓球协会主席接待了代表团。2015年7月，上奥州乒乓球队访问山东省乒乓球羽毛球训练中心并进行了训练交流活动。2015年8月，山东省体育代表团再次访问上奥州体育部，就马术、击剑等项目的深入合作进行了会谈（见图6-2）。

图 6-2　2015 年 8 月，山东省体育代表团访问上奥州击剑队

图片来源：山东省体育局对外体育交流中心。

2016—2018 年，山东省体育局与上奥州每年进行乒乓球、羽毛球项目的互访训练活动。2019 年 5 月，山东省体育局局长李政率团访问上奥州，与上奥州州长麦格·托马斯·施泰尔泽签署了《（中国）山东省体育局与（奥地利）上奥州体育局体育友好合作备忘录》（见图 6-3）。2020 年，受新冠肺炎疫情影响，双方线下交流暂停。

图 6-3　2019 年 5 月，山东省体育局局长李政与上奥州州长麦格·托马斯·施泰尔泽签署合作备忘录

图片来源：上奥州政府网站，https://www.land-oberoesterreich.gv.at/219772.htm。

2023年5月2日，山东省体育局与奥地利上奥州体育部第三次签署《（中国）山东省体育局与（奥地利）上奥州体育部体育战略合作备忘录》。山东省体育局在海外设立的第一个青少年高水平训练基地“（奥地利）上奥州体育部（中国）山东省体育局——青少年运动员高水平训练基地”为今后山东青少年运动员赴上奥州训练提供了场地支持。

### （二）与德国巴伐利亚州的交流合作

山东省与德国巴伐利亚州在体育方面交往密切，双方进行了多次互访交流。2005年7月，山东省体育局副局长张洪涛率山东省体育局代表团赴德国巴伐利亚州进行访问，由此拉开了双方体育交流的序幕。2015年6月，应德国巴伐利亚州文教、科学与艺术部邀请，山东省体育局局长张松林率团访问巴伐利亚州，双方就下一步在足球等领域的合作进行了会谈。同年7月22日，德国足球协会副主席、巴伐利亚州足球协会主席赖纳·科赫（Rainer Koch）博士、巴伐利亚州足球协会青少年女子足球队主教练弗雷德里克·克罗姆珀（Friederike Kromp）随巴伐利亚州政府团来访。其间，山东省足球运动管理中心、山东省足球运动协会与巴伐利亚州足球协会在山东省体育中心进行会谈并签署了《山东-巴伐利亚州足球合作备忘录》。会谈结束后，巴伐利亚州青少年女子足球队主教练弗雷德里克·克罗姆珀为山东省青年女子足球队进行了现场授课。

2015年11月，应德国巴伐利亚州足球协会邀请，山东省体育总会常务副主席李政等四人赴德国巴伐利亚州进行访问，就山东青年女子足球队赴德训练、聘请女足教练、派教练员赴德培训等具体合作事宜进行了协商。2016年7月15日至8月4日，山东省青少年女子足球队一行29人赴德国巴伐利亚州足球协会训练基地进行为期21天的训练活动（见图6-4）。

图 6-4　2016 年 7 月，山东省青少年女子足球队在德国巴伐利亚州足球协会训练基地训练

图片来源：山东省体育局对外体育交流中心。

2016 年 12 月，应德国巴伐利亚州田径协会邀请，山东省体育局副局长王延奎率山东省体育代表团赴巴伐利亚州进行体育交流和友好访问，并商谈合作事宜。山东省与巴伐利亚州就建立田径项目友好合作、共享双方训练资源、互派教练员和运动员比赛训练、依托巴伐利亚州田径协会建立山东-巴伐利亚州田径训练基地等进行了会谈并签署了《中国山东省体育局与德国巴伐利亚州田径协会友好合作备忘录》。此外，2018 年 2 月、2020 年 1 月、2020 年 3 月，山东省乒乓球羽毛球运动管理中心运动员受邀赴巴伐利亚州进行比赛训练活动。

### （三）与南非西开普省的交流合作

2007 年 10 月，南非西开普省政府代表团访问山东省，双方签署了合作备忘录。2012 年 11 月，山东省体育局副局长高金业率领山东省体育代表团赴南非西开普省体育娱乐事务部进行体育友好交流活动，访问期间代表团考察了体育场馆，并就强势项目合作、聘请优秀教练员来鲁执教事宜进行了洽谈。2014 年 7 月，双方再次签署体育交流合作协议，确定今后双边体育交流合作更侧重橄榄球教练互访训练、青少年运动员培养等。2016 年 9 月，双方商定继续履行已经签署的合作协议，继续加强体育高层互访交流。自 2007 年以来，双方多次互派帆船、自行车、马拉松、风筝(见图 6-5、图 6-6)等项目的运动员赴友好省州参加相关赛事。

图 6-5　2015 年 8 月,西开普省文化事务和体育部派出五名年轻水手参加在中国山东省举行的第七届青岛国际帆船周比赛

图片来源:西开普省政府网站,https://www.westerncape.gov.za/news/aspiring-wc-sailors-compete-prestigious-yacht-race-china。

图 6-6　2016 年 4 月,来自南非的阿什利(Ashley)参加潍坊国际风筝节

图片来源:西开普省政府网站,https://www.westerncape.gov.za/news/kiters-show-talent-international-kite-festivals-china。

2017 年 4 月,应南非西开普省文化事务和体育部邀请,山东省体育局副局长隋拥军等六人赴南非进行了体育友好交流活动,双方就聘请优秀橄榄球外教来鲁进行了实质性的商讨,就派代表参加 2017 年 12 月开普敦市马拉松比赛相关事宜进行了会谈。双方约定将继续加强帆船、风筝、羽毛球、体操、自行车等项目的互访交流,协商选派乒乓球教练员赴西开普省任教。

### (四)与巴西圣保罗州的交流合作

2013 年 1 月,山东省体育局局长张洪涛率团赴巴西圣保罗州进行访问,拉开了双方体育对话的序幕。2015 年 7 月,应巴西武术协会邀请,山东省武术院翟寿涛等 10 人赴巴西圣保罗州参加第一届巴西泛美传统武术锦标赛和泛美太极拳锦标赛并参加开幕表演。2015 年 10 月,应巴西圣保罗州国际关系厅邀请,山东省体育局副局长隋拥军率山东省体育代表团赴巴西圣保罗州体育、娱乐及青年厅进行访问,双方同意定期互访,在体育领域加强合作,进行乒乓球、足球、篮球、水上项目等互访比赛交流,同时确定协助山东省做好 2016 年里约奥运会山东省运动员参赛保障团的相关工作。2016 年8 月,应巴西圣保罗州体育、娱乐及青年厅邀请,第 31 届巴西里约奥运会山东省运动员参赛保障团赴里约热内卢州、圣保罗州进行了访问(见图 6-7)。

图 6-7　2016 年 8 月,里约奥运会山东省运动员参赛保障团访问圣保罗州鲁能巴西训练基地

图片来源:山东省体育局对外体育交流中心。

### (五)与美国佐治亚州、加拿大魁北克省的交流合作

2017 年 8 月,应加拿大魁北克省政府教育及高等教育部、美国佐治亚州经济发展署邀请,山东省体育局副局长王延奎率山东省体育代表团对两省州进行了访问,分别就与佐治亚州开展篮球项目交流、与魁北克省开展冰雪

项目交流进行了会谈。

## 三、山东大学与友好省州的交流合作

### (一)加拿大魁北克省蒙特利尔大学

2007年,山东大学与加拿大魁北克省蒙特利尔大学签署学术交流与合作备忘录。2019年5月,双方签署交换生项目协议。目前,山东大学已派出六名学生前往蒙特利尔大学进行交流学习。

2021年,山东大学外国语学院牵头申报的“山东大学与法语区高校国际组织后备人才联合培养项目”获得了国家留学基金管理委员会的资助。项目支持山东大学与蒙特利尔大学等国际组织人才培养方面的知名高校开展合作,培养有志于到国际组织工作的青年后备人才。

2021年7月,山东大学组织企业管理人员及教职工线上参加了蒙特利尔高等商学院举办的“可再生能源价值链讲座”。

### (二)美国佐治亚州佐治亚理工学院

2018年11月,山东大学泰山学堂与美国佐治亚理工学院签署了两校访学学生协议,每年选派泰山学堂数学方向三年级学生到佐治亚理工学院学习一个学期。目前,山东大学已派出六名学生前往佐治亚理工学院进行交流学习。此外,山东大学计算机学院学者与美国佐治亚理工学院学者共同开展了合作研究。

### (三)德国巴伐利亚州各大学

1.慕尼黑工业大学

山东大学信息学院张海霞教授与慕尼黑工业大学诺赛克(Nossek)教授共同发起创办了IEEE第一届无线通信跨层设计国际学术研讨会(IEEE IWCLD),迄今大会已在济南、巴塞罗那、雷恩和青岛成功举办四届。

2.埃尔兰根-纽伦堡大学

山东大学与埃尔兰根-纽伦堡大学在易学领域保持科研合作。2013年,山东大学易学与中国古代哲学研究中心埃尔兰根-纽伦堡大学分部成立。两校在此合作框架下开展博士生访学、专家讲学等形式的交流。每年春季，埃尔兰根-纽伦堡大学工程学系选派学生来中国考察，山东大学是其中一站。学生团在山东大学停留四天，主要活动包括与德语系学生交流、参观校园、走访在济南的德国企业、体验文化等。该项目已持续十余年。

3.慕尼黑应用语言大学

山东大学与慕尼黑应用语言大学签署了学生交流协议。山东大学德语系每年选派一名学生赴该校交流学习一年，对方选派六名学生来山东大学参加暑期学校项目。

4.奥格斯堡大学

山东大学与奥格斯堡大学艺术学院交流频繁，多次在济南、奥格斯堡两地合作举办两校师生美术作品展。山东大学德语系每年选派十余名学生赴奥格斯堡大学交流学习一学期，选派两名学生参加对方暑期学校。

5.奥格斯堡应用技术大学

山东大学与奥格斯堡应用技术大学经济学院互派交换生学习。

6.慕尼黑大学

慕尼黑大学汉学家叶翰(Hans Van Ess)教授曾多次来山东大学文艺美学研究中心讲学，且两校在汉籍整理与研究方面有着良好的合作。

## 四、山东科技大学与友好省州的交流合作

山东科技大学与德国巴伐利亚州建立了良好的合作关系。自2003年至今，山东科技大学先后与巴伐利亚州安斯巴赫应用技术大学、东拜仁雷根斯堡应用技术大学、罗森海姆应用技术大学三所高校签署了校际交流合作协议并展开合作。

### (一)德国安斯巴赫应用技术大学本科生双学位联合培养项目

德国安斯巴赫应用技术大学是在德国现代教育改革中诞生的公立应用技术大学。为了培养具有国际化视野和竞争力的高水平专业人才，给学生提供一个更广阔的发展空间，自2003年起山东科技大学与德国安斯巴赫应用技术大学开展本科生双学位联合培养项目。项目受到德国和中国各界的一致好评，被纳入中德两国政府教育合作项目。此前，项目采用的是“2+1+2”的

培养模式，即通过高考录取为普通本科生后，先在山东科技大学学习两年，再组建“中德联合培养班”在山东科技大学进行一年的德语强化训练，然后派往德国学习两年。由于在该模式下，学生完成学业的时间偏长，经双方商定，自 2011 年起采用“2＋2”的培养模式，即先在山东科技大学学习两年，其间兼修德语课程，后在安斯巴赫应用技术大学学习两年。双方学分互认，完成教学计划规定的课程和实习后，可同时取得安斯巴赫应用技术大学学士学位证书、毕业证书和山东科技大学学士学位证书、毕业证书。

自 2004 年至今，山东科技大学共派出 198 名学生赴德国安斯巴赫应用技术大学交流学习（见图 6-8）。从学成回国就业的情况看，这些学生的国际视野、专业水平、语言能力、综合素质使其在就业竞争中具有明显优势，他们得到了就业单位的认可，就业层次、薪酬待遇等非常理想。熟悉高等教育与国际交流合作的各方人士对这一独具特色的合作项目给予了很高的评价。

图 6-8　2004 年，山东科技大学留学生拜访巴伐利亚州财政部

图片来源：山东科技大学。

### （二）德国东拜仁雷根斯堡应用技术大学交换生项目

德国东拜仁雷根斯堡应用技术大学地处巴伐利亚州雷根斯堡市，是德国一所著名的公立综合类大学，文化学、经济学、信息学和生命科学等专业

是其优势专业。2019年，山东科技大学与德国东拜仁雷根斯堡应用技术大学针对师生交流和科研合作等签署了学术交流合作协议。根据协议，德国东拜仁雷根斯堡应用技术大学同意山东科技大学派遣本科生和研究生赴德学习建筑学、应用自然科学和文化研究、社会和健康管理科学、计算机科学和数学、电气工程和信息科技、机械工程等专业，学习时间通常为一个学期。学期结束后，学生在德国东拜仁雷根斯堡应用技术大学所习得的学分可在山东科技大学获得认可。

### （三）德国罗森海姆应用技术大学交换生项目

德国罗森海姆应用技术大学位于德国巴伐利亚州东南部城市罗森海姆，该校密切关注劳动市场需求，注重培养学生的实操职业技能，各层面的培训都把与经济界的深入合作摆在中心位置。2020年，山东科技大学与德国罗森海姆应用技术大学就工程领域签署了学生交流合作协议。根据协议，山东科技大学可派遣本科生和研究生赴德国罗森海姆应用技术大学学习工程学、木材工艺学与建筑学、计算机科学、管理与工程等工科专业，学习时间通常为一个学期。学期结束后，学生在德国罗森海姆应用技术大学所习得的学分可在山东科技大学获得认可。

## 五、青岛大学与友好省州的交流合作

在山东省与德国巴伐利亚州的教育合作项目框架下，青岛大学与德国巴伐利亚州的教育交流与合作蓬勃发展，青岛大学先后与拜罗伊特大学、慕尼黑应用语言大学、慕尼黑工业大学、奥格斯堡大学等高校建立了友好合作关系。近年来，随着一批批中德合作项目扎根青岛大学，青岛大学已经发展为山东省德语人才培养基地、德语教师培训基地、跨文化德语研究基地和巴伐利亚研究基地，为德语教学及中德跨文化研究培养了大批专业人才。

### （一）山东省-德国巴伐利亚州教育合作项目——青岛大学德语系

1994年，山东省省长赵志浩及德国驻华大使富泰铭（Armin Freitag）亲自为青岛大学德语系揭牌，启动了山东省人民政府和德国巴伐利亚州政府依托青岛大学实施的“鲁巴教育合作项目”。2003年，青岛大学获批德语语言文学硕士学位授权点。2004 年起,青岛大学招收跨文化交际学、德语文学、德语语言学、跨文化翻译学四个研究方向的硕士研究生,与德国拜罗伊特大学、慕尼黑应用语言大学联合培养。2017 年起,青岛大学招收翻译专业学位硕士研究生(德语笔译),与慕尼黑应用语言大学联合培养;与德国康斯坦茨应用科技大学、慕尼黑应用语言大学建立双学位项目。2019 年,德语专业入选首批国家级一流本科专业建设点。

青岛大学德语系为教育部高等学校外语教学指导委员会德语专业教学指导分委员会委员、全国翻译专业学位研究生教育指导委员会专家委员会委员、山东省本科教育非通用外国语类教学指导委员会主任委员单位。现有专职教师 11 人,其中教授 2 人、副教授 2 人,博士研究生导师 2 人、硕士研究生导师 7 人,拥有博士学位 6 人,团队成员均有德国留学经历。另外,长期聘有德国学术交流中心专家 1 人、德籍荣誉教授 3 人、国内外客座教授 5 人、翻译专业学位硕士研究生校外合作导师 2 人。

截至 2022 年 6 月,德语系已毕业 24 届本科生、16 届德语语言文学硕士研究生、4 届德语笔译专业硕士研究生,为中德两国各领域的合作与交流输送 700 余名毕业生,已成为山东省发展地方经济、开展国际合作的优质德语人才库。历届毕业生在中德政治、经济、文化及教育领域发挥着重要作用,并得到中德各文化机构及企事业单位的广泛好评。一部分毕业生在世界知名企业的管理部门任职,如梅赛德斯-奔驰、西门子、大众、奥迪等;一部分毕业生任职于中国驻德国大使馆和领事馆或德国驻中国大使馆以及各驻华文化机构;另有一部分毕业生已成为中国高校德语专业教学及科研领域的中坚力量,担任国内部分高校德语专业教授或学科负责人。

德语系现为国家级一流本科专业建设点,近 5 年承担国家社会科学基金项目 4 项、国家自然科学基金重大项目子课题 1 项、教育部人文社会科学研究项目 2 项、山东省社科重大委托项目 1 项,获批全国首批新文科研究与改革实践项目 1 项、国家级虚拟教研室建设试点 1 个、山东省教学改革重点项目 1 项、其他省部级项目 10 余项,编写出版国家级规划教材 5 部,获省级教学成果二等奖、校级教学成果一等奖各 1 项,拥有国家级一流本科课程、省级一流本科课程、省级课程思政示范课程各 1 门,获批省级智库 2 个。

### (二)学术交流

1994 年以来,青岛大学先后与拜罗伊特大学、慕尼黑应用语言大学、慕尼黑工业大学、奥格斯堡大学、汉斯·赛德尔基金会、德国学术交流中心、歌德学院、巴伐利亚州对华高教中心等建立了友好合作关系，深入开展学术交流与合作。

青岛大学德语系与拜罗伊特大学合作编译的《跨文化日耳曼学》受到中国德语界高度重视，双方合作编写的教材《中德文化比较》被国内多所高校广泛采用。青岛大学的跨文化研究引起了国内外同行的重视，得到了国内德语界权威人士的肯定。

2015年，德语系与慕尼黑应用语言大学成功申请为期五年的欧盟“伊拉斯谟＋”(Erasmus＋)项目，每年资助两名研究生赴该校学习一学期。在该项目框架内，双方还互派教师进修或短期讲学。

2016年3月，青岛大学与慕尼黑应用语言大学签署“2＋2.5”本科双学位项目合作协议。青岛大学德语系本科生在青岛大学学习两年并通过选拔考试后赴慕尼黑应用语言大学学习两年半，通过全部考试后获得青岛大学和慕尼黑应用语言大学的双学士学位。

在德国巴伐利亚州提供的全额奖学金支持下，青岛大学德语系每年选派十名左右本科生至友校学习一学期；青岛大学德语语言文学硕士研究生全部派往拜罗伊特大学研修至少一学期；青岛大学德语笔译方向专业硕士研究生经选拔，部分可获得奖学金赴慕尼黑应用语言大学学习一学期。该奖学金项目延续至今，除2020—2022年因新冠肺炎疫情未能派出学生以外，目前已先后派出全额奖学金生近300名。这样的规模在我国德语专业首屈一指。

### (三)设立山东省中德高校合作中心

随着德语系的发展，为进一步推进中国山东省高校和德国巴伐利亚州高校的交流与合作，山东省政府与巴伐利亚州政府决定分别在两省州成立高校合作中心。2007年4月，巴伐利亚州对华高教中心在拜罗伊特大学成立，同年10月，山东省中德高校合作中心在青岛大学成立。

山东省中德高校合作中心与巴伐利亚州对华高教中心积极合作，多次举办德国巴伐利亚州大学生中国国情暑期研修、山东省高校青年德语教师培训、中国跨文化日耳曼学研究会、巴伐利亚州精英学院访学、山东省大学生德国文化暑期研修等大型活动，协助安排各类赴巴伐利亚州文化、教育项目团组，成为发展山东省对德交流与合作的重要平台，进一步扩大了山东省与巴伐利亚州以及中德高校间教育、科技、文化等方面的交流合作，推动了山东省与巴伐利亚州教育合作项目的纵深发展。

### （四）设立青岛大学德福考试中心

2004 年 6 月，教育部海外考试中心与德国德福考试院共同在青岛大学设立德福考试中心（见图 6-9），这是在中国设立的第八个德福考试中心。该中心自成立以来，因出色的管理、先进的语音设备、良好的考官素养及监考人员的认真负责，很快发展为中国第三大德福考试中心，并获得德国德福考试院和广大考生的一致好评。

图 6-9　2004 年德国“德福考试”青岛大学考点揭牌仪式

图片来源：青岛大学。

### （五）设立青岛大学歌德语言中心

2010 年 9 月，青岛大学与德国歌德学院合作，成立了青岛大学歌德语言中心，该中心是德国歌德学院在中国继上海、天津、南京、西安、重庆之后成立的第六所语言中心（见图 6-10）。2016 年 3 月，青岛大学歌德语言中心以优异的成绩通过了歌德学院的全球考核，得到了歌德学院（北京）的肯定与嘉奖。截至 2020 年 4 月，青岛大学歌德语言中心已经培养了近 3800 人次的德语学习者，很多学员目前在德国攻读学位或在国内从事有关德语教学及涉德工作。在青岛地区的德语培训行业中，青岛大学歌德语言中心长期处于领头羊的位置。

图 6-10 2010 年青岛大学歌德语言中心揭牌仪式
图片来源：青岛大学。

### （六）设立青岛大学巴伐利亚研究中心

2019 年 12 月，青岛大学成立了青岛大学巴伐利亚研究中心。

2022 年 6 月 21 日，由中共山东省委宣传部、山东省委外事工作委员会办公室和青岛大学主办、巴伐利亚研究中心协办的“李希霍芬与中德文化交流研讨会暨李希霍芬《中国》翻译项目启动会”在济南举行。青岛大学巴伐利亚研究中心执行主任綦甲福教授在会上做了专题报告，介绍了李希霍芬《中国》翻译项目调研情况以及工作方案。会上，青岛大学党委书记胡金焱代表青岛大学接受了中共山东省委常委宣传部部长白玉刚签署的项目委托书。

2022 年 7 月 25 日，山东省外事研究与发展智库座谈会在山东省人民政府外事办公室举行，中共山东省委常委、秘书长张海波参加座谈会，为山东省外事研究与发展智库联盟、中德文化交流研究中心等揭牌。

2022 年 10 月 28 日至 30 日，青岛大学巴伐利亚研究中心执行主任綦甲福教授参加教育部外语教学指导委员会德语专业教学指导分委员会年会，并受邀在大会上做专题报告，介绍了青岛大学德语一流专业的发展以及青岛大学巴伐利亚研究中心、中德文化交流研究中心等的建设情况，获得了全国德语界同人及参会的德方机构——德国歌德学院、德国学术交流中心负责人的一致好评。

## 六、济南大学与友好省州的交流合作

### （一）国际友好学校建设情况

济南大学与德国巴伐利亚州的奥格斯堡大学、奥格斯堡应用技术大学，加拿大魁北克省的国立科学研究院、希尔布鲁克大学为国际友好学校。

### （二）校际合作交流情况

1.校际访问

德国巴伐利亚州。2014 年 11 月，济南大学副校长杜斌率团访问德国奥格斯堡大学。2017 年 9 月，济南大学副校长王保贤率团访问德国奥格斯堡应用技术大学。2018 年 1 月，德国奥格斯堡应用技术大学副校长曼弗雷德·克里斯丁·尤尔（Manfred Christian Uhl）率团访问济南大学。

加拿大魁北克省。2015 年 4 月，济南大学校长程新率团访问加拿大国立科学研究院，签署合作备忘录。2017 年 9 月，济南大学校长张士强率团访问加拿大希尔布鲁克大学，签署合作协议。

2.合作项目

德国巴伐利亚州。济南大学与德国奥格斯堡大学开展学生交换项目，选派德语系学生赴德国交换学习。

加拿大魁北克省。加拿大国立科学研究院费德里科·罗西（Federico Rosei）教授、维特罗内·菲奥伦扎（Vetrone Fiorenzo）教授多次来济南大学开展学术讲座。

## 七、山东农业大学与友好省州的交流合作

2017 年 10 月 13 日，山东农业大学与美国佐治亚大学签订合作框架协议。山东农业大学副校长王振林、佐治亚大学国际项目合作处主管艾默里

特·巴特(Amrit Bart)出席仪式并代表双方签约。根据协议,山东农业大学与佐治亚大学共同开展针对双方教师和学生的协作计划,在师生交流、出国学习、合作研究计划、研讨会、培训班等多个项目上开展合作。

2018 年 6 月,学校选派十名拟录取研究生赴佐治亚大学进行短期交流学习(见图 6-11)。在为期四周的学习中,通过学习英语强化课程、农业类专业课程、实地参观实验室和农场等,学生的英文水平和科研能力得到了很好的训练和提升。

图 6-11　2018 年 6 月,山东农业大学选派优秀学生赴佐治亚大学交流学习
图片来源:山东农业大学。

2019 年 12 月 8 日,中国山东农业大学-美国佐治亚大学联合科教中心在山东农业大学成立,山东农业大学党委副书记朱莉与美国佐治亚大学农学院院长助理、国际处处长艾默里特·巴特教授共同为科教中心揭牌(见图 6-12)。中国山东农业大学-美国佐治亚大学联合科教中心是佐治亚大学在国际上建立的继与意大利、乌干达、英国合作后的第四个国际合作中心,也是在亚洲建立的第一个国际合作中心。

图 6-12　2019 年 12 月 8 日，中国山东农业大学-美国佐治亚大学联合科教中心揭牌仪式

图片来源：山东农业大学。

2020 年以来，受新冠肺炎疫情影响，山东农业大学与佐治亚大学主要通过线上的方式开展合作交流。

# Chapter 6  Exchanges and Cooperation in Culture, Education, and Sports

## 6.1 Exchanges and Cooperation between Shandong Provincial Department of Culture and Tourism and Sister Provinces and States

### 6.1.1 Cultural Events in Celebration of the 30-year Partnership between Shandong Province and Bavaria, Germany

On 20 November 2017, celebrations marking the 30-year partnership between Shandong Province and Bavaria were held in Munich, Germany, which were attended by over 300 people, including Executive Vice Governor Li Qun, members of the Bavaria government and parliament, and people from all walks of life (see Figure 6-1). As a highlight of the celebrations, the *Confucius Ceremony Musical Dance* performed by Shandong Song and Dance Theater demonstrated the unique rhythm of fine traditional Chinese culture to German audiences. The "'Vision of Communication'—Photo Exhibition Celebrating the 30-year Partnership between Shandong Province and Bavaria" and "Rizhao Farmers' Art Exhibition" were also held during the celebrations.

Figure 6-1 Executive Vice Governor Li Qun attending celebrations for the 30-year partnership between Shandong province and Bavaria (20 November 2017)

Photo Credit: Foreign Exchange and Cooperation Department, Shandong Provincial Department of Culture and Tourism.

### 6.1.2 Shandong International Friendship Cities Conference for Cooperation and Development—Cultural and Tourism Cooperation Forum

On 16 October 2019, the Shandong International Friendship Cities Conference for Cooperation and Development—Cultural and Tourism Cooperation Forum were held at Jinan Nanjiao Hotel. Yu Jie, Vice Governor of Shandong Province, Christine Haberlander, Deputy Governor of Upper Austria, Austria, attended the conference and delivered speeches. Wang Lei, head of the Shandong Provincial Department of Culture and Tourism, chaired the forum. Themed "People-to-People Connectivity—Convergence of Culture and Tourism", the forum combined the promotion of cultural and tourism resources in Shandong, speeches by representatives of international sister cities, exhibitions, performances and talks to highlight the unique cultural and tourism resources and cultural customs of Shandong and various international sister cities. The forum was attended by members of delegations of international sister cities, representatives of foreign agencies stationed in China and Shandong, tourism professionals, and representatives from cultural and tourism departments and enterprises in 16 cities.

## 6.2 Exchanges and Cooperation between Shandong Administration of Sports and Sister Provinces and States

Since the establishment of the Regional Leaders' Summit, there have been frequent exchanges in the sports sector among sister provinces and states. So far, the Shandong Administration of Sports has established connections with the government sports departments or sports organizations and clubs in Upper Austria (Austria), Bavaria (Germany), Quebec (Canada), Western Cape (South Africa), São Paulo (Brazil), and Georgia (USA). It has signed the *Memorandum of Friendly Cooperation in Sports* with the Upper Austria Administration of Sport and the Sports and Recreation Department of São Paulo of Brazil, and the *Agreement for Friendly Cooperation in Sports* with the Bavarian Football Association and Bavarian Athletics Association, and conducted reciprocal visits by high-level sports personnel with Quebec (Canada), Western Cape (South Africa) and Georgia (USA).

### 6.2.1 Exchanges and Cooperation with Upper Austria, Austria

Since 2006, the Shandong Administration of Sports has conducted multiple reciprocal visits and exchanges with Austria's Upper Austria in such sports as football, table tennis, and badminton. As their exchanges in sports deepened, the two sides signed memorandums of understanding on sports exchanges three times in 2014, 2019, and 2023. In July 2006, a delegation from Shandong Province went to Upper Austria to participate in the 21st Upper Austria Cup International Youth Soccer Tournament, marking the beginning of sports exchanges and cooperation between the two sides. In April 2015, the table tennis team of Shandong Province visited Upper Austria at the invitation of the Upper Austria Table Tennis Association for training and exchanges, and was received by the deputy head of the Upper Austria Administration of Sports, Chairman of the Austrian Table Tennis Association, and Chairman of the Upper Austria Table Tennis Association. In July

2015, the Upper Austria table tennis team came to Shandong Province Table Tennis and Badminton Training Center for training and exchanges. In August 2015, a sports delegation from Shandong Province went on another visit to the Upper Austria Administration of Sports for talks on in-depth cooperation on equestrianism, fencing and other sports (see Figure 6-2).

Figure 6-2 Shandong Province sports delegation visiting the Upper Austria fencing team (August 2015)

Photo Credit: Foreign Sports Exchange Center, Shandong Administration of Sports.

From 2016 to 2018, the two sides conducted reciprocal visits and training activities for table tennis and badminton every year. In May 2019, Li Zheng, Director of the Shandong Administration of Sports, led a delegation to visit Upper Austria and signed the *Memorandum of Friendly Cooperation on Sports between the Shandong Administration of Sports (China) and the Upper Austria Administration of Sports (Austria)* with Mag. Thomas Stelzer, Governor of Upper Austria (see Figure 6-3). Since 2020, the COVID-19 has put a temporary stop to offline exchanges between the two sides.

Figure 6-3 Li Zheng, Director of the Shandong Administration of Sports, and Mag. Thomas Stelzer, Governor of Upper Austria, signing the memorandum of cooperation (May 2019)

Photo Credit: Website of the Government of Upper Austria, https://www.land-oberoesterreich.gv.at/219772.htm.

On 2 May 2023, Shandong Administration of Sports and Upper Austria Administration of Sports, Austria, signed the *Memorandum of Understanding on Strategic Cooperation in Sports between the Shandong Administration of Sports (China) and the Upper Austria Administration of Sports (Austria)* for the third time. The "Upper Austria Administration of Sports (Austria)-Shandong Administration of Sports (China)—High-level Training Base for Young Athletes", which is the first high-level youth training base established by the Shandong Administration of Sports overseas, provided venue for young athletes in Shandong in receiving training in Upper Austria in the future.

### 6.2.2 Exchanges and Cooperation with Bavaria, Germany

Shandong Province and Bavaria, Germany conduct close exchanges on sports, including multiple reciprocal visits. In July 2005, Zhang Hongtao, Deputy Director of the Shandong Administration of Sports, led a delegation from the Administration to visit Bavaria, Germany, marking the beginning of sports exchanges between the two sides. In June 2015, at the invitation of the Bavarian State Ministry for Education, Science and the Arts, Zhang Songlin, Director of the Shandong Administration of Sports, led a delegation to visit Bavaria. The two sides held talks on subsequent cooperation in football and other sports. On 22 July of the same year, Dr. Rainer Koch, Vice President of the German Football Association (DFB) and President of Bavarian Football Association, and Friederike Kromp, head coach of the Bavarian Football Association women's youth football team, came with the Bavarian State Government delegation for a visit. During this period, Shandong Football Management Center, and Shandong Province Football Association held a meeting with the Bavarian Football Association at the Shandong Sports Center and signed the *Shandong-Bavaria Memorandum for Cooperation in Football*, after which Friederike Kromp, head coach of the Bavaria women's youth football team, gave an onsite lecture to the women's youth football team of Shandong Province.

In November 2015, at the invitation of the Bavarian Football Association in Germany, a four-people delegation including Li Zheng, Executive Vice Chairman of Shandong Sports Federation, visited Bavaria to hold talks over specific matters for cooperation such as having Shandong women's youth football team go to Germany for training, hiring women's football coaches, and sending coaches to Germany for training. From 15 July to 4 August 2016, 29 members of Shandong women's youth football team went to the training base of the Bavarian Football Association in Germany for a 21-day training (see Figure 6-4).

Figure 6-4 Shandong women’s youth football team undergoing training at the training base of the Bavarian Football Association in Germany (July 2016)

Photo Credit: Foreign Sports Exchange Center, Shandong Administration of Sports.

In December 2016, invited by the Bavarian Athletics Association, Wang Yankui, Deputy Director of Shandong Administration of Sports, led a sports delegation of Shandong to Bavaria for exchanges in sports and friendly visits, and discussions of matters of cooperation. Shandong Province and Bavaria conducted talks on establishing friendly relations and cooperation on track and field events, sharing each other’s training resources, sending each other coaches and athletes for competitions and training, and building the Shandong-Bavaria track and field training base with the support of the Bavarian Athletics Association, and signed the *Memorandum of Friendly Cooperation between Shandong Administration of Sports and Bavaria Athletics Association*. In addition, in February 2018, January 2020, and March 2020, athletes from the Shandong Province Table Tennis Badminton Sports Management Center were invited to Bavaria for competitions and training.

### 6.2.3 Exchanges and Cooperation with Western Cape, South Africa

In October 2007, a government delegation from Western Cape, South Africa visited Shandong, and the two sides signed a *Memorandum of Understanding*. In November 2012, Gao Jinye, Deputy Director of Shandong Administration of Sports, led a Shandong sports delegation to the Department of Cultural Affairs and Sport of Western Cape, South Africa, to carry out friendly exchanges on sports. During the visit, the delegation inspected stadiums and gymnasiums, and held talks on cooperation in superior events and hiring excellent coaches to teach in Shandong. In July 2014, the two sides once again signed the *Sports Exchange and Cooperation Agreement* and made the decision to focus more on reciprocal visits and training of rugby coaches and the cultivation of youth athletes in subsequent bilateral exchanges and cooperation in sports. In September 2016, both sides agreed to continue performing their cooperation agreements and increase high-level reciprocal visits and exchanges in sports. Since 2007, both sides have sent athletes of such events as sailing, cycling, marathon, and kiting to participate in relevant competitions in the sister province (see Figure 6-5, 6-6).

Figure 6-5 The Department of Cultural Affairs and Sport of Western Cape sending five young sailors to participate in the seventh Qingdao International Sailing Week in Shandong, China (August 2015)

Photo Credit: Website of the Western Cape Government, https://www.westerncape.gov.za/news/aspiring-wc-sailors-compete-prestigious-yacht-race-china.

Figure 6-6 Ashley from South Africa participating in the Weifang International Kite Festival (April 2016)

Photo Credit: Website of the Western Cape Government, https://www.westerncape.gov.za/news/kiters-show-talent-international-kite-festivals-china.

In April 2017, at the invitation of the Department of Cultural Affairs and Sport of Western Cape, South Africa, a 6-person delegation including Sui Yongjun, Deputy Director of Shandong Administration of Sports, visited South Africa for friendly exchanges on sports. The two sides had substantive discussions on hiring excellent foreign rugby coaches to work in Shandong. They talked over matters in relation to sending athletes to participate in the Cape Town Marathon in December 2017. The two sides agreed to keep increasing reciprocal visits and exchanges in sports such as sailing, kiting, badminton, gymnastics, and cycling. They also discussed over selecting and sending table tennis coaches to teach in Western Cape.

### 6.2.4 Exchanges and Cooperation with São Paulo, Brazil

In January 2013, Zhang Hongtao, Director of Shandong Administration of Sports, led a delegation to visit São Paulo, Brazil, marking the beginning of dialogue on sports between the two sides. In July 2015, at the invitation of the Brazilian Confederation of Kungfu Wushu (Confederação Brasileira de

Kungfu Wushu), a ten-person delegation including Zhai Shoutao from Shandong Wushu Academy went to São Paulo, Brazil to compete in the first Annual Pan American Traditional Wushu and Taijiquan Championships and participate in the opening performance. In October 2015, invited by the Department of International Relations of São Paulo, Brazil, a Shandong sports delegation led by Sui Yongjun, Deputy Director of Shandong Administration of Sports, visited the SELJ. The two sides agreed to conduct regular reciprocal visits, strengthen cooperation in sports, and carry out reciprocal visits, competitions and exchanges in table tennis, football, basketball, and water sports. A decision was made to help Shandong with work related to the support team for Shandong athletes competing in the 2016 Rio Summer Olympics. In August 2016, at the invitation of the SELJ, the "Support Team for Shandong Athletes Competing in the 2016 Rio Summer Olympics" visited Rio and São Paulo (see Figure 6-7).

Figure 6-7 Shandong Provincial Athletes Support Team for Rio Olympics visiting Luneng Brazil Sports Center in São Paulo (August 2016)

Photo Credit: Foreign Sports Exchange Center, Shandong Administration of Sports.

### 6.2.5 Exchanges and Cooperation with Georgia (USA) and Quebec (Canada)

At the invitation of the Ministry of Education and Higher Education of

Quebec (Ministère de l'Éducation et de l'Enseignement supérieur), and the Georgia Department of Economic Development, USA, a Shandong sports delegation led by Wang Yankui, Deputy Director of Shandong Administration of Sports, visited the two regions in August 2017. Bilateral talks on conducting exchanges with Georgia on basketball, and with Quebec on winter sports were held.

## 6.3 Exchanges and Cooperation between Shandong University and Sister Provinces and States

### 6.3.1 University of Montreal, Quebec, Canada

The two universities signed a memorandum of understanding on academic exchange and cooperation in 2007, and an agreement on exchange student programs in May 2019. As of now, Shandong University has sent six students to University of Montreal for exchange study.

In 2021, the "Project for Joint Training of Reserve Talents for International Organizations between Shandong University and Universities in French-Speaking Regions" applied for by the School of Foreign Languages and Literature of Shandong University was granted funding from the China Scholarship Council. The project supports cooperation between Shandong University and University of Montreal, Canada and other universities known for cultivating talents for international organizations in cultivating young reserve talents interested in working in international organizations.

Additionally, Shandong University organized enterprise managers and faculty to attend online the "Renewable Energy Value Chain Lecture" held by HEC Montréal in July 2021.

### 6.3.2 Georgia Institute of Technology, USA

Shandong University Taishan College and Georgia Institute of Technology, USA signed an agreement on visiting students between them on November 2018, with Taishan College selecting and sending math-oriented juniors to

Georgia Institute of Technology to study for one semester every year. As of now, Shandong University has sent six students to Georgia Institute of Technology for exchange study. In addition, scholars from the School of Computer Science and Technology, Shandong University, and Georgia Institute of Technology, USA have conducted joint research.

### 6.3.3 Universities in Bavaria, Germany

#### 6.3.3.1 Technical University of Munich

Prof. Zhang Haixia from the School of Information Science and Engineering of Shandong University and Prof. Nossek from Technical University of Munich jointly launched the first IEEE International Workshop on Cross Layer Design (IEEE IWCLD), which has been successfully held in Jinan, Barcelona (Spain), Rennes (France) and Qingdao for four years.

#### 6.3.3.2 University of Erlangen-Nuremberg (FAU)

The two universities are keeping up their cooperation in Zhouyi studies. In 2013, the Center for Zhouyi & Ancient Chinese Philosophy of Shandong University established a branch at the University of Erlangen-Nuremberg. Under this cooperative framework, the two universities conduct exchanges such as doctoral student visits and lectures by experts. Every spring, the Faculty of Engineering of University of Erlangen-Nuremberg would select and send a group of students on a research tour to China, and Shandong University is one of the stops. The students will stay at Shandong University for four days, engaging in activities such as exchanging ideas with students of the Department of German Language and Literature, visiting the campus, visiting German companies in Jinan, and experiencing the local culture. This program has been ongoing for over ten years.

#### 6.3.3.3 Munich University of Applied Languages (SDI München)

Shandong University and Munich University of Applied Languages (SDI) have concluded a student exchange agreement. Every year, the Department of German Language and Literature at Shandong University will send one student to study at the SDI Munich for one year, while six students from the SDI Munich come to Shandong University to participate in the summer program.

#### 6.3.3.4 University of Augsburg

The fine art schools of Shandong University and the University of Augsburg maintain frequent exchanges and have cooperated in holding art exhibitions of teachers and students of the two schools in Jinan and Augsburg for many times. The Department of German Language and Literature at Shandong University send more than ten students to study at the University of Augsburg for one semester every year, and two students to participate in the University of Augsburg's summer program.

#### 6.3.3.5 Augsburg University of Applied Sciences

The schools of economics of Shandong University and Augsburg University of Applied Sciences exchange students to study at each other's schools.

#### 6.3.3.6 University of Munich (LMU)

Prof. Hans Van Ess, sinologist at LMU, has visited the Center for Literary Theory and Aesthetics of Shandong University several times to give lectures, and the two universities have good cooperation in the organization and research of Chinese literature.

## 6.4 Exchanges and Cooperation between Shandong University of Science and Technology (SDUST) and Sister Provinces and States

Shandong University of Science and Technology (SDUST) has established a strong partnership with Bavaria in Germany. Since 2003, SDUST has signed intercollegiate exchange and cooperation agreements to collaborate with three universities in Bavaria, including Ansbach University of Applied Sciences, Regensburg University of Applied Sciences in Eastern Bavaria (OTH Regensburg), and Rosenheim Technical University of Applied Sciences (TH Rosenheim).

### 6.4.1 Program on Joint Cultivation of Double-degree Undergraduates with Ansbach University of Applied Sciences

Ansbach University is a public university of applied sciences born in the modern educational reform in Germany. Since 2003, SDUST has been collaborating with Ansbach University of Applied Sciences to offer a double-degree undergraduate cultivation program. This program aims to cultivate high-level professionals with an international perspective and competitiveness, providing students with a broader development space. The program has won universal appraisal of all circles in Germany and China and has been included in the education cooperation programs between the two countries. Previously, the program followed a "2+1+2" model, where students were admitted as regular undergraduates through college entrance examination studied for two years at SDUST, followed by a year of German language training in a joint class, and then two years of study in Germany. However, due to the longer completion time, the program switched to a "2+2" model in 2011, where students study for the first two years at SDUST while taking German language courses, and then study for the remaining two years at Ansbach University of Applied Sciences. Upon completion of the required courses and internships, students, under the mutually recognized credit framework, will be granted with the bachelor's degree and graduation certificates from both universities.

Since 2004, SDUST has sent a total of 198 students to study at Ansbach University of Applied Sciences (see Figure 6-8). After returning China, these students have shown a significant advantage in job competition due to their international perspective, demeanor, professional level, language ability, and comprehensive quality, and they have been highly recognized by social units, with ideal position and salary. Those familiar with higher education and international exchange and cooperation spoke highly of this unique cooperation program.

Figure 6-8 International students from SDUST visiting the Bavarian State Ministry of Finance (2004)

Photo Credit: Shandong University of Science and Technology (SDUST).

### 6.4.2 Student Exchange Program of Regensburg University of Applied Sciences (OTH Regensburg), Eastern Bavaria, Germany

OTH Regensburg is a well-known public comprehensive university located in Regensburg, Bavaria, Germany. Its strengths lie in majors such as cultural studies, economics, information science, and life sciences. In 2019, SDUST signed an academic exchange agreement with OTH Regensburg regarding student and faculty exchanges and scientific collaboration. According to the agreement, OTH Regensburg agreed to accept undergraduate and graduate students from SDUST to study architecture, applied natural sciences and cultural studies, social and health management sciences, computer science and mathematics, electrical engineering and information technology, and mechanical engineering, which usually lasts for one semester. After the semester ends, the credits earned by students in Germany will be recognized by SDUST.

### 6.4.3 Student Exchange Program of Rosenheim (TH Rosenheim) Technical University of Applied Sciences, Germany

TH Rosenheim is situated in Rosenheim, a Bavarian city in southeast Germany. It pays close attention to the needs of the labor market and to cultivating students' practical vocational skills. Its training at all levels focus on in-depth cooperation with economic circles. In 2020, SDUST and TH Rosenheim signed an agreement on student exchange and cooperation in the field of engineering. According to the agreement, SDUST may send undergraduate and graduate students to study engineering, wood technology and architecture, computer science, management and engineering, and other engineering majors at TH Rosenheim, which usually lasts for one semester. After the semester ends, the credits earned by students in Germany will be recognized by SDUST.

## 6.5 Exchanges and Cooperation between Qingdao University (QDU) and Sister Provinces and States

Under the framework of the education cooperation project between Shandong Province and Bavaria (Germany), Qingdao University has seen a boom in exchanges and cooperation with educational institutions in Bavaria, and established cooperation with the University of Bayreuth, SDI München, Technical University of Munich, and University of Augsburg. In recent years, with a number of Sino-German cooperation projects taking root in Qingdao University, the university has developed into a German talent training base, a German language teacher training base, a base for cross-cultural German studies and a Bavarian research base in Shandong Province.

### 6.5.1 Shandong-Bavaria Education Cooperation Program, Department of German Language and Literature, Qingdao University

In 1994, Zhao Zhihao, governor of Shandong Province, and Armin Freitag,

German ambassador to China, inaugurated the Department of German Language and Literature at Qingdao University, marking the beginning of the “Shandong-Bavaria Education Cooperation Program” between the Shandong Provincial People's Government and the Bavarian State Government relying on Qingdao University. In 2003, the German major of Qingdao University was approved as an authorized program for a master's degree in German language and literature. Since 2004, the department has begun to enroll master's degree candidates in cross-cultural communication, German-speaking country literature, German linguistics and cross-cultural translation, and jointly trained them with University of Bayreuth. Since 2017, the department has begun to enroll graduate students in German translation with a master's degree in translation, and jointly cultivated them with University of Bayreuth and SDI München. It also established double-degree programs with Konstanz University of Applied Sciences and SDI München. In 2019, the German major was approved as one of the first national first-class undergraduate specialties.

The Department of German Language and Literature at Qingdao University is a member of the German Language Sub-committee of the National Advisory Committee on Teaching Foreign Languages to Majors in Higher Education under the Ministry of Education, an expert committee member of the China National Committee for Graduate Education of Translation and Interpreting, and a chairman member of the Shandong Advisory Committee on Teaching Non-general Foreign Languages to Undergraduates. The department currently boasts a team of 11 full-time faculty members, including two professors, two associate professors, two doctoral student supervisors, and seven postgraduate supervisors. All team members have studied in Germany, with six holding a PhD degree. Moreover, the department has entered long-term cooperation agreements with one expert from the German Academic Exchange Service (DAAD), three German emeritus professors, five visiting professors at home and abroad, and two off-campus co-advisors for postgraduate students majoring in translation.

By June 2022, the Department of German Language and Literature has witnessed the graduation of 24 cohorts of undergraduate students, 16 cohorts of German language and literature master's students, and four cohorts of master's students in German translation, and channeled over 700 graduates to the fields of cooperation and exchange between China and Germany, making it a high-quality German-speaking talent pool for boosting local economic development and conducting international cooperation in Shandong Province. Graduates from previous years have played an important role in the political, economic, cultural and educational fields of China and Germany, and have won wide acclaim from cultural institutions and enterprises in both countries. Of outstanding graduates some are employed in the management departments of world-renowned enterprises, such as Mercedes-Benz, Siemens, Volkswagen, and Audi; some work at the Chinese embassy and consulates in Germany, the Germany Embassy in China, and cultural institutions in China; and some have become the backbone of German language teaching and research in China's colleges and universities, serving as professors or discipline leaders of German major in some colleges and universities in China.

The Department of German Language and Literature is now recognized as a national first-class undergraduate specialty. In the past five years, it has undertaken four programs funded by the National Social Science Fund of China, one sub-project of the major project of the National Natural Science Foundation of China, two humanities and social sciences programs of the Ministry of Education, and one major commissioned project from the Shandong social science planning; it has one project selected into the first batch of new humanities and social sciences research and reform practice projects in China, one pilot project on the establishment of national virtual teaching and research office, one key education reform project in Shandong, and more than ten other provincial- and ministerial-level projects; it has compiled and published five national planning textbooks, and won one second prize of provincial teaching achievements and one first prize of school-level teaching achievements; it has one national first-class undergraduate course, one provincial first-class undergraduate course, one provincial ideological and political demonstration course, as well as two provincial-level think tanks.

### 6.5.2 Academic Exchanges

Since 1994, Qingdao University has established friendly and cooperative relations with the University of Bayreuth, SDI München, Technical University of Munich, University of Augsburg, German Hanns Seidel Foundation, German Academic Exchange Service (DAAD), Goethe Institute, and BayCHINA, carrying out in-depth academic exchanges and cooperation.

It jointly compiled *Cross-Cultural German Studies* with the University of Bayreuth, which has attracted great attention from the German language community in China. Additionally, the two universities have collaborated on compiling the textbook *Chinese-German Culture Comparison*, which has been widely used by many colleges and universities in China. Qingdao University's cross-cultural research has aroused the attention of domestic and foreign counterparts, and has been affirmed by the authorities in the German language community in China.

In 2015, the Department of German Language and Literature and SDI München successfully applied for a five-year Erasmus project funded by the European Union, which sponsors two postgraduate students to study at the university for one semester each year. Within the project framework, both sides also send teachers to each other for further study or short-term lectures.

In March 2016, Qingdao University signed a “2+2.5” double-degree program agreement with SDI München for undergraduate students. According to the agreement, after studying for two years at Qingdao University and passing the selection exam, undergraduate students of the Department of German Language and Literature need to go to SDI München to have a 2.5-year study of German translation. After passing all exams, they will be granted with a double bachelor's degree from both Qingdao University and SDI München.

Supported by full scholarships provided by the Bavarian government in Germany, the Department of German Language and Literature selects around ten undergraduate students each year to study for one semester at partner universities; all German language and literature master's students are sent to the University of Bayreuth for at least one semester of study; upon selection, some master's students in German translation may receive scholarships to study for one semester at the SDI München. Except for the inability to send students for exchange study due to the pandemic from 2020 to 2022, this scholarship program has been ongoing. At present, it has sent nearly 300 students with full scholarship. This scholarship program is second to none in German majors in China.

### 6.5.3 Establishment of Shandong Sino-German University Cooperation Center

With the development of the Department of German Language and Literature, in order to further promote exchanges and cooperation between colleges and universities in Shandong Province and those in Bavaria, Germany, the governments of the two regions have decided to establish a "university cooperation center" in the province and the state respectively.

In April 2007, the BayCHINA was established at the University of Bayreuth, and in October of the same year, the Shandong Sino-German University Cooperation Center (the "Sino-German Center") was established at Qingdao University.

The Sino-German Center has actively cooperated with the BayCHINA and successfully organized a range of large-scale events, including the BayCHINA Students' Summer Study Tour on Chinese Culture, the Shandong Young German Language Teachers Training Program, the China Intercultural German Studies Association Conference, the Bavarian Elite Academy Study Tour, and the Summer Study Tour of University Students from Shandong on German Culture, and helped arrange cultural and educational exchange programs to Bavaria for various groups. Given these efforts, the Sino-German Center has become an important platform for furthering exchanges and cooperation between Shandong Province and Bavaria, which has further expanded the exchanges and cooperation in education, science and technology, culture and other aspects between Shandong and Bavaria as well as Chinese and German universities, and promoted the in-depth development of Shandong-Bavaria education cooperation programs.

### 6.5.4 Establishment of TestDaF Examination Center at Qingdao University

In June 2004, the Ministry of Education's Overseas Examinations Center and the TestDaF Institute jointly established the TestDaF Center at Qingdao University, the eighth TestDaF Center in China (see Figure 6-9). Since its establishment, the center has quickly become the third largest one in China, thanks to its excellent management, advanced audio equipment, high-quality examiners, and conscientious invigilators, and is particularly well-received among TestDaF Institute and numerous candidates.

Figure 6-9 Unveiling Ceremony for TestDaF Center at Qingdao University (2004)

Photo Credit: Qingdao University.

### 6.5.5 Establishment of Goethe Language Center at Qingdao University

In September 2010, Qingdao University and Goethe Institute established the Goethe Language Center at Qingdao University, the sixth language center established by the Goethe Institute in China, following Shanghai, Tianjin, Nanjing, Xi'an, and Chongqing centers (see Figure 6-10). In March 2016, the center passed the global assessment of the Goethe Institute with excellent results, winning the affirmation and commendation of the Goethe Institute (Beijing). As of April 2020, the Goethe Language Center at Qingdao University has trained nearly 3,800 German learners, many of whom are currently studying for degrees in Germany, or engaged in German teaching and German-related work in China. It has long been a leader in the German language training industry in Qingdao.

Figure 6-10 Unveiling the nameplate of Goethe Language Center at Qingdao University (2010)

Photo Credit: Qingdao University.

### 6.5.6 Establishment of the Bavarian State Research Center at Qingdao University

In December 2019, Qingdao University established the Bavarian State Research Center.

On June 21, 2022, the "Richthofen and the Sino-German Cultural Exchange

Seminar & Launch Meeting of Richthofen's ‘China’ Translation Project”, hosted by the Publicity Department and the Office of Foreign Affairs Committee of the CPC Shandong Provincial Committee and Qingdao University, and co-organized by the Bavarian State Research Center, was held in Jinan. Prof. Qi Jiafu, executive director of the Center, delivered a special report at the meeting, introducing the research and work plan of Richthofen's ‘China’ translation project. At the meeting, Hu Jinyan, Party Secretary of Qingdao University, on behalf of Qingdao University, accepted the project commission letter signed by Bai Yugang, member of the Standing Committee of the CPC Shandong Provincial Committee and head of the Publicity Department.

On July 25, 2022, the Shandong Provincial Foreign Affairs Research and Development Think Tank Symposium was held at the Foreign Affairs Office of Shandong Provincial People's Government. Zhang Haibo, member of the Standing Committee of the CPC Shandong Provincial Committee and Secretary-General, attended the symposium and inaugurated the Shandong Provincial Foreign Affairs Research and Development Think Tank Alliance and the Sino-German Cultural Exchange Research Center, among other institutions.

From October 28 to 30, 2022, Professor Qi Jiafu, the executive director of the center, attended the annual meeting of the German Language Teaching Guidance Sub-Committee of the Ministry of Education's Foreign Language Instruction Committee and was invited to give a keynote speech, introducing the development of Qingdao University's first-class German major and the construction of think tank institutions such as the Qingdao University Bavarian Research Center and the Sino-German Cultural Exchange Research Center. His presentation received high praise from colleagues in the German language field across the country and representatives from German institutions such as the Goethe Institute and the German Academic Exchange Service.

## 6.6 Exchanges and Cooperation between the University of Jinan (UJN) and Sister Provinces and States

### 6.6.1 International Sister Universities

The University of Jinan has the University of Augsburg and Augsburg University of Applied Sciences in Bavaria, Germany as well as the National Institute of Scientific Research (INRS) and University of Sherbrooke in Quebec, Canada as its international friendship universities.

### 6.6.2 Intercollegiate Cooperation and Exchanges

#### 6.6.2.1 Visits at the University Level

Bavaria, Germany. In November 2014, Du Bin, Vice President of the University of Jinan, led a delegation to visit the University of Augsburg in Germany. In September 2017, Wang Baoxian, Vice President of the University of Jinan, led a delegation to visit Augsburg University of Applied Sciences in Germany. In January 2018, Manfred Christian Uhl, Vice President of Augsburg University of Applied Sciences, Germany, led a delegation to visit the University of Jinan.

Quebec, Canada. In April 2015, Cheng Xin, President of University of Jinan, led a delegation to visit INRS in Canada and signed a memorandum of cooperation. In September 2017, Zhang Shiqiang, President of the University of Jinan, led a delegation to visit University of Sherbrooke in Canada and signed a cooperation agreement.

#### 6.6.2.2 Cooperation Projects

Bavaria, Germany. The University of Jinan and the University of Augsburg in Germany carry out student exchange programs, and send students of the Department of German Language and Literature to Germany for exchange study.

Quebec, Canada. Prof. Federico Rosei and Prof. Vetrone Fiorenzo of National Institute of Scientific Research (INRS), Canada, have come to the University of Jinan for many times to give academic lectures.

## 6.7 Exchanges and Cooperation between Shandong Agricultural University (SDAU) and Sister Provinces and States

On October 13, 2017, SDAU signed a cooperation framework agreement with the University of Georgia (UGA). Wang Zhenlin, Vice President of SDAU, and Amrit Bart, Director of International Project Cooperation Department of UGA attended the ceremony and signed the agreement on behalf of both parties. According to the agreement, SDAU and UGA jointly develop collaborative programs for teachers and students of both sides, and cooperate in many projects such as teacher and student communication, study abroad, cooperative research programs, seminars and training courses.

In June, 2018, SDAU sent 10 graduate students to UGA for short-term exchange study (see Figure 6-11). During the four-week study, students took intensive English courses and agricultural professional courses, and visited laboratories and farms on the spot, etc., which greatly trained and improved their English level and scientific research abilities.

Figure 6-11 Outstanding students selected for communication and learning at University of Georgia (June 2018)

Photo Credit: Shandong Agricultural University (SDAU).

Shandong Agricultural University-University of Georgia Joint Research and Education Center was established at Shandong Agricultural University (SDAU) on 8 December 2019. The center was inaugurated by Zhu Li, Deputy Party Secretary of SDAU, and Prof. Amrit Bart, Assistant Dean for International Affairs at the UGA College of Agricultural and Environmental Sciences and Director of the College's Office of Global Programs (see Figure 6-12). This is the fourth cooperation center built by UGA in the world following the cooperation centers in Italy, Uganda and the UK. This is also the university's first international cooperation center in Asia.

Figure 6-12 Unveiling Ceremony for Shandong Agricultural University-University of Georgia Joint Research and Education Center (8 December 2019)
Photo Credit: Shandong Agricultural University (SDAU).

Affected by the COVID-19 pandemic, SDAU has adopted online means of cooperation and exchange with UGA since 2020.

# 第七章　科技领域交流合作

## 一、友好省州领导人峰会微小卫星论坛

2018 年，在第九次友好省州领导人峰会期间，山东省科技代表团参加了友好省州领导人峰会微小卫星论坛，交流了国际合作立方体卫星项目进展情况，并参加了开幕式、主题大会等(见图 7-1)。

5 月 17 日至 18 日，山东省科技代表团参加了微小卫星论坛的专题交流会，会议由来自德国巴伐利亚州维尔茨堡大学的克劳斯・席林(Klaus Schilling)教授主持，来自德国巴伐利亚州的弗洛伦丝・戈齐(Florence Gauzy)博士、安娜・奥曼(Anna Auman)博士，来自中国山东省的姜连祥高级工程师，来自美国佐治亚州的艾米・哈德纳尔(Amy Hudnall)教授，来自加拿大魁北克省的戴维・圣昂吉(David St-Onge)博士、汤姆・兰德里(Tom Landry)高级工程师、因吉・雅格穆尔(Inci Yagmur)主管等现场参会。

图 7-1　微小卫星论坛专题交流会参会专家合影

图片来源：山东航天电子技术研究所。

安娜·奥曼博士介绍了各参与方的项目进展情况，德国和中国明确了各研制三颗立方体卫星的任务，巴西表示正在申请研发经费，南非也计划研制一颗立方体卫星。项目应用方向包括立体测量（如火山灰观测）、洪水和火灾监测、闪电监测、海洋应用（如非法渔业、海岸线监视）、环境监测等。

随后，德国介绍了其立方体卫星的项目进展情况。山东省科技代表团成员在会上介绍了其研制的三颗立方体卫星的进展情况、零部件选用情况、能够向合作方提供的产品，以及希望从合作方采购的产品。当中国提出对地测控数传采用 X 波段时，德国对中国的产品很感兴趣，询问姿态控制系统是否采用星敏传感器，并表示对中方 80g 星敏传感器感兴趣，希望会后提供数据表。

来自南非西开普省的西亚斯·莫斯泰特（Sias Mostert）教授介绍了其载荷相机的功能、性能指标、研制周期等。艾米·哈德纳尔教授介绍了佐治亚州理工学院研制微纳卫星的现有基础。因吉·雅格穆尔主管表示会后将尽力向上级主管领导争取加拿大研制立方体卫星所需的经费。来自蒙特利尔理工学院 MIST（Making Innovative Space Technology）实验室的戴维·圣昂吉博士希望能够有机会参与该项目。

在第九次友好省州领导人峰会开幕式之后的欢迎酒会上，山东省科技代表团团员与各国与会专家、教授进行了深度交流，各方均表达了加强合作的意向。

## 二、第九次友好省州领导人峰会能源夏令营

在全球着力应对气候变化和能源危机的大背景下，实现以可再生能源为主的能源转型升级是推动能源革命和经济社会绿色低碳发展的核心举措。发展新型可再生能源技术已成为全球科学研究的重要任务之一，青年科技人员作为科技人才队伍的中坚力量，是可再生能源进入高质量发展新阶段的生力军。

2018 年 5 月 9 日至 18 日，第九次友好省州领导人峰会能源夏令营在加拿大魁北克省举行，来自七个友好省州的 20 余名青年科技人员参与其中（见图 7-2）。夏令营学员们系统学习了魁北克省能源分布情况、新能源及可再

生能源的利用情况以及加拿大在合理利用这些能源及生物质高效转化上所做的努力，对加拿大的能源利用、新能源发展有了更全面的认识。

图 7-2　夏令营团队合影
图片来源：山东省科学院能源研究所。

其间，学员听取了专家学者的报告，分别了解了巴西、德国的新能源分布、利用、开发情况及能源监测报告的生成过程，聆听了能源专家对友好省州能源网络地区的可再生能源状况的圆桌会议讨论，参观了魁北克大学三河城分校和魁北克水电研究院（见图 7-3），参加了第九次友好省州领导人峰会及能源会议的开幕式，参加了在费尔蒙芳缇娜城堡酒店举行的由七省州领导人及代表团出席的能源会议，会上以视频方式展示了各省州的能源情况及塞巴斯蒂安·戈尔斯（Sebastian Goers）博士所做的能源监测报告（见图 7-4）。

根据议程，安排学员分小组完成了各自的团队任务。来自不同地区、不同专业的学生组成三个跨区域、多学科小组，各小组选择一个区域，根据这个区域所存在的能源问题，以未来能源技术和能源效率为核心展开小组讨论，设计一套能够解决该区域能源问题的可行方案，并进行汇报。

图 7-3　夏令营学员参观魁北克水电研究院

图片来源：山东省科学院能源研究所。

图 7-4　夏令营学员与授课专家合影

图片来源：山东省科学院能源研究所。

## 三、友好省州领导人峰会科学网络新冠肺炎疫情专题线上会议

为推动多边科技合作、促进共同进步，德国巴伐利亚州牵头在友好省州领导人峰会下成立了友好省州领导人峰会科学网络，设立能源网络、全球航空航天园区、小卫星和数字化专家对话四个小组，除在峰会期间同步组织科技论坛等活动外，还在峰会闭会期间继续联络各省州组织交流活动等。

2020年9月15日至16日，“友好省州领导人峰会科学网络新冠肺炎疫情专题线上会议”举行。此次专题线上会议由奥地利上奥州主办，会议讨论了抗击新冠肺炎疫情的最佳实践、挑战和退出策略，推出了新的数字健康倡议，旨在扩大科学网络并进行跨学科研究。

### （一）新冠肺炎疫情科学圆桌会议

1.能源网络小组

塞巴斯蒂安·戈尔斯博士代表能源网络小组进行了主旨发言，介绍了“疫情期间和疫情后引导友好省州地区能源转型的方法”。友好省州领导人峰会的七个地区均在进行基于可再生能源扩张、能源储存设施开发、能源效率提高和能源节约措施实施的能源转型。能源转型将这些措施整合到应对疫情衰退期间和之后的经济复苏的全面战略中，可以在短期、中期和长期内为克服经济崩溃、创造就业机会以及实现或进一步增强经济繁荣和经济韧性做出贡献。通过友好省州领导人峰会能源网络在能源系统转型方面的跨学科和多区域合作，友好省州的政策制定者得以在新冠肺炎疫情期间和疫情之后制定出创造经济和生态红利的策略。

2.全球航空航天园区小组

全球航空航天园区（Global Aerospace Campus，GAC）首席科学家克劳斯·德雷克斯勒（Klaus Drechsler）教授进行了主旨发言，主题为“全球航空航天园区：通过教育连接地区”。克劳斯·德雷克斯勒教授就新冠肺炎疫情期间航空航天领域在线教育的发展发表了意见。

3.小卫星小组

由首席科学家克劳斯·席林教授主持的小卫星小组进行了“在疫情期间使用立方体卫星进行地球观测：远程信息处理国际任务（Telematics International Mission，TIM）视角”的主题演讲，展示了在新冠肺炎疫情期间，卫星图像如何可靠地提供关于精度和运动模式的信息，即使在访问困难和危险的情况下也是如此。该小组正在利用友好省州现有的关于微型卫星、空间通信（导航、制导、控制）、小型化和机电一体化的专业知识研发一种强大的微型卫星编队。

4.数字化专家对话小组

在数字化专家对话小组中，蒂埃里·卡尔森提（Thierry Karsenti）教授汇报了“数字时代的家庭工作和学习”研究成果。新冠肺炎疫情使得工作流程进一步数字化，以避免直接接触和进一步的传染。该小组对地方政府面临的一些基本问题进行了比较，如社会正义（包括获取、提供和教育）、商业基础设施（包括信息和网络安全产业）、社会归属和法律框架条件等。数字化加速具有一定的优势，如通过灵活性提高效率、节省成本等，同时也带来了重大的社会变革和挑战。在区域比较中，重要的是获取更多数据并更好地解释在更大社会背景下数字化的影响。

### （二）科学网络数字健康倡议启动

根据巴伐利亚州的提议，各友好省州于 2020 年 9 月 16 日启动了数字健康倡议。

在新冠肺炎疫情暴发之前，“第四次工业革命”在许多地方推动了医疗行业的重大变革。新冠肺炎疫情大大增加了对数字医疗的需求，特别是在人工智能、远程医疗和数字化医疗管理（诊所、实验室、卫生部门的数据和流程数字化）三个领域。数字医疗所带来的便利程度甚至超越了当前的紧急救护。在科学领域，区域示例展示了临床试验、疾病登记、电子健康记录和移动健康应用程序数据的自动组合将如何使研究人员快速访问大量信息，以及人工智能将如何越来越多地改变临床研究。

人工智能（Artificial Intelligence，AI）可以更可靠地分析、诊断、预测和对抗病毒，为患者提供更个性化的治疗方案。此外，人工智能可以加速药物更新，并能为追踪接触者的应用程序提供支持。从流行病学和临床研究到人工智能支持的诊断图像和文本数据评估以及患者监测等领域的成功应用已经充分证明了这一点。

数字健康是一个非常广泛的领域，目前由三大支柱组成：人工智能、医疗技术和临床研究。为了挖掘七省州的科技潜力，同时探索区域合作的特殊附加值，友好省州领导人峰会科学网络讨论了如何使联合分析方法更有意义。

在新冠肺炎疫情期间，友好省州领导人峰会科学网络在国际科学合作中表现出了极大的优势，这也说明了友好省州领导人峰会科学网络是各省州危机时期循证医学的重要资源。

## 四、友好省州领导人峰会科学网络数字周

### （一）2021 年第一次科学网络数字周

为应对新冠肺炎疫情，自 2021 年开始，友好省州领导人峰会科学网络每年举办线上数字周活动，活动每次持续五天，每天聚焦一个领域开展两个小时的科技研讨和交流。2021 年 6 月 14 日至 18 日，第一次科学网络数字周由德国巴伐利亚州主办，主题为“数据：区域资源的支撑”，七省州共计 140 余人参加。山东乾云信息科技集团、山东第一医科大学、中国科学院青岛生物能源与过程研究所的四位专家代表山东省参加数字化、数字健康和可再生能源领域活动并发表演讲。

此次科学网络数字周共包括“4＋1”个研究小组，分别是全球航空航天园区、能源网络、小卫星、数字化专家对话与数字健康倡议。

1.全球航空航天园区

全球航空航天园区小组活动拉开了会议周的序幕。应慕尼黑航空航天公司的邀请，结合其工作与此次数字周的主题，该小组探讨了“先进城市空中交通”问题。来自巴伐利亚州慕尼黑工业大学、佐治亚州佐治亚理工学院、魁北克省康考迪亚大学和圣保罗州圣保罗大学的专家就先进城市空中交通的不同方面发表了演讲，包括可持续性、社会接受度、监管和空中交通管制方面的内容。专家们回顾了各自地区先进城市空中交通的最新发展，阐述了新兴趋势以及如何在不同的文化、政治和地理背景下应对挑战。

2.能源网络

能源网络小组在2018年监测报告和2020年友好省州能源转型SWOT(Strengths、Weaknesses、Opportunities、Threats,即优势、劣势、机会、威胁)分析工作的基础上就“能源建模和系统”进行了交流。来自巴伐利亚州、佐治亚州、魁北克省、圣保罗州、山东省和上奥州的专家进行了即兴发言,讨论的议题涵盖气候变化和能源转型的大数据分析、智能电网和氢等新能源、使用生命周期分析工具进行区域建模、生物燃料以及宏观经济和社会经济指标等。

3.小卫星

小卫星组举行了内部项目会议。该小组将努力确保来自巴伐利亚州的三颗远程信息处理观察任务(Telematics Observation Mission,TOM)卫星和来自山东的三颗微型卫星在2021年发射,旨在将尽可能多的地区整合到友好省州地面站网络中。卫星连接的地面站越多,覆盖范围就越大,可以下载和分析的地球观测数据也就越多。克劳斯·席林教授展示了可以为各地区生成的各种可能的数据类型,证明了该项目为直接数据生成和分析带来的价值。

4.数字化专家对话与数字化健康倡议

数字化专家对话与数字化健康倡议小组举行了联席会议。该组报告了在“数字领域工作”方面2020年的最新情况。来自巴伐利亚州、佐治亚州、圣保罗州和山东省的专家介绍了友好省州领导人峰会七个地区在工作和商业模式方面的数字化转型,包括高等教育、网络安全、开放研究和企业方面。新兴的数字化健康倡议小组听取了巴伐利亚州、圣保罗州、山东省和上奥州的专家在电子健康平台、基于人工智能的医疗应用、大数据,以及疾病识别、验证、预测等方面的主旨发言。

5.科学网络跨学科联合会议

友好省州领导人峰会科学网络召开了主题为“数据:区域资源的支撑”的跨学科联合会议。参加本次会议的有来自“4+1”研究小组的代表以及来自科学网络政治、科学和科学管理层的代表。巴伐利亚州欧洲和国际事务部部长梅拉妮·胡姆尔(Melanie Huml)和上奥州常务副州长克里斯蒂娜·哈博兰德视频致辞。来自巴伐利亚州、魁北克省和圣保罗州的专家进行了主题演讲。与会者一致认为科学网络在友好省州领导人峰会上发挥着关键作用,其作为有效合作的稳定平台,为地区政府举措的关键领域提供了高度信任的网络。

## (二)2022年第二次科学网络数字周

2022年4月4日至8日,第二次科学网络数字周由德国巴伐利亚州主办,主题为“有韧性和可持续的地区复苏”,来自七个友好省州的112名专家学者参加了本次活动(见图7-5)。30多位专家学者进行了主旨发言,分别介绍了先进的空中交通、能源安全和系统复原力、微型卫星的数据使用可能性以及区域数字卫生举措等。山东第一医科大学人工智能与大数据学院院长于长斌教授参加了数字健康领域的研讨并演讲,对山东省开展的“网络-物理联合诊断”“基于深度学习的医学影像处理”等情况进行了推介;中国科学院青岛能源与过程研究所薛松教授参加了可再生能源领域的活动。

图7-5 2022年第二次科学网络数字周(线上)

图片来源:山东省科技厅、山东第一医科大学。

1. 联合开幕式

4月4日,友好省州领导人峰会科学网络举办了联合开幕式。巴伐利亚州欧洲和国际事务部部长梅拉妮·胡姆尔、圣保罗研究基金会科学主任路易斯·尤金尼奥·梅洛(Luiz Eugênio Mello)和上奥州新任科学网络政治协调员迈克尔·塞克莱纳(Michael Secklehner)先后致欢迎辞,强化了友好省州领导人峰会科学网络与峰会各友好省州政府之间的联系。

2.全球航空航天园区:城市和先进的空中交通

4月5日,全球航空航天园区小组展示了他们最新的电子学习课程“城市空中交通”(见图7-6)。该课程由克劳斯·德雷克斯勒教授主讲,是全球航空航天园区系列电子学习课程中的第三门课程,是来自不同地区的友好省州领导人峰会科学网络合作伙伴模块的第一门课程。“城市空中交通”可在在线教育平台(coursera)上免费获得，并将添加更多模块。全球航空航天园区小组围绕数字周主题分享了他们在城市和先进空中交通领域的专业知识，演示了数字周主题在区域层面的一系列发展。

图 7-6　全球航空航天园区小组“城市空中交通”课程(线上)

图片来源：山东省科技厅、山东第一医科大学。

3.能源网络：弹性能源系统——危机时期的能源安全和供应

4 月 6 日，能源网络小组举行了会议，围绕“弹性能源系统——危机时期的能源安全和供应”主题进行了探讨(见图 7-7)。三位发言者分别介绍了他们所在地区的能源安全经验和相关系统，列举了对矿物燃料进口的依赖、在消费者充分赋权的情况下增加系统复杂性以及输电网数量庞大等实例。在小组讨论环节，来自五个地区的专家探讨了气候变化和供应链对能源转型的影响、社会接受度和政府行动的可能性及局限性，以及对不同地区未来能源系统至关重要的因素。与会专家普遍认为，在能源话题上与公民互动是一项必要但艰巨的挑战，通过定价激励措施和其他工具增强人们的认识至关重要。

图 7-7　“弹性能源系统——危机时期的能源安全和供应”主题会议(线上)

图片来源：山东省科技厅、山东第一医科大学。

4.小卫星小组：远程信息处理国际任务和远程信息处理观察任务

4 月 6 日，克劳斯·席林教授及其团队向各地区的合作伙伴介绍了远程信息处理国际任务和远程信息处理观察任务的最新进展(见图 7-8)。巴伐利亚州的三颗远程信息处理观察任务微型卫星将于 2022 年年底发射。正在建立的友好省州地面站网络将支持卫星下载数据。在这个框架中，正在建立一个科学网络用户社区，使对即将产生的地球观测数据特别是地球科学应用感兴趣的用户参与进来。

图 7-8　小卫星：远程信息处理国际任务和远程信息处理观察任务进展汇报（线上）

图片来源：山东省科技厅、山东第一医科大学。

5.数字健康倡议：与联合路线图保持一致的区域举措

4 月 7 日，数字健康倡议小组举行了简短会议（见图 7-9）。塞巴斯蒂安·比克豪普特（Sebastian Bickelhaupt）博士回顾了小组目前所取得的进展。基于数字健康倡议的联合路线图，五个省州的代表分享了各自地区的数字健康项目和倡议的案例。在小组讨论中，发言者讨论了推动数字健康倡议向前发展的下一步计划。潜在的合作主题涵盖了数据合作（数据处理、数据库以及数据保护）、培训下一代数字健康专业人员所面临的挑战以及人工智能应用面对的全球挑战等内容。

图 7-9　数字健康倡议小组会议（线上）

图片来源：山东省科技厅、山东第一医科大学。

6.闭幕会

4 月 8 日，友好省州领导人峰会科学网络举行了联合闭幕会议，对一周的会议内容进行了总结回顾，包括四个主题会议的摘要、对此次数字周活动的反思，同时对科学网络数字周模式以及科学网络的现状进行了评估（见图 7-10）。基于 2021 年和 2022 年的经验，巴伐利亚州团队建议科学网络保留数字周的形式，将其作为新冠肺炎疫情后的年度交流工具，并鼓励其他省州举办下一届会议。随后，山东省的专家介绍了山东省 2023 年第十一次友好省州领导人峰会计划的相关信息,包括将科学网络纳入会议范畴。在闭幕辞中总结指出,科学网络在推动多区域合作、选择更紧密地参与多边框架以追求共同目标方面发挥着关键作用。

图 7-10　科学网络联合闭幕会议(线上)

图片来源:山东省科技厅、山东第一医科大学。

## (三)2023 年第三次科学网络数字周

2023 年 4 月 24 日至 28 日,第三次科学网络数字周活动由德国巴伐利亚州牵头,邀请山东省作为主要参与省份,主题为"山东和科学网络:从赫尔辛继续前行",七省州共计近 130 人参加。山东省邀请了来自山东省科学院能源研究所、山东第一医科大学、山东航天威能科技有限公司、山东航天电子技术研究所、中国科学院青岛生物能源与过程研究所等九家单位 18 位专家参加四个专题领域和一个综合领域的活动。

1.可再生能源领域

可再生能源领域的主题为"减缓气候变化——从区域角度看能源系统中的挑战与机遇"。齐鲁工业大学(山东省科学院)宋安刚教授等五位山东省专家围绕制氢技术、有机固体废弃物制备生物天然气、正极材料结构设计等进行了深度分享,对拟开展的合作项目进行了推介;来自巴伐利亚州及其他省州的专家围绕能源转型和氢能源技术进行了交流。

2.小卫星领域

小卫星领域的主题为"卫星、地面站网络和数据分析"。山东航天电子技术研究所的姜连祥等三位专家围绕基于卫星遥感图像的海洋生态环境监测、卫星众包计算与应用服务平台、山东的三颗小卫星等进行了分享,并同其他省州的专家进行了互动讨论。

3.航空航天领域

航空航天领域的主题为"运用技术创新保护环境"。山东航天威能科技有限公司张烨和烟台先进材料与绿色制造山东省实验室刘旭庆两位专家从碳减排等角度对山东省在航空航天领域的研究进行了推介分享。来自魁北克省及其他省州的专家就航空航天领域的可持续发展和城市空中交通等进行了交流。

4.数字健康领域

数字健康领域的主题为“数据在数字健康中的作用”。山东第一医科大学党委副书记刘思金、山东大学薛付忠教授两位专家围绕大数据预测和疾病预防、联邦医学科学大数据平台等进行了分享。同时，来自上奥州及其他省州的专家围绕基于人工智能的医疗数据分析、数字健康数据共享的国际模式等内容进行了交流。

5.综合领域

综合领域的主题为“山东和科学网络：从赫尔辛继续前行”。齐鲁工业大学（山东省科学院）国际合作处处长杨合同教授、山东第一医科大学医学人工智能与大数据学院于长斌教授等五位专家学者结合本次活动主题对山东省科技创新发展概况、各领域研究趋势、未来科技合作重点方向等进行了介绍与分享。

2023 年的科学网络数字周是科学网络首次将山东省作为主要参与省份举办的活动，充分展示了山东省在可再生能源、小卫星、航空航天、数字健康等领域的研究进展和成果，山东省向其他省州发出了合作邀请，为下半年由山东省主办科学网络线下活动奠定了良好基础（见图 7-11）。

图 7-11　数字周综合领域会议（线上）

图片来源：山东省科技厅、山东第一医科大学。

# Chapter 7 Exchanges and Cooperation in Science and Technology

## 7.1 RLS-Small Satellites Forum

In 2018, dring the ninth Regional Leaders' Summit, Shandong Provincial Delegation of Science and Technology participated in the Small Satellites Forum to exchange information about the progress of CubeSat projects. The delegation also attended the opening ceremony and the thematic meeting (see Figure 7-1).

The delegation participated in a symposium on small satellites from 17 to 18 May. The symposium was chaired by Prof. Klaus Schilling from University of Würzburg (JMU) in Bavaria, Germany. Participants included Dr. Florence Gauzy and Dr. Anna Aumann from Bavaria; Jiang Lianxiang, a senior engineer from Shandong; Prof. Amy Hudnall from the State of Georgia; and Dr. David St-Onge, Tom Landry, a senior engineer, and Inci Yagmur, a director, from Quebec.

Figure 7-1 Group photo of participating experts

Photo Credit: Shandong Institute of Space Electronic Technology (SISET).

Dr. Anna Aumann unveiled the project progress made by all participating parties. Germany and China had decided to develop three CubeSats each; Brazil said it was applying for research funds; and South Africa also planned to develop one CubeSat. Project applications included stereoscopic measurement (such as volcanic ash observation), flood and fire monitoring, lightning monitoring, marine application (such as illegal fishery and coastline monitoring), and environmental monitoring.

After that, the German party presented the progress of its CubeSat project. At the symposium, a member of the Shandong Provincial Delegation of Science and Technology reported the research progress of the three CubeSats undertaken by China, the selection of components and products that can be supplied for partners. When he mentioned that the X band was used for TT&C and data transmission to ground, the German party showed interest in Chinese products, asking whether star sensors were used in China's attitude control system and offering to provide relevant data sheets after the meeting if China was interested in 80g star sensors.

Prof. Sias Mostert from Western Cape, South Africa presented functions, performance indicators and development cycles of the payload camera developed by the country. Prof. Amy Hudnall briefed about the existing foundation for developing micro/nano satellites at Georgia Institute of Technology. Director Inci Yagmur said that after the meeting, he would strive for funding support from his superiors for the development of CubeSats in Canada. Dr. David St-Onge worked at MIST laboratory, Polytechnique Montreal. He also hoped to participate in this project.

At the welcome reception after the opening ceremony, members of the Shandong Provincial Delegation of Science and Technology had in-depth exchanges with experts and professors from other countries. They all expressed intention to strengthen cooperation.

## 7.2 International Summer School on Renewable Energy of the RLS-Energy Network (ISS-RLS Energy 2018)

Amid global efforts to address climate change and energy crisis, achieving energy transition and upgrading based on renewable energy is the core measure to promote the energy revolution and the green and low-carbon economic and social development. Developing new types of renewable energy technology has become an important task of global scientific research. As the backbone of technological personnel, young technicians play a key role when renewal energy ushers in a new stage of high-quality development.

International Summer School on Renewable Energy of the RLS-Energy Network (ISS-RLS Energy 2018) took place in Quebec, Canada from 9 to 18 May 2018. More than 20 young technicians from the seven RLS regions participated in the activity (see Figure 7-2). Students systematically studied the distribution of energy and the utilization of new and renewable energy in Quebec, as well as the efforts made by Canada in rational use of these resources and efficient conversion of biomass. They acquired more comprehensive information about resource utilization and new energy development in Canada.

Figure 7-2 Group photo of summer team

Photo Credit: Energy Research Institute, Shandong Academy of Sciences.

During the event, students listened to lectures by professors and scholars. They understood the situation of new energy distribution, utilization and development in Brazil and Germany, as well as the process of generating energy monitoring reports. They listened to roundtable discussions by energy experts on the situation of renewable energy in the RLS-Energy Network. Besides, students visited University of Quebec at Trois-Rivieres (UQTR) and Hydro-Quebec Research Institute (IREQ) (see Figure 7-3), attended the opening ceremony of the ninth RLS and its energy conference, and participated in the energy conference for leaders and delegations from the seven RLS regions at the Fairmont Le Chateau Frontenac. At the conference, the situation of energy in the RLS regions and an energy monitoring report by Dr. Sebastian Goers were presented via video link (see Figure 7-4).

Students completed their respective tasks by group according to the agenda. Students from different regions and majors formed three trans-regional and multidisciplinary groups. Each group carried out discussions based on existing energy problems in the selected region, focusing on future energy technology and energy efficiency, and worked out a feasible solution to these problems, which was reported in the PPT format.

Figure 7-3 Students visiting IREQ

Photo Credit: Energy Research Institute, Shandong Academy of Sciences.

Figure 7-4 Group photo of students and lecturers

Photo Credit: Energy Research Institute, Shandong Academy of Sciences.

## 7.3 RLS-Sciences Virtual Symposium on COVID-19

Led by Bavaria, the RLS-Sciences network was established under the Regional Leaders' Summit to promote multilateral scientific and technological cooperation and common progress. The network was comprised of four groups: energy network, global aerospace campus, small satellites, and expert dialogue on digitalization. It organized scientific and technological forums and other activities during the summit and carried out intersessional exchange activities in connection with the RLS regions.

RLS-Sciences Virtual Symposium on COVID-19 took place from 15 to 16 September 2020. Best practices, challenges and exit strategies for combatting the COVID-19 pandemic were discussed during the virtual symposium, which was hosted by Upper Austria. And a new RLS-Digital Health Initiative was launched with the aim of expanding the scientific network and conducting interdisciplinary research.

### 7.3.1 RLS-Sciences Round Table on COVID-19

#### 7.3.1.1 RLS-Energy Network

On behalf of the Energy Network, Dr. Sebastian Goers presented “Approaches for Navigating the RLS Regions' Energy Transition during and after the COVID-19 Crisis”. In the seven RLS partner regions, energy transition based on the expansion of renewable energy combined with the development of energy storage facilities, the increase in energy efficiency and the implementation of energy saving measures are ongoing. By integrating these into a comprehensive strategy for economic recovery during and after the COVID-19 recession, energy transition measures can contribute in the short, medium and long term to overcoming the economic collapse, creating urgently needed jobs and achieving or further strengthening prosperity and resilience. Through the interdisciplinary and multi-regional cooperation in the RLS Energy Network on energy system transformation, strategies for the simultaneous creation of economic and ecological dividends during and after the COVID-19 crisis are being derived for the political decision makers of the RLS partner regions.

#### 7.3.1.2 Global Aerospace Campus

Prof. Klaus Drechsler, lead scientist of the Global Aerospace Campus (GAC), delivered a keynote speech "Global Aerospace Campus: Connecting Regions Through Education". Prof. Klaus Drechsler offered insights into the developments of online education in the aerospace sector during the pandemic.

#### 7.3.1.3 Small Satellites

Presented by lead scientist Prof. Klaus Schilling, the Small Satellites group presentation, "Earth Observation with CubeSats in Times of COVID-19: Perspectives from the Telematics International Mission (TIM)" demonstrated how during the COVID-19 pandemic, satellite images reliably provided information on precise areas and movement patterns-even where access was difficult and dangerous. The research group is working on a powerful formation of pico-satellites in orbit, using the expertise on pico-satellites, space communication (navigation, guidance, control), miniaturization and mechatronics available in the RLS regions.

#### 7.3.1.4 RLS-Expert Dialogue on Digitalization

For the RLS-Expert Dialogue on Digitalization group, Prof. Thierry Karsenti presented "Working and Learning from Home in a Digital Era". The COVID-19 crisis has suddenly led to further digitalization of work processes in order to avoid direct contacts and further contagion. The group developed their comparison of which fundamental questions of social justice (access, provision and education), business infrastructure (existence of an ICT and cybersecurity industry), social affiliation and legal framework conditions are facing regional governments. The accelerated digitalization of the world of work holds potential (efficiency through flexibility, cost savings, etc.) and also significant social changes and challenges. In a regional comparison, it is important to obtain further data and to better interpret the effects in the larger social context.

### 7.3.2 Launch of the RLS-Digital Health Initiative

Following a Bavarian proposal, the RLS regions launched the Digital Health Initiative on 16 September, 2020.

Before the COVID-19 crisis, significant changes in the health sector were underway in many places in the course of the fourth industrial revolution. The pandemic massively accelerated the demand for digital healthcare solutions, particularly in the three areas of Artificial intelligence (AI), telemedicine and digitalized healthcare management (digitalization of data and processes in clinics, practices, laboratories and health authorities). They showed the opportunities that digital healthcare offers, even beyond the current emergency. In the scientific field, regional examples show how the automated combination of data from clinical trials, disease registries, electronic health records and mobile health applications will give researchers rapid access to a wealth of information, and how AI will increasingly transform clinical research.

AI allows the virus to be analyzed, diagnosed, predicted and combatted more reliably, with more individualized treatments for affected patients. In addition, AI supports faster ways of drug and medication development and provides the basis for various apps for contact tracing. This is already demonstrated by successful applications in the seven regions-from epidemiology and clinical research to AI-supported diagnostic image and text data evaluation and patient monitoring.

Digital health is a very broad field and currently consists of three pillars: AI, MedTech and clinical research. In order to exploit the scientific and technological potential of the seven regions and at the same time to sound out the particular added-value of regional cooperation, the RLS-Sciences network discussed possibilities to analyze more closely where exactly a joint approach would make the most sense.

The international scientific cooperation in the RLS-Sciences network demonstrated its strengths during the COVID-19 pandemic, and showed that the network is an important resource for evidence-based policy in times of crisis at the regional level.

## 7.4 RLS-Sciences Digital Week

### 7.4.1 RLS-Sciences Digital Week 2021

Affected by the COVID-19, the RLS-Sciences network met every year at the five-day digital week starting 2021 to discuss and exchange views about scientific and technological topics with a focus on one area for two hours per day. From 14 to 18 June 2021, Bavaria hosted the first RLS-Sciences Digital Week with the theme "Data as a Resource for the Regions". Over 140 participants joined, representing all the seven RLS partner regions. On behalf of Shandong, four experts from Shandong MASSCLOUDS Information Technology Group, Shandong First Medical University (SDFMU) and the Qingdao Institute of Bioenergy and Bioprocess Technology (QIBEBT) of the Chinese Academy of Sciences (CAS) participated in activities on digitalization, digital health and renewable energy and delivered speeches.

The RLS-Sciences Digital Week 2021 was comprised of 4+1 research groups—Global Aerospace Campus, Energy Network, Small Satellites and the RLS-Expert Dialogue on Digitalization with the RLS-Digital Health Initiative.

#### 7.4.1.1 RLS-Global Aerospace Campus

The RLS-Global Aerospace Campus kicked off the conference week. At the invitation of Munich Aerospace, the group brought together their work and the conference theme by addressing "Advanced (Urban) Air Mobility". Presentations were given by experts from Technical University of Munich in Bavaria, Georgia Institute of Technology, Concordia University in Quebec and University of São Paulo on the differing facets of advanced urban air mobility, including sustainability, social acceptance, regulation, and air traffic control considerations. Providing a review of the latest developments in advanced urban air mobility in their respective regions, the experts elaborated on emerging trends and how challenges are being addressed in different cultural, political and geographic contexts.

#### 7.4.1.2 RLS-Energy Network

The RLS-Energy Network met to exchange on “Energy Modelling and Systems”, building upon their work in the 2018 Monitoring Report and the 2020 SWOT (Strengths, Weaknesses, Opportunities, Threats) Analysis of energy transition in the RLS regions. Experts from Bavaria, Georgia, Quebec, São Paulo, Shandong and Upper Austria delivered keynote speeches on issues ranging from big data analysis for climate change and energy transition to smart grids and new energy sources like hydrogen through to regional modelling with life cycle analysis tools and biofuels as well as macro and socioeconomic indicators.

#### 7.4.1.3 RLS-Small Satellites

The RLS-Small Satellites group met for an internal project meeting. The group was working to ensure the launch of three TOM satellites from Bavaria and three pico-satellites from Shandong in 2021, with the aim to integrate as many regions as possible into an RLS ground station network. The more ground stations the satellites can connect to, the better the coverage will be and the more Earth observation data can be downloaded and analyzed. Prof. Schilling (Bavaria) showed a variety of possible data types which could be generated for the regions, demonstrating the value the project brings for direct data generation and analysis.

#### 7.4.1.4 RLS-Expert Dialogue on Digitalization and RLS-Digital Health Initiative

The RLS-Expert Dialogue on Digitalization held a joint session together with the new RLS-Digital Health Initiative. The group reported on updates from their 2020 work in the field of “Work in the Digital Area”, with presentations from Bavaria, Georgia, São Paulo and Shandong on the digital transformation taking place in the seven RLS regions in the way of working and doing business, including higher education, cybersecurity, open research and enterprises. The emerging Digital Health group heard contributions from Bavaria, São Paulo, Shandong, and Upper Austria on e-health platforms, AI based medical applications, big data and disease identification, verification and prediction.

#### 7.4.1.5 RLS-Sciences Joint Interdisciplinary Session

The RLS-Sciences network convened a joint interdisciplinary session on the topic "Data as a Resource for the Regions". This session included representatives from the 4 + 1 research groups, as well as the political, scientific and science management levels of RLS-Sciences. The session was opened with video greetings from Melanie Huml, Bavarian Minister for European and International Relations, and Christine Haberlander, Deputy Governor of Upper Austria. Experts from Bavaria, Quebec and São Paulo delivered keynote speeches. Participants unanimously agreed that RLS-Sciences plays a key role in the Regional Leaders' Summit, serving as a stable platform for effective collaboration across regions which is of key relevance for regional government initiatives.

### 7.4.2 RLS-Sciences Digital Week 2022

The RLS-Sciences Digital Week 2022 took place from 4 to 8 April 2022, hosted by Bavaria. The theme for the week was "Sustainable and Resilient Regional Recoveries". Altogether, a total of 112 participants from all the seven RLS partner regions joined to listen to over 30 speakers who presented on advanced air mobility, energy security and system resilience, data use possibilities for pico-satellites and regional digital health initiatives (see Figure 7-5). Prof. Yu Changbin, Dean of the SDFMU College of Artificial Intelligence and Big Data for Medical Sciences (AIMS), attended the Digital Health Initiative session and delivered a speech to recommend "network-physics joint diagnosis" and "medical image processing based on deep learning", which were performed in Shandong; Prof. Xue Song from the Qingdao Institute of Bioenergy and Bioprocess Technology, Chinese Academy of

Sciences participated in the activities in the Renewable Energy Session.

Figure 7-5 The Second RLS-Sciences Digital Week of 2022 (online)

Photo Credit: Department of Science & Technology of Shandong Province, Shandong First Medical University.

#### 7.4.2.1 Joint Opening Ceremony

The RLS-Sciences held a joint opening ceremony for the RLS-Sciences Digital Week on April 4. Welcoming messages from Bavaria's Minister of State for European and International Affairs, Melanie Huml, the São Paulo Research Foundation's Scientific Director, Prof. Luiz Eugênio Mello, and Upper Austria's new RLS-Sciences Political Coordinator, Michael Secklehner, reinforced the connection between RLS-Sciences and the regional governments of the Regional Leaders' Summit.

#### 7.4.2.2 Global Aerospace Campus: Urban and Advanced Air Mobility

On April 5, the Global Aerospace Campus group offered a sneak preview of their latest e-Learning offering "Urban Air Mobility" (see Figure 7-6). The course, presented by Prof. Klaus Drechsler, is the third in a series of e-Learning courses from the Global Aerospace Campus, and the first to include modules from RLS-Sciences partners in different regions. "Urban Air Mobility" is freely available online on the coursera platform, and further modules will be added throughout the year. The speakers for the Global Aerospace Campus session shared their expertise in the field of urban and advanced air mobility in connection with the overall April Digital Week theme of "Resilient and Sustainable Regional Recoveries". The presentations demonstrated the range of developments in the topic at the regional level.

Figure 7-6 E-Learning offering "Urban Air Mobility" by the Global Aerospace Campus group

Photo Credit: Department of Science & Technology of Shandong Province, Shandong First Medical University.

#### 7.4.2.3 RLS-Energy Network: Resilient Energy Systems-Energy Security and Supply in Times of Crisis

The Energy Network met on April 6 to explore the theme "Resilient Energy Systems-Energy Security and Supply in Times of Crisis" (see Figure 7-7). Three speakers presented their regional energy security experiences and related systems, where references to dependency on fossil fuel imports, increasing system complexity without sufficient consumer empowerment, and sheer volume of transmission grids were shared as examples. The session culminated with a panel of high-level experts from five regions, who explored the implications of climate change and supply chains on energy transition, the possibilities and limits of social acceptance and government action, and considered what will be critical for future energy systems in different regions. The panel generally agreed that engaging with citizens on energy topics is a necessary but difficult challenge, and opportunities to increase awareness through pricing incentives and other tools are of critical importance.

Figure 7-7 Online symposium on "Energy Network: Resilient Energy Systems-Energy Security and Supply in Times of Crisis"

Photo Credit: Department of Science & Technology of Shandong Province, Shandong First Medical University.

#### 7.4.2.4 Small Satellites: Telematics International Mission (TIM) and Telematics Observation Mission (TOM)

On April 6, Prof. Klaus Schilling and his team presented updates on the status of the Telematics International Mission (TIM) and the Telematics Observation Mission (TOM) to partners in the regions (see Figure 7-8). Three Bavarian pico-satellites (TOM) would be launched at the end of 2022. A ground station network, ranging across the RLS partner regions, was being established and would support the downlinking of data generated by the satellites. In this framework, an RLS-Sciences User Community was being established to identify interested users of the earth observation data which would be generated, especially for geosciences applications.

Figure 7-8 Online progress report on "Small Satellites: Telematics International Mission (TIM) and Telematics Observation Mission (TOM)"

Photo Credit: Department of Science & Technology of Shandong Province, Shandong First Medical University.

#### 7.4.2.5 RLS-Digital Health Initiative: Regional Initiatives Aligning to the Joint Roadmap

The RLS-Digital Health Initiative met on April 7 in a short session (see Figure 7-9). The session kicked off with a review by Dr. Sebastian Bickelhaupt of the steps made so far in the group. Based on the joint roadmap of the RLS-Digital Health Initiative, representatives from five regions then shared examples of digital health projects and initiatives out of their regions. In a panel discussion, the speakers engaged with the question of what the next steps should be to move the Digital Health Initiative forward. Potential cooperation topics ranged from data cooperation, including data processing and databases together with data protection, to the challenges associated with training the next generation of digital health professionals, and to applying AI to urgent global challenges.

Figure 7-9 RLS-Digital Health Initiative Panel Meeting (Online)

Photo Credit: Department of Science & Technology of Shandong Province, Shandong First Medical University.

#### 7.4.2.6 Closing Session

To bring the week to a close, the RLS-Sciences network met for a Joint Closing Session on 8 April. A panel of RLS Sciences representatives offered their perspectives on the week, including summaries of the four thematic sessions, reflections on the week as a whole, and assessments of the RLS-Sciences Digital Week model as well as the current stage of the network (see Figure 7-10). Based on their 2021 and 2022 experience, the Bavaria team recommended the network keep the Digital Week format as a yearly working instrument beyond the pandemic, and encouraged other regions to host the next edition. Presenters from Shandong Province shared information about Shandong's plans for the eleventh Regional Leaders' Summit in 2023, including the inclusion of RLS-Sciences. Closing remarks stated the key role that RLS-Sciences network plays in driving multiregional cooperation, and that choosing to engage more closely in a multilateral framework to pursue common goals is of increasing benefit and importance.

Figure 7-10 Joint Closing Session (online) of RLS-Sciences network

Photo Credit: Department of Science & Technology of Shandong Province, Shandong First Medical University.

### 7.4.3 The Third RLS-Sciences Digital Week in 2023

From 24 to 28 April 2023, the third RLS-Sciences Digital Week was led by Bavaria, who invited Shandong as the main participating province under the theme “Shandong in RLS-Sciences: Forward from Herrsching”, with nearly 130 participants from seven provinces and states. Shandong Province invited 18 experts from nine units, including the Energy Research Institute of Shandong Academy of Sciences, Shandong First Medical University, Shandong Aerospace Weineng Technology Co., Ltd., Shandong Institute of Space Electronic Technology (SISET) and Qingdao Institute of Bioenergy and Bioprocess Technology (QIBEBT), Chinese Academy of Sciences (CAS), to participate in four thematic areas and one comprehensive area.

#### 7.4.3.1 Renewable Energy

The theme is “Mitigating Climate Change—A Regional Perspective on Challenges and Opportunities in the Energy System”. Five scholars including Prof. Song Angang from Qilu University of Technology (Shandong Academy of Sciences) shared their in-depth views on hydrogen production technology, production of bio-natural gas from multiple organic solid waste, structural design of cathode materials, etc., and promoted the proposed cooperation projects. Experts from Bavaria and other regions exchanged views on energy transition and hydrogen energy technology.

#### 7.4.3.2 Small Satellites

The theme is “Satellites, Ground Station Network, and Data Analysis”. Three experts, including Jiang Lianxiang from Shandong Institute of Space Electronic Technology (SISET), shared their views on marine ecological environment monitoring based on satellite remote sensing images, satellite crowdsourcing computing and application service platform, and three small satellites in Shandong, and had discussions with experts from other provinces and states.

#### 7.4.3.3 Global Aerospace Campus

The theme is “Protecting our Environment with Technological Innovation”.

Zhang Ye of Shandong Aerospace Weineng Technology Co., Ltd. and Liu Xuqing of Shandong Laboratory of Yantai Advanced Materials and Green Manufacturing shared their research in this field from the perspective of carbon emission reduction. Experts from Quebec and other regions exchanged views on sustainable development in the field of space and urban air mobility.

#### 7.4.3.4 Digital Health

The theme is "The Role of Data in Digital Health". Liu Sijin, Deputy Secretary of Shandong First Medical University, and Prof. Xue Fuzhong of Shandong University, shared their views on big data prediction and disease prevention, and the federal medical science big data platform. Experts from Upper Austria and others exchanged views on AI-based medical data analysis and international models for digital health data sharing.

#### 7.4.3.5 Joint Interdisciplinary Session

The theme is "Shandong and RLS-Sciences: Forward from Herrsching". Five experts and scholars, including Prof. Yang Hetong, Director of the International Cooperation Office of Qilu University of Technology (Shandong Academy of Sciences) and Prof. Yu Changbin of the SDFMU College of Artificial Intelligence and Big Data for Medical Sciences, introduced and shared their views on the overview of the development of technological innovation in Shandong Province, research trends in various fields and key directions for future science and technology cooperation under the theme.

The Digital Week in 2023 was the first time that Shandong Province was invited as the main participating province, fully showcasing the research progress and achievements of Shandong Province in the fields of renewable energy, small satellites, aerospace and digital health, extending invitations for cooperation to other provinces and states, and laying a good foundation for the RLS-Sciences offline events to be hosted by Shandong Province in the second half of the year (see Figure 7-11).

Figure 7-11 Joint Interdisciplinary Session of the Digital Week (Online)

Photo Credit: Department of Science & Technology of Shandong Province, Shandong First Medical University.

# 第八章　产业项目交流合作

## 一、“中德土地整理与村庄革新”项目

南张楼村位于山东省潍坊市青州市何官镇，距离市区约40公里，是一个不靠城、不靠海、无大企业、无交通要道、无矿产资源、人多地少的典型的北方平原村落。1988年，全村共有1028户4159人，耕地6309亩，人均耕地约1.52亩，村内基础设施落后，无硬化道路，生产生活条件差，土地利用率低，农业种植结构单一，村民人均年收入1125元。

1987年，山东省与德国巴伐利亚州建立友好省州关系，德方支持中方的项目中有一个农业项目，德方要在山东找一个村庄搞“城乡等值化”试验，意在解决农村发展不充分、城乡发展不平衡等问题。经过努力，南张楼村争取到了这个项目。1988年，项目签订，项目名称为“中德土地整理与村庄革新”，一开始主要是借鉴德国村庄革新经验，逐步使南张楼村变成一个布局合理、功能齐全、生活舒适的乡村。该项目的德方合作者为德国巴伐利亚州汉斯·赛德尔基金会，这也是中国第一个土地整理项目(见图8-1)。

图 8-1　南张楼土地整理工作现场

图片来源：张文波：《南张楼土地整治模式对我国农村发展的启示》，《中国村庄》2022年第8期。

1997 年，为了更好地促进农村发展，双方商定将项目名称改为"中德土地整理与农村发展"，开始整合国土、农业、林业、水利、教育、建设等多个部门的项目和政策，开展了田、水、路、林、村综合整治，南张楼村成为全国新农村建设的典型。

2004 年，为了更好地实现对土地整理的研究与合作，汉斯·赛德尔基金会在中国山东省潍坊市青州市建立了"中德土地整理与农村发展培训中心"，同时将该中心作为山东省以及国土资源部在全国开展土地整理专业活动的培训基地。中德土地整理与农村发展培训中心离南张楼村很近，培训中心的建立不仅有利于南张楼村的进一步发展，而且有利于在更广的范围内开展专业的土地整理培训。

2018 年，乡村振兴战略实施以来，南张楼村与德方又共同编制了新一轮项目发展规划。按照"一个中心、八大板块"的总体功能布局，以农民合作社为主体，打造生态环保、乡村文明、宜居宜业、全民富裕、共融发展的最美田园综合体。综合体面积达 3.8 万亩，辐射带动南张楼村周边 16 个村。中德合作南张楼项目由 1.0 版升级到 2.0 版。

南张楼村实施"中德土地整理与村庄革新"项目的目标是增加耕地面积、提高耕地质量、改善农业基础设施条件和生产条件、统筹城乡经济发展。

借鉴德国土地整理、村庄革新的理念，南张楼村坚持政府主导、规划先行、多元投资、分类实施的原则，一张蓝图绘到底，推动山、水、林、田、湖、草全要素综合治理，形成了分区整治、集约利用、生态优先、全域等值的整治模式。

南张楼村对全村进行了功能分区：村南村西是工业区，村东是大田区，村北是文教卫生区，村中心是两个生活区。同时，保留传统农村建筑，不大拆大建，避免了重复建设造成的资源浪费，解决了过去村民生产生活混杂、村庄布局杂乱的问题。村庄建有社区服务中心、文化中心、集贸市场、小学、幼儿园、医院、超市、民俗博物馆、文化广场、休闲公园及其他公共设施，成为一个特色鲜明的村庄。

通过土地整理与村庄革新项目，南张楼村的道路全部实现了硬化，6309亩耕地实现了“旱能浇、涝能排”，水肥一体化使农业生产效率得到大大提升。目前，全村共种植了1000亩绿色韭菜、3000亩胡萝卜和山药、809亩大棚蔬菜以及1500亩优质粮食作物。同时，项目大大促进了国际交流合作。目前，全村共有630多人去国外留学、读研、打工，这不仅开阔了村民们的视野，而且壮大了集体经济，使村庄走上了一条可持续发展的道路，有力地推动了乡村振兴和生态文明建设。

## 二、潍柴动力收购奥地利VDS控股项目

潍柴动力股份有限公司成立于2002年(见图8-2)，由潍柴控股集团有限公司作为主发起人、联合境内外投资者创建而成，是中国内燃机行业在香港H股上市的企业，也是由境外回归内地实现A股再上市的公司。2022年，企业实现营业收入1751.6亿元，归母净利润49.1亿元。公司始终坚持产品经营、资本运营双轮驱动的运营策略，致力于打造具备品质、技术和成本三大核心竞争力的产品，成功构筑起了动力总成(发动机、变速箱、车桥、液压)、整车整机、智能物流等产业板块协同发展的格局，拥有“潍柴动力发动机”“法士特变速器”“汉德车桥”“陕汽重卡”“林德液压”等知名品牌。

潍柴动力股份有限公司拥有内燃机与动力系统全国重点实验室、国家商用汽车动力系统总成工程技术研究中心、国家商用汽车及工程机械新能源动力系统产业创新战略联盟、国家专业化众创空间等研发平台，设有博士后工作站等研究基地，建有国家智能制造示范基地。在中国上海、重庆、

潍坊、西安、扬州等地建有研发中心，并在全球多地设立了前沿技术创新中心，搭建起了全球协同研发平台，确保企业技术水平始终紧跟世界前沿。

奥地利威迪斯（Variable Drive Systems，VDS）公司成立于2009年，是一家专门从事车辆驱动系统开发的技术公司，其设计开发的液压变速箱、功率分流器等产品系列丰富，广泛应用于拖拉机、装载机、市政车辆、新能源公交车等。同时，该公司具备较强的产品设计、研发和测试能力，可提供从设计方案到样机生产的研发全过程咨询服务。

潍柴动力股份有限公司收购奥地利威迪斯公司51%的股份，旨在通过大马力无级变速（Continuously Variable Transmission，CVT）技术方面的合作，填补农业装备CVT动力系统关键技术领域的空白，打造潍柴液压CVT高端动力装备总成。2020年1月15日，在山东省相关领导及媒体代表的共同见证下，潍柴动力股份有限公司与奥地利威迪斯公司在山东济南签署了战略合作协议。双方约定，潍柴动力股份有限公司成功取得奥地利威迪斯公司51%的股权，成为控股股东（见图8-3）。协议的签署意味着双方正式开启深度合作的新征程。

图8-2　潍柴动力股份有限公司

图片来源：潍柴动力股份有限公司。

图 8-3　奥地利威迪斯公司
图片来源：潍柴动力股份有限公司。

## 三、济南圣泉集团股份有限公司增资巴西圣泉项目

济南圣泉集团股份有限公司始建于1979年，沪市主板上市企业，建有国家级企业技术中心，拥有科研人员500余人，年研发投入4.2亿元。产业覆盖合成树脂及复合材料、铸造材料、生物质精炼等领域。主导产品呋喃树脂和酚醛树脂的产销规模居全球首位。

1995年，济南圣泉集团股份有限公司开始拓展海外业务，至今已经在"走出去"的国际化道路上耕耘了近30年。公司在德国、波兰、法国、西班牙、俄罗斯、巴西、日本、韩国、印度等地建有子公司和办事处。

济南圣泉集团股份有限公司增资全资子公司巴西圣泉化学品贸易有限公司(Brazil Shengquan Chemicals Trading Co., LTD)(见图8-4)，注册资本1653274雷亚尔，主要从事以铸造业用化学品为主的工业品的进口、出口和仓储等，防护用品、食品及添加剂等系列产品的进出口贸易服务，纸及纸浆、树脂、涂料、化工产品等系列产品的批发销售。

济南圣泉集团股份有限公司为项目增资538.81万雷亚尔，项目建设地点为巴西圣保罗州圣保罗市。公司依托巴西现有客户资源，不断加大该市场的培育及开拓，加强品牌宣传，注重本土化建设，努力提高目标市场的占有率以降低项目的经营风险。截至2022年，公司收入、利润稳步增长。

图8-4　巴西圣泉化学品贸易有限公司
图片来源：济南圣泉集团股份有限公司。

## 四、海信集团美国分公司

2001年海信集团美国分公司于加利福尼亚州洛杉矶市成立，2007年搬迁至佐治亚州亚特兰大市(见图8-5)。海信集团美国分公司现有员工122人，主营业务涵盖海信电视、激光电视、冰箱、冷柜、空调、厨电产品等，现已进驻沃尔玛(Walmart)、百思买(Best Buy)、开市客(Costco)、塔吉特(Target)、亚马逊(Amazon)等主流渠道。海信电视在美国的市场占有率达13.7%，位列行业第二，已成为当地知名产品。

海信多年来坚持多品牌和全品类发展，在北美逐步建立起完善的研产销体系，不断推动规模增长。同时，自2023年起，海信正式成为北美地区美国职业篮球联赛(National Basketball Association，NBA)的官方合作伙伴(见图8-6)。

图 8-5 海信集团美国分公司办公楼(佐治亚州亚特兰大市)
图片来源:海信集团。

图 8-6 海信成为北美地区美国职业篮球联赛的官方合作伙伴
图片来源:海信集团。

## 五、山东七河生物在美投资食用菌项目

山东七河生物科技股份有限公司在美国投资的食用菌项目位于佐治亚州汉普顿市,计划投资 300 万美元,建设 3000 平方米杏鲍菇出菇间、6000 平方米平菇出菇间、50 栋日光温室。目前,项目已建设完成 11 栋日光温室,年产香菇、杏鲍菇、平菇 30 万斤(见图 8-7)。

图 8-7　山东七河生物在美投资的食用菌项目生产车间

图片来源：山东七河生物科技股份有限公司。

# Chapter 8 Exchanges and Cooperation in Industrial Projects

## 8.1 "Sino-German Land Consolidation and Village Renovation" Project

Nanzhanglou Village is located in Heguan Town, Qingzhou City, Shandong Province, about 40 kilometers from the city, and is a typical northern plain village far from the city and the sea, with no large enterprises, no major traffic routes, no mineral resources, but a large population and little farmland. In 1988, there were 1,028 households, 4,159 residents in the village, and 6,309 mu of arable land, with a per capita arable land of about 1.52 mu. The village had poor infrastructure, no hard surfaced roads, poor living and production conditions, low land utilization, a single agricultural planting structure and an annual per capita income of RMB 1,125.

In 1987, when Shandong Province and the Bavaria State of Germany established the sister province and state relationship, one of the projects supported by the German side was an agricultural project in which they wanted to find a village in Shandong to carry out a "rural-urban equivalence" experiment, with the intention of solving the problems of inadequate rural development and imbalance between urban and rural development. After much effort, Nanzhanglou Village obtained this project. The project was signed in 1988 under the name of "Sino-German Land Consolidation and

Village Renovation” and was initially aimed at transforming the village into a well-organized, functional and comfortable village, drawing on the German experience of village renovation. The German partner in the project was the Hans Seidel Foundation of Bavaria, and this was the first land consolidation project in China (see Figure 8-1).

Figure 8-1 Worksite of the Nanzhanglou Village renovation project

Photo Credit: Zhang Wenbo. Implications of the Nanzhanglou Village land improvement model for China's rural development [J]. China villages. 2022(8).

In order to better promote rural development, in 1997, the two sides agreed to rename the project the Sino-German Land Consolidation and Rural Development, and began to integrate the projects and policies of various departments, such as land, agriculture, forestry, water conservancy, education and construction, to carry out comprehensive improvement of fields, water, roads, forests and villages, making Nanzhanglou Village a typical example of new rural development in China.

In 2004, Hanns Seidel Foundation established the Sino-German Training Center for Land Consolidation and Rural Development in Qingzhou City, Shandong Province, China, as a training base for the professional activities of land consolidation in Shandong Province and the Ministry of Land and

Resources throughout the country, in order to better implement research and cooperation on land consolidation. The center is located very close to Nanzhanglou village and its establishment in Qingzhou will not only benefit the further development of the village but also facilitate professional land consolidation training for a wider range.

Since the implementation of the national rural revitalization strategy in 2018, Nanzhanglou Village and the German side have jointly prepared a new round of project development planning, in accordance with the overall functional layout of "one center and eight plates", with farmers' co-operatives as the main body, to create the most beautiful rural complex of ecological and environmental protection, rural civilization, livability and workability, prosperity for all, and inclusive development. The project will cover an area of 38,000 mu, radiating 16 villages around Nanzhanglou Village, and upgrading the Sino-German cooperation project from version 1.0 to version 2.0.

The objective of the "Sino-German Land Consolidation and Village Renovation" in Nanzhanglou Village is to increase the area and improve the quality of arable land, enhance agricultural infrastructure and production conditions, and integrate urban and rural economic development. Drawing on the German concept of land consolidation and village renovation, Nanzhanglou Village adheres to the principle of "government-led, planning first, diversified investment and categorical implementation", draws a complete blueprint and promotes the comprehensive management of all factors of "mountains, water, forests, fields, lakes and grasses", forming a model of "functional-based division, intensive use, ecological priority, the whole area of equal value".

The village is divided into several parts according to their functions: south and west of the village are the industrial zone, east of the village is the large field zone, north is the cultural, educational and health zone, and the center are two living areas, and the traditional residential areas are preserved without demolition or construction on a large scale, avoiding the waste of resources caused by unneeded development projects and eliminating the mixed production and life of villagers and disorganized village layout in the past. The village has a community service center, a cultural center, a market, a primary school, a kindergarten, a hospital, a supermarket, a folklore museum, a cultural square, a leisure park and other public facilities, making it a village with distinctive features.

Through land consolidation and village renovation, all roads in Nanzhanglou Village have been hardened, 6,309 mu of fertile fields can be watered in droughts and drained in floods, and the integration of water and fertilizer has greatly improved the efficiency of agricultural production. At present, 1,000 mu of green leeks, 3,000 mu of carrots and yams, 809 mu of greenhouse vegetables and 1,500 mu of quality grain crops are grown in the village. At the same time, the project has greatly facilitated international exchanges and cooperation in the village. At present, more than 630 residents in the village have gone abroad for study including postgraduate studies and work, which has not only broadened their vision but also strengthened the collective economy, setting the village on a path of sustainable development and giving a strong impetus to the revitalization of the rural areas and the ecological civilization.

## 8.2 Weichai Power's Acquisition of Austrian VDS Holdings Limited

Weichai Power Co., Ltd. was founded in 2002 by the main sponsor (see Figure 8-2), Weichai Holding Group Co., Ltd. and qualified domestic and foreign investors. It is the combustion engine company listed in Hong Kong stock market, as well as the company returning to China mainland stock market. In 2022, Weichai's sale revenue reached RMB 175.16 billion, and the net income attributable to parent reached RMB 4.91 billion. Weichai has always adhered to the product-driven and capital-driven operation strategy, and is committed to developing products with three core competences: quality, technology and cost. It has successfully built the synergetic development pattern among powertrain (engine, transmission, axle/hydraulics), vehicle and machinery, intelligent logistics and other segments. The Company owns famous brands such as "Weichai Power Engine""Fast Gear""Hande Axle""Shacman Heavy Truck" and "Linder Hydraulics".

Weichai pays high attention to science and technology innovation, and owns State Key Laboratory of Engine and Powertrain System, National Engineering Technology Research Center for Commercial Vehicle's Powertrain, National Commercial Vehicle and Construction Machinery New Energy Power Innovation Strategic Alliance, National Professional Makers' Space, "Post-doctoral Workstation" and other R&D platforms. The Company has the national intelligent manufacturing model base, as well as established R&D centers in Weifang, Shanghai, Xi'an, Chongqing, Yangzhou, etc. in China, built cutting-edge technology innovation centers in many places around the world, and set up a global collaborative R&D platform to make sure that the technology stays at global leading level.

Established in 2009, VDS is a technical company specializing in the vehicle drive systems. It designs and develops a wide range of products such as hydraulic transmissions and power dividers, which are widely used in tractors, loaders, municipal vehicles, new energy buses and other applications. At the same time, the company features great product design, R&D and testing capabilities and can provide consulting services for the whole R&D process from design solutions to prototype production.

Weichai Power Co., Ltd. acquired 51% of the shares of VDS, aiming to effectively fill the key technology gap in CVT power systems for agricultural equipment through cooperation in high-horsepower CVT technology, and to create a Weichai high-end hydraulic CVT powertrain. Weichai Power Co., Ltd. and VDS signed a strategic cooperation agreement in Jinan, Shandong Province on 15 January 2020, witnessed by officials from Shandong Province as well as press representatives. The two sides agreed that Weichai Power successfully acquired 51% of the equity of VDS and became the controlling shareholder (see Figure 8-3). The signing of the agreement signifies the start of a new journey of in-depth cooperation between the two companies.

Figure 8-2 Weichai Power Co., Ltd.
Photo Credit: Weichai Power Co., Ltd.

Figure 8-3 Austrian VDS Holdings Limited
Photo Credit: Weichai Power Co., Ltd.

## 8.3 Capital Increase of Jinan Shengquan on its Brazilian Project

Jinan Shengquan Group Share-Holding Co., Ltd., founded in 1979, was listed on the main board of Shanghai Stock Exchange. It has built a national enterprise technology center, with more than 500 researchers and an annual investment of RMB 420 million in R&D. Its business map covers synthetic resin and composites, foundry materials, biorefinery, etc. The production and sales volume of main products, namely, furan resin and phenolic resin, rank among the top in the world.

Since 1995, Shengquan Group has been developing its overseas business and since then it has devoted itself to globalization for nearly thirty years. Subsidiaries and offices were established in Germany, Poland, France, Spain, Russia, Brazil, Japan, South Korea and India.

Jinan Shengquan Group Share-Holding Co., Ltd. increased the capital of its wholly owned subsidiary, Brazil Shengquan Chemicals Trading Co., Ltd. (see Figure 8-4), with a registered capital of R$1,653,274, is mainly engaged in the import, export and storage of industrial products, mainly chemicals for the foundry industry; import and export trade services for products such as protective articles, foodstuffs and additives; wholesale and sales of paper and pulp, resins, paints, chemical products and other products.

The project, with a capital increase of R$5,388,100, was built in São Paulo City, São Paulo, Brazil. Relying on the existing customer resources in Brazil, the Company has kept on expanding the market, strengthening brand promotion, focusing on localization, and striving to increase the share of the target market to mitigate the operational risks of the project. By 2022, the Company's revenue and profit have been growing steadily.

Figure 8-4 Brazil Shengquan Chemicals Trading Co., Ltd.
Photo Credit: Jinan Shengquan Group Share-Holding Co., Ltd.

## 8.4 Hisense USA

Hisense USA was established in 2001 in Los Angeles, and relocated to Atlanta, Georgia in 2007 (see Figure 8-5). Hisense USA has 122 employees, with its main businesses covering Hisense TVs, Laser TVs, refrigerators, freezers, air conditioners, kitchen appliances, etc. By now, it has entered mainstream channels such as Walmart, Best Buy, Costco, Target and Amazon. Hisense TV has a market share of 13.7% in the US market, ranking second in the market, and it has become a well-known local brand.

Over the years, Hisense has insisted on multi-brand and full-category development, and has gradually established a comprehensive system covering research, production, and sales in North America, further promoting the growth of scale. In 2023, Hisense becomes an official partner of National Basketball Association (NBA) in North America (see Figure 8-6).

Figure 8-5 Office Building of Hisense USA (Atlanta, Georgia)
Photo Credit: Hisense Group Co., Ltd.

Figure 8-6 Hisense as an official partner of NBA in North America
Photo Credit: Hisense Group Co., Ltd.

## 8.5 Edible Fungi Project of Shandong Qihe Biotech in the US

The edible fungi project is located in Hampton, Georgia, USA, with a planned investment of US $ 3 million to build 3,000 square meters of mushroom production rooms for the king oyster mushroom, 6,000 square meters of oyster mushroom and 50 solar greenhouses. At present, 11 solar greenhouses have been completed, which can produce 300,000kg of shiitake mushroom, king oyster mushroom and oyster mushroom annually (see Figure 8-7).

Figure 8-7　Production plant for Qihe Biotech's edible fungi project in the US

Photo Credit: Shandong Qihe Biotechnology Co., Ltd.

# 第九章　行政学院交流合作

## 一、山东行政学院与巴伐利亚行政学院合作概况

德国巴伐利亚行政学院是巴伐利亚州公务员培训机构，隶属于巴伐利亚州内务部。1994—1997年，山东行政学院与巴伐利亚行政学院开展了代表团互访、专家授课等交流活动。2016年，在山东省人民政府外事办公室、德国巴伐利亚州内务部等的多方推动和帮助下，山东行政学院与巴伐利亚行政学院建立了友好合作长效机制，开启了长期、友好的合作。

## 二、山东行政学院与巴伐利亚行政学院重点合作项目

### （一）山东行政学院常务副院长王卫东率团访问巴伐利亚行政学院

2016年12月4日至8日，山东行政学院代表团拜访巴伐利亚州内务部、汉斯·赛德尔基金会，与巴伐利亚行政学院董事会主席迈克尔·汉斯·约阿希姆·沃纳（Michael Hanns Joachim Werner）先生进行了座谈（见图9-1），签署了联合备忘录（见图9-2）。双方明确了在1994年9月24日签署的《山东行政学院与巴伐利亚行政学院关于建立校际友好关系的备忘录》的基础上，在五个方面展开新的合作，包括校领导互访、人才培养和继续教育方面的措施、双方教师互访、参加对方的论坛或座谈会以及其他协商后的合作项目等；商定了2017年的具体合作项目，包括领导人互访、进一步相互了解、有针对性地交流学习等；确定2018年的合作项目，德方派遣教师到山东行政学院授课，山东行政学院派公务员到德方做精准交流。

图 9-1　2016 年 12 月，山东行政学院常务副院长王卫东率团访问巴伐利亚行政学院

图片来源：山东行政学院。

图 9-2　2016 年 12 月，山东行政学院与巴伐利亚行政学院签署联合备忘录

图片来源：山东行政学院。

## (二)巴伐利亚行政学院董事会主席到访山东行政学院

2017 年 5 月 8 日至 12 日，巴伐利亚行政学院董事会主席迈克尔・汉斯・约阿希姆・沃纳先生到访山东行政学院。访问期间，迈克尔・汉斯・约阿希

姆·沃纳先生为山东行政学院教职工举办了“德国公务员培训经验分享——以巴伐利亚行政学院为例”讲座，与有关处室开展了学术研讨活动，在联合备忘录的基础上签署了《山东行政学院与巴伐利亚行政学院领导人互访合作协议》和《山东行政学院派遣教师赴德访问合作协议》。访问期间，沃纳先生还参加了山东省与巴伐利亚州结好30周年庆祝活动。

### （三）应急处置精准交流项目

2017年11月5日至8日，山东行政学院、山东省人民政府外事办公室和县（市、区）分管应急管理工作的负责人共计20人赴德国进行应急处置精准交流。

山东行政学院对此次应急处置精准交流进行了周密设计和组织，第一次采用“三段式”培训模式。第一阶段，在国内进行一周专题培训。通过系统学习公共安全风险管理、欧盟风险管理与民事保护机制、德国应急管理体系等课程，学员们掌握了有关公共安全风险管理和应急处置的理论框架，了解了欧盟、德国的基本应急管理体系，并且特别注重通过课堂互动、学员结构化研讨等形式聚焦问题，带着问题参加精准交流。第二阶段，预培训。中共山东省委组织部、山东省人民政府外事办公室相关处室围绕具体的纪律要求、学习要求和德国的基本情况、涉外礼仪，对学员进行了行前预培训。第三阶段，赴德国精准交流。其间，学员先后到巴伐利亚州消防学校学习了其公共安全风险管理和应急管理，参观了巴伐利亚州应急调度中心，现场观摩了巴伐利亚州消防学校的消防演练（见图9-3），到黑森州布朗菲尔斯市学习了解了当地公共安全应急管理实务（见图9-4）。

图 9-3　山东行政学院考察巴伐利亚州消防学校

图片来源：山东行政学院。

图 9-4　山东行政学院与德国黑森州布朗菲尔斯市政府座谈

图片来源：山东行政学院。

### (四)山东行政学院常务副院长徐闻率团访问巴伐利亚行政学院

2018年12月12日至16日,山东行政学院代表团在巴伐利亚行政学院开展了公务员培训和智库建设的交流与合作,访问了汉斯·赛德尔基金会、费尔达芬培训中心、巴伐利亚州消防学校、施达因加登镇。

巴伐利亚行政学院院长莫妮卡·维娜尔(Monika Werner)与山东行政学院常务副院长徐闻就双方签订的《山东行政学院与巴伐利亚行政学院领导人互访合作协议》和《山东行政学院派遣教师赴德访问合作协议》内容进行了深入交流,并达成了一致意见。巴伐利亚行政学院进修教育处处长塞巴斯蒂安·潘格尔(Sebastian Panger)先生介绍了制订与实施公务员培训计划、兼职教师管理制度等方面的经验和做法。代表团实地参观了费尔达芬培训中心实训基地、巴伐利亚州消防学校综合调度员培训中心和消防实训基地。

### (五)巴伐利亚行政学院院长一行到访山东行政学院

2019年5月13日至15日,巴伐利亚行政学院院长莫妮卡·维娜尔、副院长罗斯维塔·菲佛(Roswitha Pfeiffer)、教育顾问克里斯汀·尼德迈耶(Christine Niedermeyer)一行三人到访山东行政学院,进行了为期四天的访问、交流、授课,围绕巴伐利亚行政学院的教学理念、教学方法、领导力培训等内容做了三场专题报告,开展了学习类型测试、法学案例分析等互动式教学活动,演示了有关课程建设规划。山东行政学院全体教师及部分从事教学管理、师资培训工作的人员,部分市行政学院的教师代表等260余人参加了培训交流活动(见图9-5)。

图 9-5　培训活动现场
图片来源：山东行政学院。

### (六)山东行政学院教师代表团赴巴伐利亚行政学院学习交流

2019 年 11 月 18 日至 22 日，根据双方签署的合作协议，山东行政学院选派六位教师赴巴伐利亚行政学院进行了学习交流，就共同关心的教学规律、教学方式等进行了交流研讨，并实地参观了巴伐利亚行政学院慕尼黑总部及霍尔茨豪森培训中心的硬件设施和数字化教学环境(见图 9-6)。

此次与巴伐利亚行政学院主要领导及教师进行的座谈有利于深入、全面地了解巴伐利亚行政学院数字化教学的特点、流程及运用，为山东行政学院制定数字化战略、实现数字化教学目标、提高办学水平提供了新的思路和借鉴。双方探讨了在教学、科研、管理等方面实现优势互补、资源共享的可行性，充分表达了以交流促合作、以合作促发展的共同愿望，为今后双方开展更加广泛、深入的交流与合作奠定了坚实的基础。

图 9-6 巴伐利亚行政学院数字化教学学习交流现场
图片来源:山东行政学院。

## (七)山东行政学院致信巴伐利亚行政学院祝贺其建校 100 周年

2020 年 9 月,正值巴伐利亚行政学院建校 100 周年之际,山东行政学院通过发送贺信及庆祝照片向友校致以诚挚的问候和祝贺(见图 9-7、图 9-8)。

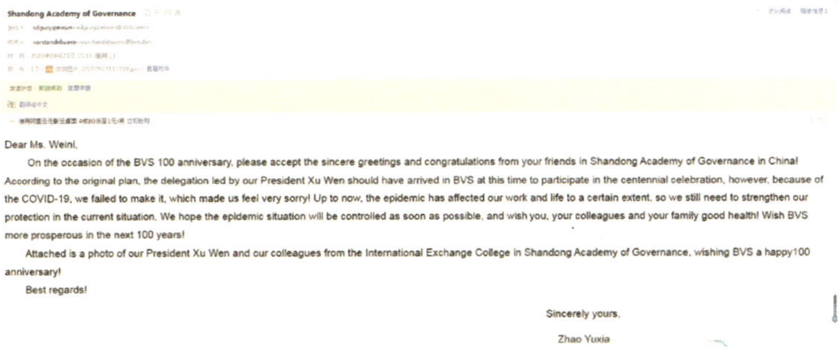

Shandong Academy of Governance

Dear Ms. Weinl,

On the occasion of the BVS 100 anniversary, please accept the sincere greetings and congratulations from your friends in Shandong Academy of Governance in China! According to the original plan, the delegation led by our President Xu Wen should have arrived in BVS at this time to participate in the centennial celebration, however, because of the COVID-19, we failed to make it, which made us feel very sorry! Up to now, the epidemic has affected our work and life to a certain extent, so we still need to strengthen our protection in the current situation. We hope the epidemic situation will be controlled as soon as possible, and wish you, your colleagues and your family good health! Wish BVS more prosperous in the next 100 years!

Attached is a photo of our President Xu Wen and our colleagues from the International Exchange College in Shandong Academy of Governance, wishing BVS a happy100 anniversary!

Best regards!

Sincerely yours,

Zhao Yuxia

图 9-7 山东行政学院祝贺巴伐利亚行政学院成立 100 周年贺信邮件
图片来源:山东行政学院。

图 9-8　庆祝巴伐利亚行政学院成立 100 周年
图片来源：山东行政学院。

### (八)山东行政学院与巴伐利亚行政学院院长见面会暨云上课堂活动

新冠肺炎疫情期间，山东行政学院与巴伐利亚行政学院的线下活动被迫中断。2021 年 12 月 15 日，山东行政学院与巴伐利亚行政学院举行双方院长见面会暨云上课堂活动(见图 9-9)。巴伐利亚行政学院院长莫妮卡·维娜尔、山东行政学院常务副院长徐闻出席活动并致辞。

巴伐利亚行政学院数字学习负责人弗洛里安·格劳普(Florian Glaup)以“翻转课堂——巴伐利亚行政学院的综合学习”为题进行了线上授课，授课过程面向山东省全省行政学院系统同步直播，共有 738 名教研人员参加。

图9-9　山东行政学院与巴伐利亚行政学院院长见面会暨云上课堂
图片来源：山东行政学院。

# Chapter 9 Exchanges and Cooperation between Shandong-Bavaria Administrative Institutions

## 9.1 Cooperation Overview of Shandong-Bavaria Administrative Institutions

The Bavarian Administrative School (the BVS for Bayerische Verwaltungsschule) is a civil servant training institution in Bavaria and is under the administration of the Bavarian State Ministry of the Interior. From 1994 to 1997, the Shandong Academy of Governance and the BVS carried out exchange activities such as reciprocal visits of delegations and lectures by experts. In 2016, with the help of the Foreign Affairs Office of Shandong Provincial People's Government and the Bavarian State Ministry of the Interior, the two institutions established a long-term mechanism for friendly cooperation, starting a long-term and friendly cooperation.

## 9.2 Key Cooperation Projects of Shandong-Bavaria Administrative Institutions

### 9.2.1 Visit to BVS by a Delegation led by Wang Weidong, Executive Vice President of Shandong Academy of Governance

The delegation visited the Bavarian State Ministry of the Interior and the Hanns Seidel Foundation from 4 to 8 December 2016. The delegation had a meeting with Mr. Michael Hanns Joachim Werner, Chairman of the Board of Directors of the BVS (see Figure 9-1), and signed a *Joint Memorandum* (see Figure 9-2) clarifying the new cooperation between the two parties on the basis of the *Memorandum of Understanding between the Shandong Academy of Governance and the Bavarian Academy of Governance on the Establishment of Friendly Relations* signed on 24 September 1994, in five areas, including: the reciprocal visits of school leaders, measures on personnel training as well as continuing education, reciprocal visits of teachers from both sides, mutual participation in each other's forums or symposiums, and other negotiated cooperation projects. Specific cooperation projects for 2017 were agreed upon, including: 1) reciprocal visits of leaders and personnel from both sides to further promote mutual understanding and targeted exchanges and learning, and to identify cooperation projects for 2018; 2) sending German teachers to teach at the Shandong Academy of Governance; 3) sending civil servants from the Shandong Academy of Governance for precise exchanges with the BVS.

Figure 9-1 Visit to BVS by a delegation led by Wang Weidong, Executive Vice President of Shandong Academy of Governance (December 2016)

Photo Credit: Shandong Academy of Governance.

Figure 9-2 Shandong Academy of Governance and BVS signing a *Joint Memorandum* (December 2016)

Photo Credit: Shandong Academy of Governance.

### 9.2.2 Visit of the Chairman of the Board of Directors of the BVS to Shandong Academy of Governance

From 8 to 12 May 2017, Mr. Michael Hanns Joachim Werner, Chairman of the Board of Directors of the BVS, visited the Shandong Academy of Governance. During the visit, Mr. Werner gave a lecture on "Sharing of German Civil Servant Training Experience—Take BVS as an Example" to the faculty of Shandong Academy of Governance, and held academic seminars with relevant departments. On the basis of the *Joint Memorandum*, the *Agreement on Reciprocal Visits between the Leaders of Shandong Academy of Governance and the Bavarian Administrative School* and the *Agreement on Cooperation in Sending Teachers to Germany by Shandong Academy of Governance* were signed. During the visit, Mr. Werner participated in the celebrations of the 30th anniversary of the Shandong Province and Bavaria.

### 9.2.3 Targeted Exchange Project of Emergency Response

From 5 to 8 November 2017, 20 officials from Shandong Academy of

Governance, Foreign Affairs Office of Shandong Provincial People's Government and counties (cities and districts) of Shandong Province in charge of emergency management went to Germany for a targeted exchange on "emergency response".

Shandong Academy of Governance has conducted a comprehensive design and organization for this project. For the first time, a "three-phase" training model was adopted. In the first phase, a one-week training was held in China. Through systematic learning of public safety risk management, risk management and civil protection mechanisms in the European Union, and emergency management systems in Germany, participants were able to master the theoretical framework of public safety risk management and emergency response as well as European Union and Germany's basic emergency management systems. Classroom interaction and structured seminars were designed for participants to focus on professional issues, so that they could participate in questions-oriented exchanges. The second phase was pre-training. Relevant departments of the Organization Department of the CPC Shandong Provincial Committee and the Foreign Affairs Office of Shandong Provincial People's Government conducted pre-departure training for the participants on specific disciplinary requirements, study requirements and the basic situation in Germany and foreign-related etiquette. The third phase was to carry out targeted exchanges in Germany. During this period, participants went to the Bavarian Fire Fighting School to learn about its public safety risk management and emergency management, visited the Bavarian Emergency Dispatch Center and observed the fire drills of the School on site (see Figure 9-3); and went to the city of Braunfels in Hessen to learn about local public safety emergency management practices (see Figure 9-4).

Figure 9-3 Visit to Bavarian Fire Fighting School by Shandong Academy of Governance

Photo Credit: Shandong Academy of Governance.

Figure 9-4 Discussion between Shandong Academy of Governance and the Municipality of Braunfels, Hessen, Germany

Photo Credit: Shandong Academy of Governance.

### 9.2.4 Visit to BVS by a Delegation Led by Xu Wen, Executive Vice President of Shandong Academy of Governance

From 12 to 16 December 2018, the delegation carried out exchanges and cooperation in civil servant training and think tank building at the BVS, visiting the Hans Seidel Foundation, the Feldafing Training Center, the Bavarian Fire Fighting School and the town of Steingaden.

Monika Werner, President of the BVS, and Xu Wen, Executive Vice President of the Shandong Academy of Governance, had an in-depth exchange of views and reached agreements on the contents of the signed *Agreement on Reciprocal Visits between the Leaders of Shandong Academy of Governance and the Bavarian Administrative School* and the *Agreement on Cooperation in Sending Teachers to Germany by Shandong Academy of Governance*. Mr. Sebastian Panger, Director of the Further Education Department of the BVS, presented his experience and practices in the development and implementation of training programmes for civil servants and the management system for part-time teachers. The delegation paid a site visit to the training base of the Feldafing Training Center, the integrated dispatcher training center of the Bavarian Fire Fighting School and the fire training base.

### 9.2.5 Visit to Shandong Academy of Governance by President of the BVS and His Delegation

From 13 to 15 May 2019, a three-member delegation of Monika Werner, President of the BVS, Roswitha Pfeiffer, Vice President, and Christine Niedermeyer, Education Consultant, visited Shandong Academy of Governance for a four-day communication and delivered lectures. Three lectures were made on the teaching philosophy, teaching methods and leadership training of the BVS, interactive teaching activities such as learning type tests and legal case studies were carried out, and plans for the relevant course development were demonstrated. More than 260 participants attended the training, including all teachers of Shandong Academy of Governance and some of those engaged in teaching management and teacher training, as well as teachers from other municipal academies of governance (see Figure 9-5).

Figure 9-5 Training activities

Photo Credit: Shandong Academy of Governance.

### 9.2.6 Governance Visit to BVS by a Delegation of Teachers from Shandong Academy of Governance for Study and Communication

From 18 to 22 November 2019, according to the cooperation agreement, six teachers from the Shandong Academy of Governance were sent to the BVS for study and communication. They shared views on issues of common interest such as the laws and ways of teaching and also took a site visit to the hardware facilities and digital teaching environment of the headquarters in Munich and the Holzhausen Training Center (see Figure 9-6).

This visit enabled teachers from Shandong to discuss with the leaders and teachers of BVS, to gain an in-depth and comprehensive understanding of the characteristics, processes and use of digital teaching in BVS, which offered new ideas and references for Shandong Academy of Governance to develop digital operation, achieve digital teaching and improve their education quality. The two sides discussed the feasibility of complementing each other and sharing resources in teaching, scientific research and management, fully expressing their common desire to promote cooperation and communication, laying a solid foundation for more extensive and in-depth exchanges and cooperation in the future.

Figure 9-6 Teachers from Shandong learning and discussing about digital teaching at the BVS

Photo Credit: Shandong Academy of Governance.

### 9.2.7 Letter from Shandong Academy of Governance to the BVS to Congratulate Its 100th Anniversary

In September 2020, on the occasion of the 100th anniversary of the BVS, Shandong Academy of Governance sent its sincere greetings and congratulations by sending a congratulatory letter and celebratory photos (see Figure 9-7, 9-8).

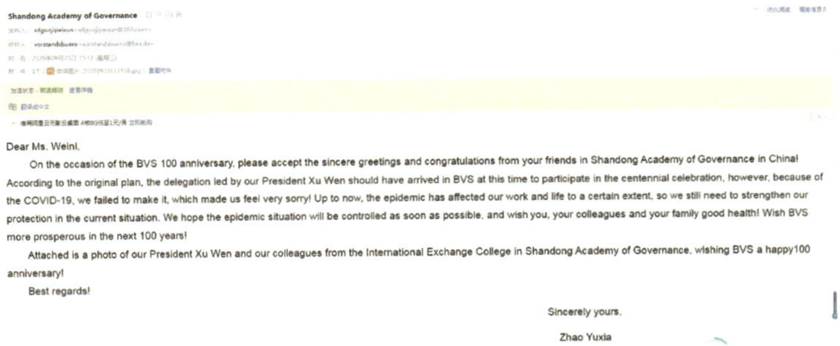

Shandong Academy of Governance

sdguojipeixun

vorstandsbuero

Dear Ms. Weinl,

On the occasion of the BVS 100 anniversary, please accept the sincere greetings and congratulations from your friends in Shandong Academy of Governance in China! According to the original plan, the delegation led by our President Xu Wen should have arrived in BVS at this time to participate in the centennial celebration, however, because of the COVID-19, we failed to make it, which made us feel very sorry! Up to now, the epidemic has affected our work and life to a certain extent, so we still need to strengthen our protection in the current situation. We hope the epidemic situation will be controlled as soon as possible, and wish you, your colleagues and your family good health! Wish BVS more prosperous in the next 100 years!

Attached is a photo of our President Xu Wen and our colleagues from the International Exchange College in Shandong Academy of Governance, wishing BVS a happy100 anniversary!

Best regards!

Sincerely yours,

Zhao Yuxia

Figure 9-7 E-mail from Shandong Academy of Governance to congratulate BVS on its 100th anniversary

Photo Credit: Shandong Academy of Governance.

Figure 9-8 Celebrating the 100th anniversary of the BVS

Photo Credit: Shandong Academy of Governance.

## 9.2.8 Online Meeting of Presidents and a Cloud Classroom

During the outbreak of the COVID-19 pandemic, offline communications had to be interrupted. On 15 December 2021, Shandong Academy of Governance and BVS held a presidents meeting and cloud classroom (see Figure 9-9). Monica Werner, President of the BVS, and Xu Wen, Executive Vice President of Shandong Academy of Governance, attended and delivered speeches.

Florian Glaup, head of Digital Learning at the BVS, gave an online lecture on the topic of *Flipped Classroom—Integrated Learning at the BVS*, which was broadcast live for the province's governance academies, with a total of 738 teaching and research staff attending.

Figure 9-9 Presidents meeting and cloud classroom of Shandong Academy of Governance and BVS

Photo Credit: Shandong Academy of Governance.

# 第三篇 展望篇

## 第十章 友好省州交流合作面临的新形势

友好省州是不同省州之间建立友好合作关系的一种形式。尽管全球化作为经济发展的必然趋势不会终结,但全球化发展进入深度调整期已成共识。友好省州间的交流与合作既面临新挑战,又面临新机遇。

### 一、国际格局变化带来新挑战

当今世界正在经历百年未有之大变局,国际格局和国际体系发生深刻变化,全球治理体系发生深刻变革。各国间的联系和依存日益加深,但也面临诸多共同挑战。

#### (一)国际经济形势冲击友好省州交流合作的基础

随着国际局势的急剧变化,全球化趋势受阻,国际合作出现新的困难,基于全球产业链分工的国际贸易体系受到冲击。发达经济体与新兴经济体复苏分化,经济增长和发展不平衡的问题更加突出,全球经济增长不稳定、不确定性加大,可能会使一些友好省州间的交流合作计划受到一定的影响。一些国际经济贸易活动可能被取消或推迟,一些跨国合作项目可能受到政治和经济环境的影响而暂停或终止。

#### (二)非传统风险需要高度关注

气候变化、信息科技等非传统风险交织叠加。近几年,各种严重自然和环境灾害发生的概率和频率越来越高,对经济金融造成了突发性冲击,要高度关注气候与环境恶化带来的风险。粮食和能源危机此起彼伏，要高度关注投资环境不稳定带来的风险。

全球在享受信息化、数字化红利的同时，也面临新的社会稳定挑战和治理难题，需要高度关注新兴技术带来的风险。新兴技术所具备的创新性、颠覆性以及未来发展的未知性共同构成了其本身的不确定性，给技术发展和全球商业活动带来了巨大的风险。业内专家强调，物联网将打破物理世界和虚拟世界之间的界限，病毒、蠕虫和特洛伊木马过去只在虚拟世界中攻击，实际上也会在现实世界中造成损害。[①]

### （三）组织协调难度增大

国际局势的变化导致友好省州之间组织与协调的难度增大，需要健全组织机构，强化统筹协调与合作。友好省州之间的交流互动需要更为高效具体的机制支持，如经济贸易合作与投资项目、科学网络、人员往来、交换学生、互派文化交流团、体育项目交流等。这些组织机构和机制的健全完善需要多方共同努力。

## 二、全球科技革命和产业变革带来新机遇

当前，全球新一轮科技革命和产业变革加速酝酿，全球经济处于新旧动能转换和结构调整关键期，孕育着新的重大机遇。

### （一）技术进步和产业升级带来更多合作机会

全球化遭遇逆流和新冠肺炎疫情的反复冲击虽然影响了国际贸易投资的发展，但是也催生了大量新技术、新业态、新场景、新模式，以 5G 技术、数字经济、人工智能、新能源汽车等为代表的新增长点蓬勃兴起。主要经济体强化转型战略布局，加快新基础设施建设，加大技术创新和产业升级支持力度，推动新兴技术迭代更新和跨产业协同，新的投资热点不断涌现。根据中国信息通信研究院 2022 年 12 月 7 日发布的《全球数字经济白皮书（2022

① 参见《专家警告：新兴技术带来的风险正在上升》，2020 年 8 月 14 日，https://cloud.tencent.com/developer/news/676582。

年)》统计的 47 个国家的情况，2021 年数字经济增加值规模同比名义增长 15.6%，占 GDP 的比重为 45%，全球面向实体经济的工业与产业互联网平台快速发展，释放数据要素价值成为各国共同的探索方向。

### (二)绿色转型和可持续发展促进能源环境领域务实合作

近年来，全球极端天气频繁发生，气候变化已经成为各国面临的紧迫现实危机。积极应对气候变化，推动绿色转型和可持续发展已成为国际社会的广泛共识，全球正迎来一场以绿色低碳为特征的产业和技术变革。主要经济体纷纷推出绿色转型和可持续投资计划，共商绿色转型和可持续发展，建立绿色发展伙伴关系，搭建多边合作平台，举办绿色发展支持活动，凝聚绿色发展国际共识，深化能源绿色低碳领域务实合作，提升国家生态环境保护能力，为全球可持续发展提供有力支持和强劲动力。

## 三、地方政府国际合作提供新支撑

随着全球化进程的调整，国际交往正在发生转型，地方政府的国际往来日益活跃，地方政府间国际合作成为新型国际交流合作形式，一个以民族国家为中心的“全球层面—民族国家层面—次国家行为体层面”多层互动的立体网络正在形成，地方政府正是这一立体网络中的一个重要行为体。① 因为地方政府的卷入，全球化出现了一个新的现象，即“全球地方化”(Glocalization)，这意味着地方与全球的连接成为国际社会的新现象，全球化因为地方与全球的结合而呈现出与以前大不相同的地域特性。国际地缘格局、经济的同质性与互补性、共同的政策目标、领导者的强力推动和有利的国际环境共同构成了地方政府跨国合作的动力系统，地方政府在上述因素下做出跨国合作的理性选择有助于形成地方政府跨国合作的制度性集体行动框架。②

当前，各国都面临国内经济社会发展、应对气候变化与环境保护等诸多方面的巨大压力，需要寻求外部支持和合作，借助两种资源、开拓两个市场成为地方政府利益最大化的必然路径，区域合作受到更大青睐，地区间高质

① 参见王立军：《全球化背景下的中国地方政府国际合作》，山东大学博士学位论文，2012 年。

② 参见胡佳、王开茹：《地方政府跨国合作的动力机制与约束条件——“一带一路”背景下中国-东盟的案例研究》，《地方治理研究》2019 年第 2 期。

量的互联互通格局初现轮廓[①]，这为友好省州的合作提供了新的支撑。

地方政府在国家整体外交框架下也有差异化的发展目标和国际交流合作需求，需要基于自身实际采取相应行动。特别是对发展导向的各友好省州来说，通过友好省州领导人峰会推动相互间经济贸易往来和人文、社会等各领域交流合作，可以实现精准对接、优势互补，强化经济社会发展的国际要素资源支撑。

① 参见刘融、蔡子畅、李亚楠等：《共建“一带一路”为区域合作添动力》，《人民日报》2022 年 9 月 19 日。

# Part Ⅲ Outlook

## Chapter 10 The New Situation of Exchanges and Cooperation between Sister Provinces and States

Sister province-state relations are a form of friendship and cooperation among different provinces and states. In the post-pandemic era, although globalization as an inevitable trend of economic development will not come to an end, there is a consensus that the development of globalization has entered a period of in-depth adjustments. Exchanges and cooperation between sister provinces and states are facing both new challenges and new opportunities.

### 10.1 Changes in the International Landscape Bringing New Challenges

The world today is undergoing major changes unprecedented in a century, with profound evolutions in the international landscape and the international system, and far-reaching transformations in the global governance system. While the ties and interdependence among countries are deepening, they are also facing many common challenges.

#### 10.1.1 International Economic Situation Shocking the Foundation of Exchanges and Cooperation among Sister Provinces and States

With the acute changes in the international situation, globalization has been seriously hampered, new difficulties have emerged in international cooperation, and the international trade system based on the division of labour in the global industrial chain has been greatly impacted. The divergence in recovery between developed and emerging economies, the more prominent problems of uneven economic growth and development, and the increased instability and uncertainty in global economic growth may cause some impact on friendship cities exchange and cooperation programmes. Some international economic and trade activities may be cancelled or postponed, and some cross-border cooperation projects may be suspended or terminated as a result of the political and economic environment.

### 10.1.2 Non-traditional Risks Requiring Significant Attention

Non-traditional risks such as climate change and information technology are intertwined. In recent years, the probability and frequency of various serious natural and environmental disasters have been increasing, causing sudden shocks to the economy and finance, and the risk of climate and environmental deterioration requires high attention. As food and energy crises are emerging, close attention should be paid to the risk of an unstable investment environment.

As the world enjoys the dividends of information technology and digitalization, it also faces new challenges to social stability and governance, and the risks posed by emerging technologies require great attention. The innovative and subversive emerging technologies, together with their unknown development trends cause the uncertainty and pose huge risks to technological development and global business activities. An expert (Zhou Hongyi, 2020) highlighted that the IoT will break down the boundaries between the physical and virtual worlds, and viruses like worms and Trojan that used to attack only in the virtual world, will actually cause damage in the real world.[①]

### 10.1.3 Increased Difficulty in Organization and Coordination

As changes in the international situation have made it more difficult to organize and coordinate communications among sister provinces and states, we need to make exchanges more organized and cooperate in a more coordinated way. The interaction needs to be supported by more efficient and concrete mechanisms, such as economic and trade cooperation and investment projects, RLS-Sciences, personnel exchanges, student exchanges, cultural exchange delegations, and sports exchanges. The improvement of these structures and mechanisms requires the joint efforts of many parties.

## 10.2 Global Technological and Industrial Changes Bringing New Opportunities

At present, a new round of global sci-tech revolution and industrial transformation is accelerating, and the global economy is in a critical period of replacement of old growth drivers with new ones and structural adjustment, giving birth to major new opportunities.

### 10.2.1 Technological Advancement and Industrial Upgrading Bringing More Opportunities for Cooperation

Despite the headwinds of globalization and the recurring impact caused by the pandemic, which affected the development of international trade and investment, a large number of new technologies, business models, scenarios and modes have emerged, with new growth points represented by 5G technology, digital economy, AI and new energy vehicles flourishing. Major economies are strengthening the strategic plan for transformation,

① "Warning by Experts: Risk Brought by Emerging Technologies Is Rising", https://cloud.tencent.com/developer/news/676582, 14 August, 2020.

accelerating the construction of new infrastructure, increasing support for technological innovation and industrial upgrading, and promoting updates on emerging technology and cross-industry synergies. As a result, new investment hotspots are emerging. According to the statistics on 47 countries in the *White Paper on Global Digital Economy* (2022) released by the China Academy of Information and Communications Technology on 7 December 2022, the value added of the digital economy increased by 15.6% in 2021, accounting for 45% of GDP, and the global industrial internet platforms for the real economy developed rapidly, making the release of the value of data elements a common exploration direction for all countries.

### 10.2.2 Green Transformation and Sustainable Development Promoting Practical Cooperation in the Energy and Environment Sector

In recent years, extreme weather has occurred frequently around the world, and climate change has become an urgent and real crisis for all countries. It has become a broad consensus in the international community to actively respond to climate change and promote green transformation and sustainable development, and the world is witnessing an industrial and technological transformation characterized by green and low-carbon development. Major economies have launched investment plans, discussed and established partnerships on green transformation and sustainable development. They have built multilateral cooperation platforms and organized green development support activities to forge international consensus and deepen practical cooperation in the field of green and low-carbon energy as well as enhance ecological and environmental protection capacity of participating countries, thus providing strong support and vigorous momentum for global sustainable development.

## 10.3 International Cooperation among Local Governments Providing New Support

With the adjustment of the globalization process, international exchanges are undergoing a transformation with local governments becoming increasingly active, and cooperation among local governments acting as a new form of international exchange and cooperation. A three-dimensional network of interaction at the global, nation-state and sub-national levels, with the nation-state at the center, is forming, and local governments are an important actor in this three-dimensional network.① A new phenomenon of globalization has emerged because of the engagement of the local, i.e. glocalization, which means that the connection between the local and the global has become a new phenomenon in the international community, and globalization has assumed a very different geographical character owing to this connection. The international geopolitical landscape, economic homogeneity and complementarity, common policy goals, strong leadership and a favourable international environment together constitute the driving force of transnational cooperation among local governments. The rational choice of local governments to cooperate across borders in the light of the above factors contributes to the formation of an institutional framework of their collective actions. ②

All countries are facing enormous pressure in domestic economic and social development, climate change and environmental protection, and need to seek external support and cooperation. Leveraging domestic and international resources and expanding markets at home and abroad have

---

① Wang Lijun, "International Cooperation between Local Governments in China under the Backgrcund of Globalization," Dissertation, Shandong University (2012).

② Hu Jia, Wang Kairu, "The Dynamic Mechanism and Constraints of Local Government's Transnational Cooperation: A Case Study of China-ASEAN under the Background of 'The Belt and Road Initiative'," *Local Governance Research*, no. 2 (2019), pp.13-15,78,79.

become an inevitable path for local governments to make the most of their interests, and regional cooperation has become more favoured, with the pattern of high-quality interconnectivity among regions emerging,① providing new support for cooperation among sister provinces and states.

Within the framework of overall national diplomacy, local governments also have differentiated development goals and needs for international exchanges and cooperation, and need to take corresponding actions based on their own realities. Especially for development-oriented sister provinces and states, promoting mutual economic and trade exchanges and cooperation in various fields such as humanities and society through the Regional Leaders' Summit can provide targeted connections and complement each other's strengths, and strengthen the support of international factors and resources for economic and social development.

① Liu Rong, Cai Zichang, Li Yanan, et al., “Jointly Build the ‘Belt and Road’ to Add Power to Regional Cooperation,” *People's Daily* (9 September, 2022).

# 第十一章　友好省州交流合作的未来展望

在当今时代，各国利益交融、命运休戚与共是大势所趋，不断创造更加美好的生活是各国人民的共同期待。[①] 各友好省州应携手同行、共创未来，围绕可持续发展主题，进一步深化务实合作，共享发展机遇，共同面对挑战，实现合作共赢，推动发展进步。

## 一、坚持可持续发展主题

实现可持续发展是世界各国的共同任务。当前，可持续发展面临人口急剧增长与老龄化并存、水资源紧缺、森林缩减、能源危机、环境污染等一系列挑战。友好省州领导人峰会应围绕可持续发展主题加强交流与合作，增进对全球性问题的共识，继续采取有效措施推动经济高质量发展，提高能源生产效率，增加可再生能源的使用等，积极应对人口变化、气候变化、环境保护、城市安全等，共同推动和实现可持续发展。

## 二、加强重点领域务实合作

第一，加强政府间合作。在友好省州领导人峰会机制下，加强各友好省州政府间高层对话与互访，促进各层级人员往来，推动经贸、科技、人文、能源和基础设施等重点领域的合作，提升合作水平。

---

① 参见《习近平主席向 2019 年"读懂中国"广州国际会议致贺信》，2019 年 10 月 26 日，https://www.gov.cn/xinwen/2019-10/26/content_5445217.htm。

第二，深化民间合作。从民间交往方面拓展省州和城市之间的联系，拓宽民间交往渠道，积极宣传推广国际友好城市合作，通过增加民间交往来加深对不同文化的理解，消除彼此之间交流合作的制约因素。①

第三，强化经贸合作。强化友好省州经贸合作的基础作用，持续优化营商环境，促进企业在友好省州产业项目上的投资合作，推动经贸与投资合作不断迈上新台阶，共享发展机遇，实现互利互惠和共同繁荣发展。

第四，促进文化和体育交流合作。友好省州之间的文化和体育交流活动可以促进友好省州相互了解，增进彼此友谊，拓宽人们的视野和认知，相互借鉴、取长补短，有助于保持各地区文化的创新性、创造力。

第五，推动绿色发展领域务实合作。聚焦清洁交通、绿色金融、绿色科技等领域，不断拓展能源转型和绿色环保等产业的投资边界，推动政府、金融机构、企业等各相关方的对接合作，挖掘合作潜能，深化能源绿色低碳领域务实合作，实现绿色发展优势互补。

第六，深化科技创新交流合作。将科学和创新视为实现经济社会现代化的载体，承认创新对经济社会发展的重要性，加强友好省州间交流与合作，实现知识互通、创意联通、创新共享。②

第七，加强人才教育培训合作。依托各友好省州强大的教育培训资源，推动各省州高校、培训机构开展各类人才交流活动和培训项目，加强人才交流与培养合作，培养具有国际视野的掌握前沿知识、理念和技术的国际化高端人才。

## 三、深挖产业升级及经贸互补发展潜力

经贸往来和产业合作是国际交往的核心，相比政治和文化，地区间的联系更加依靠经济。世界各国和各地方政府都在寻求经济及先进生产技术的支持，以促进本国经济和社会快速发展。

① 参见马学广、孟颖焘：《中国国际友好城市发展演变及影响因素分析》，《中国名城》2016 年第 10 期。

② 参见《第九次峰会能源转型联合宣言》，2018 年 5 月 18 日，加拿大魁北克省。

友好省州各具特色、优势互补，既面临不同问题又面临共性挑战，加强合作基础深厚、前景广阔。未来，友好省州应继续挖掘已有产业与经贸合作资源潜力，深化相互间在经贸、投资、科技以及教育、旅游、人文等领域的实质性交流与合作，促进产业升级和经贸互补；推进诸如生态城市、智慧城市、数字城市等绿色科技领域的交流合作，深化互学互鉴，共享知识、技术和资源，倡导绿色、低碳、循环、可持续的发展方式，推动绿色发展，共创美好未来。

## 四、优化国际营商环境

各友好省州都是经济强省州，持续提升国际营商环境建设，以更开放、更国际化的营商环境推动相互间产业与企业经贸投资合作，对各省州深度参与全球产业分工和合作、维护多元稳定的国际经济格局和经济贸易关系具有深刻的现实意义。要积极顺应国际经济贸易格局发展趋势，在贸易、投资和人员流动等方面进一步加大开放力度，实现程序、标准和规则的接轨，推动各类生产要素跨境流动，加大对外商投资权益和知识产权的保护，促进跨境投资自由化和贸易便利化。

## 五、推动国际人员交流

进一步加强人员互访，广泛开展文化交流、学术交流、人才交流、媒体合作、青少年交往、志愿者服务等多种形式的交流活动，为深化友好合作奠定更加坚实的民意基础。特别要着力加强青少年交往，使青年一代成为传统友谊的参与者、传承者和开拓者，实现友好交往持续深入发展。

## 六、完善国际合作机制

创新友好省州合作机制，复制和推广以友好省州领导人峰会机制为核心的各项合作新机制、新模式，共同打造更广阔的交流平台，铺就高水平合作之路，拓宽合作领域，提升合作层次。有计划地组织专题交流与研讨，建立常态化沟通联络机制，加强沟通与研判，积极搭建经贸、文化、教育等领域的交流合作平台，确保友好省州合作始终走在良性轨道上。

对于友好省州领导人峰会达成的各项共识与交流合作事项，要强化后续的落实执行。应加大相关项目与活动的经费支持力度，统筹协调各项资源保障，创造充分的条件以确保议定事项落实落地。

# Chapter 11 Outlook for Exchanges and Cooperation among Sister Provinces and States

Nowadays, it is a general trend that the interests and shared future of countries across the globe are more intertwined, and the common expectation of all peoples is to continually create a better life.[①] Sister provinces and states should work together for the common future. Focusing on sustainable development, they should further deepen practical cooperation, share development opportunities and face challenges together, to achieve win-win cooperation and promote development and progress.

## 11.1 Staying Committed to Sustainable Development

Achieving sustainable development is a common task for all countries in the world. At present, "sustainable" development is faced with a series of challenges such as rapid population growth and aging, water scarcity, forest depletion, energy crisis and environment pollution. The summit should continue to strengthen exchanges and cooperation on the theme of sustainable development, and reinforce the consensus on global issues. To this end, sister provinces and states should take effective measures to promote

---

① "President Xi Jinping Sends Congratulatory Letter to the 2019 Understanding China Conference in Guangzhou", https://www.gov.cn/xinwen/2019-10/26/content_5445217.htm, 26 October, 2019.

quality economic development, improve energy production efficiency, and use more renewable energy, so as to actively respond to demographic change, climate change, environmental protection and urban safety challenges, and jointly promote and achieve sustainable development.

## 11.2 Enhancing Practical Cooperation in Key Areas

First, sister provinces and states should strengthen inter-governmental cooperation. Relying on the leaders' summit mechanism, sister provinces and states aim to strengthen high-level dialogue and reciprocal visits between their governments, promote people-to-people exchanges at all levels, foster cooperation in key areas such as economy and trade, science and technology, humanities, energy and infrastructure, and raise the cooperation quality.

Second, sister provinces and states should intensify non-government cooperation. Connections and channels of sister provinces/states and cities can be broadened through non-government cooperation. Sister provinces and states should actively promote international sister city cooperation to deepen understanding of different cultures and remove constraints through increased people-to-people contacts.①

Third, sister provinces and states should reinforce economic and trade cooperation. Efforts should be made to strengthen the basic role of economic and trade cooperation among sister provinces and states, continue to optimize the business environment, and encourage enterprises to increase investment in industrial projects in sister provinces and states, for the purpose of pushing economic, trade and investment cooperation to a higher level, sharing development opportunities, and achieving mutual benefits and common prosperity and development.

---

① Ma Xueguang, Meng Yingtao, “The Evolution and Influencing Factors Analysis of International Sister Cities in China,” China Ancient City, no. 10 (2016), pp.4-14.

Fourth, sister provinces and states should promote cultural and sports exchanges and cooperation. Cultural and sports exchanges among sister provinces and states can promote mutual understanding and mutual friendship, broaden people's horizons and knowledge. Through the communication, people from different regions will learn from each other and maintain the innovation and creativity of their own culture.

Fifth, sister provinces and states should boost practical cooperation in green development. Focusing on clean transport, green finance, green technology and other fields, sister provinces and states will continue to expand the investment boundary in energy transition and green environmental protection industries, promote the government, financial institutions, enterprises and other relevant parties to match their demands, explore the potential for cooperation, and deepen pragmatic cooperation in the field of green and low-carbon energy, accelerating the implementation of complementary advantages in green development.

Sixth, sister provinces and states should deepen exchanges and cooperation in technological innovation. Science and innovation should act as vehicles for the modernization of the economy and society. Sister provinces and states need to understand the importance of innovation to economic and social development, share knowledge and support creativity and innovation through strengthened exchanges and cooperation.①

Seventh, sister provinces and states should enhance cooperation in personnel education and training. Relying on their abundant education and training resources, sister provinces and states will promote various personnel exchanges and training programmes by universities and training institutions in the provinces and states, and foster their cooperation, so as to broaden their international horizons, help them master cutting-edge knowledge, concepts and technologies, and train internationalized high-end personnel.

---

① Joint Declaration on Energy Transition of The 9th Regional Leaders' Summit. Quebec, Canada. 18 May, 2018.

## 11.3 Tapping into the Potential of Industrial Upgrading and Complementary Economic and Trade Development

Economic and trade exchanges and industrial cooperation are the core of international exchanges, and inter-regional ties are relying more on global economic ties that transcend political and cultural factors. Countries and local governments around the world are seeking strong economic and advanced production technology to support the rapid development of their economies and societies.

With their distinctive features and complementary advantages, the sister provinces and states face different problems and common challenges, and have a deep foundation and broad prospects for strengthening cooperation. In the future, sister provinces and states should continue to explore the potential of their existing industrial and economic and trade cooperation resources, deepen practical exchanges and cooperation in the fields of trade, investment, science and technology, as well as education, tourism and humanities, and promote industrial upgrading and economic and trade complementarity. They should also promote exchanges and cooperation in green technology areas such as eco-cities, smart cities and digital cities, deepen mutual learning from each other, and through the sharing of knowledge, technology and resources, jointly advocate a green, low-carbon, circular and sustainable development approach to promote green development and create a better future.

## 11.4 Optimizing International Business Environment

As the sister provinces and states are economically robust, it is of profound practical significance to continuously optimize the internationalized business environment and to promote economic, trade and investment cooperation among industries and enterprises with a more open and internationalized business environment, so as to enable the provinces and states to participate deeply in the global industrial division of labour and cooperation and to maintain a diversified and stable international economic pattern and economic and trade relations. Sister provinces and states should actively follow the development trend of the international economic and trade, further intensify opening up in trade, investment and the mobility of people, realizing the alignment of procedures, standards and rules and promoting the cross-border mobility of various production factors. Furthermore, the protection of the rights and interests of foreign investment and intellectual property rights should be intensified, only by doing so can they promote cross-border investment liberalization and trade facilitation.

## 11.5 Promoting International Personnel Communication

Reciprocal visits will be increased including exchanges in the fields of culture, academia, personnel, media cooperation, youth, and volunteer services, to lay a more solid public opinion foundation for deepening friendship and cooperation. In particular, efforts should be made to strengthen youth communication, so that the young generation can become participants, inheritors and pioneers of traditional friendship, and to achieve sustained and in-depth development of friendly communication.

## 11.6 Improving International Cooperation Mechanisms

Sister provinces and states should seek a new cooperation mechanism, promote and replicate various new mechanisms and models of cooperation with the leaders' summit mechanism as the core, jointly create more exchange platforms, in order to pave the way for high-level cooperation, broaden the scope and raise the level of cooperation. It is important to organize themed exchanges and seminars in a planned manner, establish a regular communication and liaison mechanism, strengthen communication and evaluation, and actively build platforms for exchanges and cooperation in the fields of economy, trade, culture and education to ensure that the cooperation among sister provinces and states is always on a positive track.

The implementation of the agreements, exchanges and cooperation reached at the summit should be strengthened by providing sufficient guarantee such as intensified financial support and coordinated resources.

# 附　录

## 中国山东省概况

山东省地处中国东部沿海、黄河下游，省会济南市，人口超过1亿，陆域面积15.58万平方千米，下辖16个地级市，经济总量位居全国第三。山东省作为人口大省、经济大省、文化大省，是中国重要的工业基地和北方地区经济发展的战略支点。林武任中共山东省委书记，周乃翔任山东省省长。

近年来，山东省推进中国式现代化“山东实践”、实施黄河重大国家战略获得重大进展，加快新旧动能转换取得重大成效，绿色低碳高质量发展先行区实现重大突破，全省经济社会发展取得显著成就。

2022年，山东省地区生产总值达8.74万亿元，农业总产值率先突破万亿元，市场主体超过1400万家，进出口规模突破3万亿元。山东省工业门类齐全、产业基础雄厚。山东省持续培育壮大新一代信息技术、高端装备、新能源新材料等“十强产业”，海洋经济总量位居全国第二，海洋生物医药等产业增加值位居全国第一，国家级海洋牧场示范区数量占全国的近40%；港口货物吞吐量稳居全球第一，集装箱吞吐量位居全球第三。未来，山东省将加快构建现代化产业体系，打造世界级先进钢铁、高端铝业、现代轻工纺织基地和绿色化工产业集群。

山东省历史悠久、底蕴深厚，是儒家思想的发源地，是中华文明的重要发祥地之一，素有“孔孟之乡，礼仪之邦”的美誉。泰山被联合国教科文组织列为世界文化与自然双重遗产，曲阜孔庙、孔林、孔府和京杭大运河山东段、齐长城被联合国教科文组织列为世界文化遗产。山东省是教育大省，目前拥有各级各类学校3.87万所，普通高等学校153所，其中本科院校70所、高职院校83所，研究生培养机构35处，在校生2200多万人。

“绿水青山就是金山银山。”山东省统筹推进生态优先、节约集约、绿色低碳发展，节能减排目标全面完成，新能源、可再生能源发电装机占比39.3%。2022年，国家赋予山东省建设绿色低碳高质量发展先行区的重大历史使命。未来，山东省将实施碳达峰“十大工程”和能源转型发展“九大工程”，协同推进降碳、减污、扩绿、增长，促进经济社会发展全面绿色转型。

山东省努力打造对外开放新高地，充分用好自由贸易试验区、中国—上海合作组织地方经贸合作示范区等开放平台，自由贸易试验区实际使用外资年均增长率达61.4%。上海合作组织青岛峰会、跨国公司领导人青岛峰会、儒商大会、世界入海口城市合作发展大会等影响广泛。山东省已与世界上94个国家建立了623对友好城市和友好合作关系城市。“选择山东、创业齐鲁”越来越成为世界各国的共识。

# 德国巴伐利亚州概况

巴伐利亚，又称“拜恩”“拜仁”，位于欧洲腹地，阿尔卑斯山北麓，地处德国东南部，东倚捷克，南邻奥地利、瑞士；面积 70552 平方公里，约占全国的 19.7%，是德国面积最大的州；拥有人口 1314 万，位居德国第二；首府是慕尼黑市；现任州长为马库斯·索德尔。2022 年，巴伐利亚州国内生产总值达 7168 亿欧元，几乎占德国经济总量的 1/5，超过全球 90%以上国家的国内生产总值。

巴伐利亚州在航空航天、生物及基因工程、传媒、信息和电信技术等领域处于德国领先地位，在金融、保险、会展、物流、出版、专利、科研等领域的国际地位突出。巴伐利亚州产生过众多震惊世界的技术发明和创造，如鲁道夫·狄塞尔（Rudolf Diesel）发明了柴油发动机，卡尔·林德（Carl von Linde）研究出了空气液化技术等。30 多位诺贝尔奖获得者出生在巴伐利亚州或在巴伐利亚州接受大学教育、从事科研和教学，其中最著名的有发明伦琴射线的首届诺贝尔物理学奖得主威廉·康拉德·伦琴（Wilhelm Conrad Röntgen），1973 年诺贝尔和平奖得主、1923 年出生于巴伐利亚州菲尔特市的美国前国务卿亨利·基辛格（Henry Alfred Kissinger）等。

巴伐利亚州拥有一批世界一流的大学和科研机构，共有 11 所综合性大学、24 所应用技术大学，其中实力最强和最具代表性的大学是慕尼黑大学和慕尼黑工业大学，国际顶尖科研机构如拥有 70 多年历史、总部位于慕尼黑、从事基础科学研究的马克斯·普朗克科学促进协会（下设 86 个研究所及研究机构），欧洲最大的从事应用技术研究的弗朗霍夫研究院（下设 74 个研究所及研究机构）。此外，欧洲专利局也在巴伐利亚州首府慕尼黑。

巴伐利亚州有一大批著名的跨国大公司，如阿迪达斯、奥迪、宝马、欧洲航空防务航天公司以及西门子等。德国股票交易所计入成分股指的大型上市公司中有1/4总部设在巴伐利亚州。巴伐利亚州是世界领先的工业基地之一，产品包罗万象，其中汽车、机械和电子产品约占工业总产值的40%。巴伐利亚州的制造业比重超过了德国平均水平，制造业总量占德国总量的20.6%。

巴伐利亚州作为德国强大的经济中心，与世界众多国家和地区建立了贸易联系，产品往来交易密切。2022年，巴伐利亚州产品出口总额约2164亿欧元，进口总额2505亿欧元。巴伐利亚州的进出口产品种类繁多，从制造业到轻工业都有涉及。产品出口量排名前三的产品依次为汽车、电气产品及机械设备，三者出口之和占出口总量的一半。电气、汽车及机械设备同样也是巴伐利亚州最青睐的进口产品。巴伐利亚州的企业比其他地方的企业有更强的抗危机能力。2022年，巴伐利亚州的破产率仅为0.35%（德国为0.46%）。德国股票指数（Deutscher Aktienindex，DAX）中的40家公司有9家总部设在巴伐利亚州，微软、英特尔、谷歌和苹果等大型国际公司也将德国总部甚至欧洲总部设在巴伐利亚州。

巴伐利亚州的经济支柱是中小企业，巴伐利亚州是德国中小企业第一州。巴伐利亚州的约61.4万家企业中，99.6%为中小企业。中小企业为巴伐利亚州提供了约430万个就业岗位，占全部就业市场的75%以上；同时提供了约19万个培训岗位，占巴伐利亚培训岗位的80%以上。中小企业的年营业额接近4320亿欧元，占据了巴伐利亚州工业总产值的近38%。

# 美国佐治亚州概况

佐治亚州地处美国东南部，东临大西洋，东北部与南卡罗来纳州接壤，北接田纳西州和北卡罗来纳州，西接亚拉巴马州，南邻佛罗里达州。佐治亚州总面积为15.39万平方公里，约占全国总面积的2.5%，总人口约为1071万。2022年，佐治亚州地区生产总值约为7556亿美元，居全国第八位。佐治亚州首府为亚特兰大市，1996年第26届夏季奥运会在亚特兰大举办。佐治亚州全州有159个县，535个市、镇。现任州长是共和党人布莱恩·坎普(Brian Kemp)。

19世纪上半叶，佐治亚州依靠棉花种植业成为美国南方最富有的州之一。20世纪以来，佐治亚州经济逐步向多元化发展，其传统产业如农业、造纸、纺织、制造业等实力雄厚，新兴产业如生命科学、能源、航空航天、金融服务、旅游业等发展迅速，多次被评为美国最适宜从事商业活动的州。可口可乐、联合包裹等多家世界500强企业的总部设在佐治亚州。

佐治亚州农业发达，全州有约6万家农场，花生产量占美国产量的一半；资源丰富，森林面积占全州面积的67%；中部瓷土含量丰富，北部盛产大理石和花岗岩，为美国建筑石料的主要来源之一，匹根斯县是世界上主要的大理石产地之一；拥有锰矿、铝土矿、煤矿等丰富的矿产资源。

佐治亚州工业体系完备，纺织业占有突出位置，地毯占全国总产量的一半以上；汽车和飞机制造集中于亚特兰大；金融服务、建筑设计、法律咨询、物流零售等服务业是佐治亚州经济的重要组成部分；互联网、软件通信和生命科学等高科技产业发达。佐治亚州交通便捷，亚特兰大国际机场是世界上最繁忙的机场之一，拥有两个通往大西洋的深水良港——萨凡纳港和布伦斯威克港。

佐治亚州教育发达，拥有佐治亚大学、佐治亚理工学院和佐治亚州立大学等高校。佐治亚州旅游业发达，是著名黑人民权运动领袖马丁·路德·金(Martin Luther King)的故乡、著名小说《飘》(*Gone with the Wind*)的故事发生地，拥有历史名城萨凡纳、石山公园等。

# 加拿大魁北克省概况

魁北克省总面积为167万平方公里，占加拿大国土面积的近1/6，位居加拿大第一。2022年魁北克省总人口约为870万，位居加拿大第二，全省人口主要集中在南部地区，特别是圣劳伦斯河及其支流沿岸。魁北克省官方语言为法语，讲法语的居民约占85%。魁北克省省会为魁北克市，全省分为17个行政地区，下设88个县、市，1128个市、镇。现任省长为魁北克未来联盟党领袖弗朗索瓦·勒戈(François Legault)。

魁北克省是加拿大经济强省，拥有广阔的地域和多样化的经济，2022年地区生产总值约为2898亿美元，经济总量位居加拿大第二。近年来，魁北克省的服务业发展迅速，创新型经济得到发展，高新技术产业获得支持，航空航天、软件及信息科技、生命科学、信息通信、清洁能源等发展较好。

魁北克省资源丰富，森林面积广阔，淡水和海水资源充足，气候环境良好，农业发达，农业种植以玉米、大豆、蔬菜为主，是世界上最大的枫糖产地，拥有丰富的矿产资源。

航空产业是魁北克省经济的重要组成部分，魁北克省拥有庞巴迪等一批知名公司。魁北克省在生命科学领域处于北美洲领先地位。此外，魁北克省在通信技术、微电子、半导体、动画、游戏开发等领域有独特优势。

魁北克省教育发达，有拉瓦尔大学、蒙特利尔大学、希尔布鲁克大学、麦吉尔大学、康科迪亚大学、魁北克大学等高校。魁北克省既有北美社会的特征，又是美洲主要的法语社会，欧洲文化与北美文化的汇合赋予了魁北克创作人员源源不断的灵感以及广阔的市场，如太阳马戏团(Cirque du Soleil)、歌唱家席琳·迪翁(Celine Dion)等。

魁北克省蒙特利尔市是加拿大第二大城市，超过65个国际组织将总部设在蒙特利尔市。魁北克省省会魁北克市成立于1608年，是北美洲最古老的城市之一，魁北克古城被联合国教科文组织列为世界文化遗产。

# 巴西圣保罗州概况

圣保罗州位于巴西东南部，东临大西洋，总面积约为24.82万平方公里，约占巴西国土面积的3%，总人口约为4442万，设645个市，首府为圣保罗市，现任州长为塔尔西奥·德弗雷塔斯（Tarcísio de Freitas）。作为南美洲国际化程度最高的州之一，圣保罗州有来自70多个不同国家的约300万移民，是巴西人口最多样化的地区。

圣保罗州资源丰富、基础设施完备、产业齐全、科技水平和劳动力素质高，是巴西经济实力最雄厚的州，被称为巴西的“经济发动机”。2020年，圣保罗州地区生产总值约为2.44万亿雷亚尔，约占全国的1/3，位居巴西第一。圣保罗州服务业占比高达65.64%，工业占比17.07%，农牧业占比1.41%。

圣保罗州经济多元，是巴西其他地区和国外消费品、资本货物、服务的主要供应地，其中食品、化学、焦炭及石油、生物燃料、汽车、机械设备制造等行业产值尤为突出，超过了巴西一半的金融机构产值和30.3%的工业加工产值。同时，圣保罗州也是巴西最大的消费市场。以甘蔗衍生物和水力发电为主的可再生能源在圣保罗州能源结构中占据重要地位，非可再生能源主要为石油和天然气。巴西国家生物乙醇科技实验室位于圣保罗州。

圣保罗州拥有巴西规模最大、质量最佳的基础设施，有30多个机场，公路里程达3.7万公里，公路、铁路和水路等多种联运方式带动了圣保罗州的出口。桑托斯港是拉丁美洲最重要的港口之一，港口进出口额占巴西贸易量的近30%。

圣保罗州30%的面积被大西洋森林覆盖，州海岸线长约622公里，拥有30多个州级生态保护区，70多万公顷的完整自然保护单位被用于保护、研究及旅游。旅游资源丰富，旅游基础设施较为完善。

圣保罗州人类发展指数（Human Development Index，HDI）达0.806，就

业人口的教育水平高于全国平均水平，圣保罗大学在QS（Quacquarelli Symonds，夸夸雷利·西蒙兹）世界大学排名和泰晤士高等教育世界大学排名中位列拉丁美洲第一。圣保罗州文化丰富多元，人文旅游景点众多，音乐厅及剧院数量位居巴西第一，手工艺品富有特色、行业成熟，传统节庆活动众多、特色鲜明。

圣保罗州首府圣保罗市人口约为1145万，面积约为1521平方公里，是巴西的工业、服务业和商业活动中心。圣保罗市展会众多，是巴西主要的商务旅行目的地，2014年巴西世界杯开幕式在圣保罗市举办。此外，圣保罗时装周和艺术双年展等也享有盛誉。

# 奥地利上奥州概况

上奥州位于奥地利西北部，西邻德国巴伐利亚州，北接捷克共和国。上奥州总面积为1.2万平方公里，占奥地利国土面积的14.3%，位列奥地利第四。上奥州总人口约为149.5万，位列奥地利第三。上奥州下设18个地市、442个乡镇，首府为林茨市。上奥州实行议会制，州议会是州的立法机构。现任州长为麦格·托马斯·施泰尔泽。

上奥州政府所在地林茨市是上奥州政治、经济、文化中心，面积96平方公里，人口20.7万。林茨市是在罗马古城的遗址上发展起来的城市，位于多瑙河右岸。古代林茨市是通商要道的交叉点，地理位置十分重要，现在林茨市仍然是运输枢纽，是多瑙河的重要码头、奥地利最大的河港。林茨市还是奥地利重要的工业中心，其黑色金属冶炼、化学工业、机器制造、纤维、香烟等行业都很发达。

上奥州是奥地利的重工业生产基地，是奥地利9个联邦州中国民经济工业化程度最高、经济实力最强的州。2022年，上奥州地区生产总值为763亿欧元，位居奥地利第二。上奥州工业经济占国民经济的36.6%，冶金(炼钢)、汽车制造、能源、机电、建材、造纸、环保是其支柱产业，在规模上和技术上具有较强实力和显著优势。上奥州在能源和环保领域处于领先地位，有34.7%的能源为可再生资源。

# 南非西开普省概况

西开普省位于非洲大陆西南端，西面和南面分别为大西洋和印度洋所环绕，本格拉寒流为西海岸带来了丰富的渔业资源，印度洋暖流为南部沿海地区带来了丰沛的降水。西开普省总面积为 12.9 万平方公里，占南非国土面积的 10.6%，位居南非第四。2022 年西开普省总人口为 721.2 万，占南非人口的 11.9%。西开普省的官方语言是南非荷兰语、英语、科萨语。西开普省下辖一个大都市、五个区，分别是开普敦大都市、西海岸区、瓦恩兰角区、奥弗贝格区、花园大道区和中卡鲁区，地区政府下辖 24 个市镇，省会为开普敦市。现任省长为艾伦·温迪(Alan Winde)。

西开普省经济发展水平较高，2022 年地区生产总值为 500 亿美元，是南非最发达的省份之一；西开普省经济富有活力、产业门类齐全、发展比较均衡，是南非造船业中心；经济以服务业、制造业、贸易、旅游业和农业为主；信息通信技术是发展最快的产业之一，服装纺织业是主要的就业领域；旅游业资源、林业资源和植物花卉资源丰富，矿产资源贫乏；主要出口商品为水果、酒类、海产品、机械产品和钢铁制品。

西开普省是南非的农业大省，生产了南非 46%的农产品，是南非最重要的“菜篮子”之一。小卡鲁地区还有大规模的鸵鸟农场，鸵鸟肉和皮制品是重要的产业。西开普省葡萄酒产量占南非葡萄酒产量的 95%，产量位居世界第七。西开普省盛产水果、蔬菜、驼鸟、猪肉、牛肉、羊肉、绵羊毛、美利奴羊种羊、赛马种马、肉食鸡、鸡蛋、乳品、黄木、臭木、白梨木等；渔业资源十分丰富，渔业产量占南非渔业总产量的 85%；海产品种类丰富，包括开普龙虾、鲍鱼、金枪鱼、章鱼、牡蛎、贻贝等，西海岸地区的深海和远洋渔业资源尤其丰富。

西开普省的旅游资源十分丰富，旅游业是促进西开普省经济增长的重要产业，每年前往西开普省旅游度假的游客超过 800 万人，著名的旅游景点有好望角、开普敦国家植物园、桌山、企鹅滩、海豹岛、葡萄园、钻石城等。

西开普省的工业和第三产业较发达，如制酒业、渔业、家具业、旅游业、制造业、珠宝业、造船业、印刷包装业、医疗业、化工业、金融业和影视、电信、高科技产业等，制衣和纺织业是西开普省主要的劳动力就业行业。

西开普省比较重要的贸易投资促进机构和商会有西开普省贸易投资发展局和开普地区商会。西开普省贸易投资发展局是西开普省官方投资和促进机构，负责招商引资、对外贸易和树立西开普省商业形象。开普地区商会主要负责维护会员利益，改善商业环境，与政府、工会等公共部门进行协调，同时为会员提供广告、咨询、会展等服务。

西开普省的主要文化机构有南非国家美术馆、南非博物馆、开普艺术公司、开普敦城市芭蕾舞团、开普爱乐乐团、南非国家图书馆等。

西开普省的教育水平较高，公民受教育程度位居全国第一，有开普敦大学、斯泰伦布什大学和西开普大学等著名高校，此外还有两所技术学院和多所培训中心。

西开普省与美国的佛罗里达州、德国的巴伐利亚州、奥地利的上奥州、突尼斯的突尼斯省、葡萄牙的马德拉自治区、中国的山东省建立了友好省州关系。

# Appendix

## A Brief Introduction to Shandong Province, China

Shandong, sitting on the lower reaches of the Yellow River, is a coastal province with a population of over 100 million in eastern China. It covers a land area of 158,000 square kilometers, accounting for about 1.6% of the country's total land area, and its economic volume is the third largest in China. Subdivided into 16 cities, with Jinan as the capital city, Shandong remains a populous, cultural and economic powerhouse, an important industrial base in China, and a strategic support for the economic development in the northern region. The current Secretary of the CPC Shandong Provincial Committee is Lin Wu, and the Governor is Zhou Naixiang.

In recent years, Shandong has made significant progress in the advancement of the "Shandong Practice" of Chinese modernization and the implementation of the major national strategy for the protection of the Yellow River, achieved significant results in expediting the replacement of old growth drivers with new ones, and realized major breakthroughs as a pioneer in pursuing green, low-carbon and high-quality development.

In 2022, Shandong's GDP reached RMB 8.74 trillion, with an average annual growth rate of 5.4%, the gross output value of agriculture taking the lead in exceeding RMB 1 trillion, the number of market players exceeding 14 million, and the total imports and exports exceeding RMB 3 trillion. Shandong possesses complete industrial categories which constitute a strong industrial base. It continues to foster and strengthen the “Top 10 Industries”, such as the new generation of information technology, high-end equipment and new energy & materials. Meanwhile, both the total volume of its marine economy and the added value of its industries such as marine biopharmaceuticals rank first in the country, and its national-level marine ranch demonstration areas account for nearly 40% of the country's total. Its port cargo throughput sits on top of the world, and its container throughput ranks third in the world. In the future, Shandong will accelerate its efforts to build a modern industrial system, world-class advanced bases for steel, high-end aluminum, and modern light and textile industries, as well as a green chemical industry cluster.

With a long and profound history, Shandong is the birthplace of Confucianism and one of the centers of Chinese civilization, and has been known as the “Hometown of Confucius and Mencius” and the “Land of Etiquette”. Mount Tai has been listed as both World Natural Heritage and World Cultural Heritage by the United Nations Educational, Scientific, and Cultural Organization (UNESCO), and the three Confucian scenic spots (i.e., the Temple and Cemetery of Confucius and the Kong Family Mansion) in Qufu, the Grand Canal and the Great Wall of Qi have also been inscribed on the UNESCO World Heritage List. Shandong is a major province of education, with 38,700 schools of various levels and categories, including 153 regular institutions of higher education (comprising 70 undergraduate colleges and universities and 83 higher vocational colleges), and 35 institutions of postgraduate education, with a total of more than 22 million students enrolled.

Adhering to the concept of “Lucid waters and lush mountains are invaluable assets”, Shandong has coordinated and accelerated its efforts to prioritize ecological protection, conserve resources and use them efficiently, and pursue green and low-carbon development. It has fully accomplished its energy conservation and emission reduction targets, with its installed capacity of power generation from new and renewable energy accounting for 39.3%. In 2022, China bestowed on Shandong a major historical mission to build itself into a pioneer for green, low-carbon and high-quality development. In the future, Shandong will implement ten major projects to ensure carbon peaking and nine major projects to ensure energy transition and development, and promote concerted efforts to cut carbon emissions, reduce pollution, expand green development, and pursue economic growth, to advance the all-round green transition in economic and social development.

Shandong strives to build new highland for opening up, fully utilizing the Pilot Free Trade Zone, the China-SCO Local Economic and Trade Cooperation Demonstration Area, and other new open platforms, with the average annual growth rate of actual use of foreign capital in the Pilot Free Trade Zone reaching 61.4%. The SCO Qingdao Summit, the Qingdao Multinationals Summit, the Conference of Great Business Partners, and the World Estuarine Cities Conference for Cooperation and Development held in Shandong have a profound influence. In addition, Shandong has established sister-city relations and friendly cooperation with 623 cities in 94 countries around the world. "Select Shandong, Start a Business in Qilu" has further become the consensus worldwide.

# A Brief Introduction to Bavaria, Germany

Bavaria, also known as Bayern, is situated in the south-east of Germany, lying at the heart of Europe and the northern foot of the Alps, and bordered by the Czech Republic to the east and Austria and Switzerland to the south. With an area of 70,552 square kilometers, about 19.7% of the country's total area, it is the largest of the 16 federal states of Germany. It has a population of 13.14 million, the second largest in Germany. The capital city is Munich. In 2022, Bavaria reached a GDP of EUR 716.8 billion, which was almost one fifth of the German economic aggregate, outperforming more than 90% of the countries worldwide. The current Minister President of Bavaria is Markus Söder, Chairman of the German Christian Social Union (CSU).

Bavaria secures the leading position in Germany in the fields of aerospace, biological and genetic engineering, media, information and telecommunication technology, etc., and is also internationally recognized in the fields of finance, insurance, conventions & exhibitions, logistics, publishing, patents, scientific research, etc. Bavaria has produced numerous world-shattering technological inventions and creations, such as the diesel engine invented by Rudolf Diesel and the air liquefaction process devised by Carl Von Linde. More than 30 winners of the Nobel Prizes in physics, chemistry, medicine, literature and peace were born in Bavaria or received their college education here, or were engaged in research and teaching here. The most famous of them include Wilhelm Conrad Röntgen, winner of the first Nobel Prize in Physics, who invented the X-ray, and Henry Kissinger, born in 1923 in Fürth, Bavaria, winner of the Nobel Peace Prize in 1973 and former US Secretary of State.

Bavaria has a number of world-class universities and research institutes, with a total of 11 comprehensive universities, of which University of Munich and Technical University of Munich are the most powerful and representative, as well as 24 universities of applied sciences. It has two world-leading research institutes, i.e., the Max Planck Institute (having 86 institutes and research institutions), which has a history of more than 70 years, is headquartered in Munich and engages in research in basic sciences, and the Fraunhofer Institute (having 74 institutes and research institutions), which is the largest institute for applied technology in Europe. In addition, the European Patent Office is also situated in Munich, the capital of Bavaria.

Bavaria is home to a large number of well-known multinational giants such as Adidas, Audi, BMW, European Aeronautic Defence and Space Company (EADS), MAN and Siemens. A quarter of the large companies listed on the Deutsche Börse Group, which are included in the constituent index, are headquartered in Bavaria. Bavaria is one of the world's leading industrial locations, with a wide range of products, among which the automobiles, machinery and electronics account for around 40% of its total industrial output value. Its share of manufacturing exceeds the German average, with total manufacturing accounting for 20.6% of the total of Germany's 16 federal states.

As a strong economic center of Germany, Bavaria has made connections and traded with many countries and regions around the world. In 2022, the total exports of its products reached about EUR 216.4 billion and imports totaled EUR 250.5 billion. Bavaria imports and exports a wide variety of products ranging from manufacturing to light industry. The top three exports are automobiles, electrical products, and mechanical equipment, which together account for half of the state's total exports. These three categories are likewise Bavaria’s most favored imports. Bavarian companies are more crisis-resistant than elsewhere. In 2022, the bankruptcy rate in Bavaria was merely 0.35% (Germany: 0.46%). Nine of the German DAX 40 companies are headquartered in Bavaria (including BMW, Siemens, Adidas and Audi), while major international companies such as Microsoft, Intel, Google, and Apple also have their German and even European headquarters in Bavaria.

The backbone of the Bavarian economy is small- and medium-sized enterprises (SMEs): Bavaria is known as No.1 state for SMEs in Germany. 99.6% of its approximately 614,000 enterprises are SMEs. SMEs provide around 4.3 million jobs in Bavaria, which account for over 75% of the total job market, as well as around 190,000 training positions, which account for over 80% of the total trainees in Bavaria. The annual turnover of SMEs is approximately EUR 432 billion, accounting for nearly 38% of Bavaria’s industrial output value.

# A Brief Introduction to Georgia, the United States

Georgia lies in the southeastern United States, bordering the Atlantic Ocean to the east, South Carolina to the northeast, Tennessee and North Carolina to the north, Alabama to the west, and Florida to the south. It covers a total area of 153, 900 square kilometers, about 2.5% of the country's total area, and has a population of about 10.71 million. In 2022, its GDP was about US $ 755.6 billion, ranking 8th in the country. With Atlanta as the capital, which hosted the 26th Summer Olympics in 1996, Georgia has 159 counties and 535 municipalities. The current governor is Brian Kemp, a member of the Republican Party (US).

In the first half of the 19th century, Georgia became one of the wealthiest states in the South, relying on cotton planting. Since the 20th century, it has gradually moved towards a diversified economy. Georgia has been recognized many times as the best state in the United States to do business for its great strength in traditional industries such as agriculture, papermaking, textiles, and manufacturing, and its rapid growth in emerging industries such as life sciences, energy, aerospace, financial services and tourism. Several Fortune 500 companies, such as Coca-Cola and United Parcel Service (UPS), have their headquarters here.

Georgia is agriculturally advanced, with a total of about 60,000 farms, which produces half of the peanuts produced in the country; it is rich in resources, with forests covering 67% of its total area; its central part is rich in kaolin, the northern part is rich in marble and granite, one of the major sources of building stone in the country, and Pickens County is one of the major producers of marble in the world. In addition, Georgia is blessed with other rich mineral resources such as manganese ore, bauxite, and coal.

Georgia has a complete industrial system. Its textile industry occupies a prominent position, with carpet production accounting for more than half of the country's total; automobile and aircraft manufacturing is primarily in Atlanta; services such as finance, architectural design, legal counseling, logistics and retailing are important components of the state's economy; the state also has advanced high-tech industries in the fields of the Internet, software communications, life sciences, etc.; and it has easy access to transportation, including the Hartsfield-Jackson Atlanta International Airport, one of the world's busiest airports, and two deep-water ports to the Atlantic Ocean, i.e., Savannah and Brunswick.

Georgia has enlightened education systems, represented by University of Georgia, Georgia Institute of Technology, Georgia State University, etc. Furthermore, it has a flourishing tourism as it is the hometown of Martin Luther King, Jr., who led the American civil rights movement, and the setting of the famous novel *Gone with the Wind*, and boasts Savannah, a historic district, Stone Mountain Park, and other scenic spots.

# A Brief Introduction to Quebec, Canada

With an area of 1.67 million square kilometers, Quebec occupies nearly one-sixth of Canada's territory, being the largest in the country. It has a population of about 8.7 million (2022), the second largest in Canada, of which French-speaking residents account for about 85%. Quebec is populated mainly in the southern region, especially along the St. Lawrence River and its tributaries. The official language is French. The provincial capital is Quebec City. The province of Quebec is divided into 17 administrative regions with 88 counties and 1,128 municipalities. The current Premier is Francois Legault, leader of the Coalition Avenir Quebec (CAQ).

As Canada's economic powerhouse, Quebec has a vast geographic area and a diversified economy, with its GDP of approximately US $ 289.8 billion in 2022 and economic volume ranking second in the country. In recent years, while its service sector has been growing rapidly, Quebec has made great efforts to develop an innovative economy and to support high-tech industries, achieving desirable development in aerospace, software and information technology, life sciences, information and communications, clean energy, etc.

Quebec possesses rich resources, vast forests, plenty of fresh and sea water, and a favorable climate. Its agriculture is well-developed, with corn, soybeans, vegetables as main crops. Besides, it is the world's largest maple sugar producer, and it is also rich in mineral resources.

With the aviation industry as an important part of its economy, Quebec has a number of well-known companies such as Bombardier. It is also a leader in North America in the field of life sciences. In addition, Quebec has unique advantages in the fields of communication technology, microelectronics, semiconductors, animation, game development, etc.

And it has enlightened education systems, represented by Laval University, University of Montreal, University of Sherbrooke, McGill University, Concordia University, University of Quebec, etc. Quebec is the main Franch-speaking society with the characteristics of a North American society in the Americas. The convergence of European and North American cultures has given the creators in the province an unfailing source of inspiration and a broad market, with representative cultural symbols such as Cirque du Soleil and famous singer Celine Dion.

The Montreal is the second largest city in Canada and is home to the headquarters of more than 65 international organizations. Quebec City, the capital of the province of Quebec, founded in 1608, is one of the oldest cities in North America, with the District of Old Quebec having been listed as a World Heritage Site by the UNESCO.

# A Brief Introduction to São Paulo, Brazil

São Paulo is located in southeastern Brazil, bordering the Atlantic Ocean to the east, and covers an area of approximately 248,200 square kilometers, accounting for about 3% of the country's total area. It has a total population of about 44.42 million and is divided into 645 municipalities. The capital city is São Paulo. The current Governor is Tarcísio de Freitas, a member of the Republican Party. As one of the most internationalized states in South America, São Paulo hosts about 3 million immigrants from more than 70 countries, making it the most demographically diverse region in Brazil.

With rich resources, self-contained infrastructure, all categories of industries, high level of science and technology and high-quality labor force, São Paulo is considered as the state with the most economic strength in Brazil, and is known as the "Economic Powerhouse" of Brazil. In 2020, it had a GDP of about R$ 2.44 trillion, accounting for about one-third of the country's, ranking first. Its services, industry and agriculture account for 65.64%, 17.07% and 1.41%, respectively.

São Paulo has a diversified economy, with a particularly prominent output in sectors such as food, chemicals, coke and petroleum products, biofuels, automobiles, and mechanical equipment manufacturing. It is the major supplier of consumer goods, capital goods and services to the rest of Brazil and abroad, concentrating more than half of the output of financial institutions in Brazil and 30.3% of the country's industrial processing output. It is also the largest consumer market in Brazil. Renewable energy sources, dominated by sugarcane derivatives and hydropower, occupy an important position in São Paulo's energy mix, and the main sources of its non-renewable energy include oil and natural gas. The Brazilian Bioethanol Science and Technology National Laboratory (CTBE) is situated in São Paulo.

São Paulo has one of the largest and best-quality infrastructures in Brazil, and its exports have been boosted by multimodal transport such as highways, railways and waterways. The Port of Santos is one of the most important ports in Latin America, with imports and exports accounting for nearly 30% of Brazil's trade volume. The state has more than 30 airports and 37,000 kilometers of highways.

São Paulo has 30% of its area covered by the Atlantic Forest, a total coastline of about 622 kilometers, more than 30 state ecological reserves, as well as more than 700,000 hectares of intact nature conservation units used for conservation, research, and tourism. It is rich in tourism resources and its tourism infrastructure is relatively sufficient.

The São Paulo has a human development index of 0.806, and the educational attainment of the employed population is higher than the national level. University of São Paulo (USP) is ranked first in Latin America on the QS (Quacquarelli Symonds) World University Rankings and the Times Higher Education (THE) World University Rankings. São Paulo possesses a rich and diverse culture, many cultural tourist attractions, the highest number of concert halls and theaters in the country, a distinctive and well-established handicraft industry, as well as a number of traditional festivals with distinctive characteristics.

The city of São Paulo, as the capital, has a population of about 11.45 million and an area of about 1,521 square kilometers, of which the São Paulo Metropolitan Area is the fourth largest urban agglomeration in the world, and is the center of the industrial, service and commercial activities in Brazil. It hosts numerous exhibitions and is a major business travel destination in Brazil. It hosted the opening ceremony of the 2014 FIFA World Cup. In addition, events such as the São Paulo Fashion Week and the Art Biennial enjoy a high reputation.

# A Brief Introduction to Upper Austria, Austria

Upper Austria is located in northwestern Austria, bordered by Bavaria, Germany to the west and the Czech Republic to the north. It covers an area of 12,000 square kilometers, accounting for 14.3% of the total area of Austria, ranking fourth, and has a population of about 1,495,000, ranking third in Austria. With Linz as the capital city, Upper Austria is divided into 18 municipalities, of which Linz, Steyr and Wels are municipalities directly under the central government, with a total of 442 towns. Upper Austria has a parliamentary system and its legislature is the statehouse. The current Governor is Thomas Stelzer, a member of the Austrian People's Party.

Linz, the seat of the Government of Upper Austria, is the political, economic and cultural center of the state, with an area of 96 square kilometers and a population of 207,000. Developed from the remains of the Ancient Roman City and located on the right bank of the Danube, Linz used to occupy an important geographical position at the crossroads of ancient major trade routes. As of today, it remains a transportation hub, an important dock on the Danube and the largest river port in Austria. In addition, Linz is an important industrial center in Austria, with flourishing ferrous metal smelting, chemical industry, machine building, fibers, cigarettes, etc.

Upper Austria is the heavy industry production base in Austria, and has the highest degree of industrialization of the national economy and the best economic strength among Austria’s nine federal states. In 2022, Upper Austria had a GDP of EUR 76.3 billion, ranking only second to Vienna region. With metallurgy (steelmaking), automobile manufacturing, energy, electromechanics, building materials, papermaking and environmental protection as its pillar industries, Upper Austria has strengths and advantages in terms of industrial scale and technology, and its industrial economy accounts for 36.6% of the national economy. In addition, Upper Austria is leading in the fields of environmental protection and energy, with 34.7% of its energy coming from renewable sources.

# A Brief Introduction to Western Cape, South Africa

The Western Cape is located on the southwestern tip of the African continent and is surrounded by the Atlantic and Indian Oceans to the west and south, respectively. The Benguela Current flows along its west coast, bringing abundant fishery resources, and the Warm Indian Ocean Current brings abundant rainfall for its southern coastal area. The province covers an area of 129,000 square kilometers, accounting for 10.6% of South Africa's territory, ranking fourth. It has a population of 7,212,000 (2022), accounting for 11.9% of the national total. The official languages are Afrikaans, English and Xhosa. The provincial capital is Cape Town. The Western Cape comprises one metropolitan city and five districts, i. e., the Cape Town Metropolitan Area, the West Coast District, the Cape Winelands District, the Overberg District, the Garden Route District and the Central Karoo District, with 24 municipalities under the regional government. The current Premier is Alan Winde, a member of the Democratic Unionist Party.

As one of the most developed provinces in South Africa, the Western Cape has a high level of economic development, with a GDP of US $ 50 billion in 2022. It has a dynamic economy with a wide range of industries, dominated by services, manufacturing, trade, tourism and agriculture, which are relatively balanced in development. Information and communication technology is one of its fastest growing industries, and the garment and textile industry is the main area of employment in the province. It is rich in resources such as tourism, forestry and plants and flowers, and lacks mineral resources. Its exports mainly include fruit, wine, seafood, machinery products and steel products. It is the center of South Africa's shipbuilding industry.

The Western Cape is leading agriculture in South Africa, producing 46% of the country's agricultural products, and is known as one of the country's most important "food baskets". The Little Karoo has large ostrich farms, with ostrich meat and leather products as an important industry. The Western Cape is the seventh largest producer of wine in the world, producing 95% of the country's total wine. It yields abundant fruit, vegetables, ostriches, pork, beef, mutton, sheep's wool, breeding merino sheep, racehorse studs, broiler chickens, eggs, dairy products, yellowwood, stinkwood, and white pear wood, etc. The Western Cape Province is rich in fishery resources, with its fishery production accounting for 85% of South Africa's total, and its seafood categories include lobsters, abalones, tunas, octopus, oysters, mussels, etc. In particular, the West Coast District is rich in deep-sea and pelagic fishery resources.

The province is also rich in tourism resources, and tourism is an important industry that contributes to the growth of the provincial economy, hosting more than 8 million tourists every year. Famous tourist attractions include the Cape of Good Hope, the National Botanical Garden, the Table Mountain, the Penguin Beach, the Seal Island, the Vineyard, and the Diamond Museum.

In the Western Cape, the industrial and tertiary sectors are relatively developed, and the garment and textile industry is the major labor-employing sector. Major industries include winemaking, fishery, furniture, tourism, manufacturing, jewelry, shipbuilding, printing and packaging, medical care, chemical, finance, film & TV, telecommunications, and high-tech industries.

Major trade and investment promotion organizations and chambers of commerce in the Western Cape include Wesgro (the official Investment and

Trade Promotion Agency for the Western Cape) and the Cape Regional Chamber of Commerce and Industry. Wesgro is responsible for attracting investment, promoting foreign trade and building the business image of the Western Cape. The Cape Regional Chamber of Commerce and Industry is primarily responsible for safeguarding the interests of its members, improving the business environment, coordinating with the public sector, such as the government and the trade union, and providing advertising, consulting and exhibition services for its members.

Major cultural organizations in the Western Cape include the South African National Gallery, the South African Museum, Cape Arts Corporation, the Cape Town City Ballet, the Cape Town Philharmonic Orchestra and the National Library of South Africa.

The Western Cape has a high level of education, with its citizens being the best educated in the country. It is home to prestigious universities such as University of Cape Town, Stellenbosch University and University of the Western Cape, as well as two technical colleges and a number of training centers.

The Western Cape has established friendly inter-provincial relations with Florida in the United States, Bavaria in Germany, Upper Austria in Austria, Tunis Governorate in Tunisia, the Autonomous Region of Madeira in Portugal, and Shandong Province in China.

# 参考文献


1.《第一次友好省州领导人峰会联合宣言》,德国巴伐利亚州,2002 年 1 月 31 日。

2.《第三次友好省州领导人峰会联合宣言》,奥地利上奥州,2006 年 7 月 12 日。

3.《第四次友好省州领导人峰会联合宣言》,山东省济南市,2008 年 8 月 7 日。

4.《第六次友好省州领导人峰会联合宣言》,巴西圣保罗州,2012 年 4 月 12 日。

5.《第八次友好省州领导人峰会联合宣言》,德国巴伐利亚州,2016 年 7 月 15 日。

6.《第九次友好省州领导人峰会能源转型联合宣言》,加拿大魁北克省,2018 年 5 月 18 日。

7.《第十次友好省州领导人峰会宣言》,奥地利上奥州,2021 年 11 月 11 日。

8.王立军:《全球化背景下的中国地方政府国际合作》,山东大学博士学位论文,2012 年。

9.刘融、蔡子畅、李亚楠等:《共建"一带一路"为区域合作添动力》,《人民日报》2022 年 9 月 19 日。

10.董礼智:《巨大的差异,共同的主题——慕尼黑五国友好省州首脑大会纪事》,《走向世界》2002 年第 2 期。

11.胡佳、王开茹:《地方政府跨国合作的动力机制与约束条件——"一带一路"背景下中国—东盟的案例研究》,《地方治理研究》2019 年第 2 期。

12.马学广、孟颖焘:《中国国际友好城市发展演变及影响因素分析》,《中国名城》2016 年第 10 期。

13.山东省人民政府外事办公室课题组:《新形势下山东省与欧洲友好省(州)合作现状与对策》,《山东经济战略研究》2011 年第 12 期。

14.鞠川江:《山东省省长郭树清率团访美:鼓励美国企业投资山东战略性新兴产业》,2014 年 6 月 1 日,http://cnews.chinadaily.com.cn/2014-06/01/content_17556591.htm。

15.李杨:《"云话山东"走进潍坊青州南张楼村　中德合作项目绘就乡村新画卷》,2021 年 7 月 8 日,http://weifang.iqilu.com/wfyaowen/2021/0708/4901614.shtml。

16.满倩倩:《山东将于 2023 年举办第十一次友好省州领导人峰会》,2021 年 12 月 7 日,https://sd.dzwww.com/sdnews/202112/t20211207_9529234.htm。

17.张宇鸿、王亚楠、朱殿封:《第四届世界太阳城大会通过〈德州宣言〉》,2010 年 9 月 19 日,http://paper.dzwww.com/dzrb/data/20100919/html/2/content_10.html。

18.中国信息通信研究院:《全球数字经济白皮书(2022 年)》,2022 年 12 月 7 日,http://www.caict.ac.cn/english/research/whitepapers/202303/P020230316619916462600.pdf? eqid=a12c38b10015ecc1000000026488df4e。

19.《习近平主席向 2019 年"读懂中国"广州国际会议致贺信》,2019 年 10 月 26 日,https://www.gov.cn/xinwen/2019-10/26/content_5445217.htm。

20.《第四次友好省州领导人峰会 8 月 5 日至 7 日举行》,2008 年 7 月 31 日,http://www.dzwww.com/shandong/sdnews/200807/t20080731_3804742.htm.

21.《专家警告:新兴技术带来的风险正在上升》,2020 年 8 月 14 日,https://cloud.tencent.com/developer/news/676582。

# References

1.*Joint Declaration of the First Regional Leaders' Summit*. Bavaria, Germany. 31 January, 2002.

2.*Joint Declaration of the Third Regional Leaders' Summit*. Upper Austria, Austria. 12 July, 2006.

3.*Joint Declaration of the Fourth Regional Leaders' Summit*. Jinan, Shandong. 7 August, 2008.

4.*Joint Declaration of the Sixth Regional Leaders' Summit*. São Paulo, Brazil. 12 April, 2012.

5. *Joint Declaration of the Eighth Regional Leaders' Summit*. Bavaria, Germany. 15 July, 2016.

6. *Joint Declaration on Energy Transition of the Ninth Regional Leaders' Summit*. Quebec, Canada. 18 May, 2018.

7.*Joint Declaration of the Tenth Regional Leaders' Summit*. Upper Austria, Austria. 11 November, 2021.

8.Wang Lijun, "International Cooperation between Local Governments in China under the Backgrcund of Globalization," Dissertation, Shandong University (2012).

9.Liu Rong, Cai Zichang, Li Yanan, et al., "Jointly Build the 'Belt and Road' to Add Power to Regional Cooperation," *People's Daily* (9 September, 2022).

10.Dong Lizhi, "Great Difference and Common Purpose: Minutes of the Summit of the Five Sister Provinces and States in Munich," *Openings*, no. 2 (2002), pp.36-37.

11.Hu Jia, Wang Kairu, "The Dynamic Mechanism and Constraints of Local Government's Transnational Cooperation: A Case Study of China-ASEAN under the Background of 'The Belt and Road Initiative'," *Local Governance Research*, no. 2 (2019), pp.13-15,78,79.

12.Ma Xueguang, Meng Yingtao, "The Evolution and Influencing Factors Analysis of International Sister Cities in China," *China Ancient City*, no. 10 (2016), pp.4-14.

13.Research Group of Foreign Affairs Office of Shandong Provincial People's Government, "The Current Situation and Countermeasures of Cooperation between Shandong Province and Sister Provinces and States in Europe under the New Situation," *Shandong Economic Strategy Research*, no. 12 (2011), pp. 21-24.

14.Ju Chuanjiang, "Governor Guo Shuqing of Shandong Province Leads a Delegation to America: Encourage American Companies to Invest in Strategic Emerging Industries in Shandong", http://cnews.chinadaily.com.cn/2014-06/01/content_17556591.htm, 1 June, 2014.

15. Li Yang, "'Yun Hua Shandong' in South Zhanglou Village of Qingzhou, Weifang • Sino-German Cooperation Project Paints a New Picture of Rural Areas", http://weifang.iqilu.com/wfyaowen/2021/0708/4901614.shtml, 8 July, 2021.

16.Man Qianqian, "Shandong is Going to Hold the 11th Regional Leaders' Summit in 2023", https://sd.dzwww.com/sdnews/202112/t20211207_9529234.htm, 7 December, 2021.

17. Zhang Yuhong, Wang Yanan, Zhu Dianfeng, "The Fourth ISCI Congress Passes the *Dezhou Declaration*", http://paper.dzwww.com/dzrb/data/20100919/html/2/content_10.html, 19 September, 2010.

18.China Academy of Information and Communications Technology, *White Paper on Global Digital Economy* (2022), http://www.caict.ac.cn/english/research/whitepapers/202303/P020230316619916462600.pdf? eqid=a12c38b10015ecc1000000026488df4e, 7 December, 2022.

19. “President Xi Jinping Sends Congratulatory Letter to the 2019 Understanding China Conference in Guangzhou”, https://www.gov.cn/xinwen/2019-10/26/content_5445217.htm, 26 October, 2019.

20. “The Fourth Regional Leaders’ Summit to be Held in 5 to 7 August”, http://www.dzwww.com/shandong/sdnews/200807/t20080731_3804742.htm, 31 July, 2008.

21. “Warning by Experts: Risk Brought by Emerging Technologies Is Rising”, https://cloud.tencent.com/developer/news/676582, 14 August, 2020.

# 后　记

友好省州领导人峰会作为国际友好城市合作机制的典范，自2002年首次举行以来，为各友好省州加强相互了解、深化交流合作做出了很好的探索和示范，值得深入研究和总结。为系统梳理友好省州领导人峰会20年来的历程，总结20年来的探索经验，同时服务于2023年9月在山东济南举行的2023友好省州领导人峰会，山东行政学院国际友城研究院围绕“山东省与‘友好省州领导人峰会’20年历程”开展了一系列研究，本书是系列研究成果之一。

山东行政学院作为承担政府公务员培训的机构，历任领导都非常重视国际交流合作，设立国际交流学院专职从事国际学术交流与涉外培训工作，设立国际友城研究院开展国际友城相关研究。2023年，山东行政学院领导提出将打造国际友城研究平台作为学院重点工作之一。本书是山东行政学院2023年度重大项目攻关创新科研支撑项目“山东省国际友城间交往模式研究”的阶段性成果。

经过周密的调研和系统的梳理，课题组成员深入探讨、多次修改，先后数易其稿，历时半年，形成了本书的最终稿。其中，写作提纲由赵玉霞、孙秀亭、王朝华拟定，第一章、第八章由朱晓静撰写，第二章、第十章、第十一章由孙秀亭撰写，第三章由孙秀亭、朱晓静撰写，第四章由刘彦梅撰写，第五章由张慧卿撰写，第六章由刘彦梅、孙秀亭撰写，第七章由孙秀亭、谭晓文撰写，第九章由赵玉霞撰写，附录由朱晓静、刘彦梅、张慧卿、谭晓文搜集梳理。赵玉霞、孙秀亭、王朝华对全书进行统稿，房蕊、李磊负责对外联络和调研资料搜集工作。

在本书的撰写过程中，山东省科学技术厅、山东省住房和城乡建设厅、山东省文化和旅游厅、山东省体育局、山东省能源局等单位，山东大学、山东科技大学、青岛大学、济南大学、山东农业大学、山东第一医科大学、山东省科学院能源研究所、中国科学院青岛生物能源与过程研究所等高校、科研机构，山东能源集团、潍柴动力股份有限公司、济南圣泉集团股份有限公司、山东七河生物科技股份有限公司等企业积极配合调研，提供了大量第一手资料和图片，在此一并致谢！

感谢山东大学出版社对本书出版提供指导服务，感谢山东大学出版社编辑们专业细致地工作以推动本书出版。

由于水平所限，书中难免存在遗漏和不足之处，敬请读者批评指正。书中涉及的有关文献和观点，我们尽可能详尽地列出出处，如有遗漏或影响到作者的权益，在此致歉并请随时联系我们。

本书撰写组

2023 年 6 月

# Postscript

As an exemplary mechanism for international sister cities cooperation, the Regional Leaders' Summit has made good explorations and demonstrations for sister provinces and states to enhance mutual understanding and deepen exchanges and cooperation since its first session in 2002, which deserves further study and summary. In order to systematically review the 20-year history of the Regional Leaders' Summit, summarize the exploration experience during this period, and serve the eleventh Regional Leaders' Summit to be held in Jinan, Shandong in September 2023, the Institute of International Friendship Cities of the Party School of CPC Shandong Committee (Shandong Academy of Governance) has conducted a series of researches on "A Review of Shandong's Exploration and Practice to Regional Leaders' Summit over the Past Two Decades". This book is part of the research findings.

As an institution undertaking the training of government civil servants, Shandong Academy of Governance has always attached great importance to international exchanges and cooperation. It has established the College of International Exchange dedicated to international academic exchanges and foreign-related training, as well as the Institute of International Friendship Cities for research on international sister cities. In 2023, the leadership of the Academy proposed that building an international sister cities research platform is one of its key tasks. This book presents the phased results of "Research on the Interaction Patterns between International Sister Cities of Shandong" which is an innovative research support project for major challenges of 2023 of the Academy.

After thorough research and systematic review, the members of the research group conducted in-depth discussions, made multiple revisions, and changed their manuscripts several times successively. The final draft was formed six months later. The Outline is drafted by Zhao Yuxia, Sun Xiuting and Wang Zhaohua; Chapters 1 and 8 are presented by Zhu Xiaojing, and Chapters 2, 10 and 11 by Sun Xiuting. Chapter 3 is co-authored by Sun Xiuting and Zhu Xiaojing. Chapter 4 is written by Liu Yanmei, and Chapter 5 by Zhang Huiqing. Chapter 6 is co-authored by Liu Yanmei and Sun Xiuting, and Chapter 7 by Sun Xiuting and Tan Xiaowen. Chapter 9 is finished by Zhao Yuxia. The data collection and organization of the Appendix is done by Zhu Xiaojing, Liu Yanmei, Zhang Huiqing, and Tan Xiaowen. Zhao Yuxia, Sun Xuting, and Wang Zhaohua are responsible for the final compilation and editing of the entire book. Fang Rui and Li Lei are responsible for external liaison and research data collection.

We appreciate the cooperation of various organizations such as the Department of Science & Technology of Shandong Province, Housing and Urban-Rural Development Department of Shandong Province, Shandong Provincial Department of Culture and Tourism, Shandong Administration of Sports, the Energy Administration of Shandong Province, as well as universities and colleges and scientific research institutions such as Shandong University, Shandong University of Science and Technology, Qingdao University, University of Jinan, Shandong Agricultural University, Shandong First Medical University, Energy Research Institute of Shandong Academy of Sciences, Qingdao Institute of Bioenergy and Bioprocess Technology, Chinese Academy of Sciences. Last but not least, we would like to thank enterprises such as Shandong Energy Group, Weichai Power Co., Ltd., Jinan Shengquan Group, Shandong Qihe Biotechnology Co., Ltd., for their active collaboration and provision of abundant first-hand materials.

We are grateful to Shandong University Press for providing guidance services for the publication of this book, and to the editors of the press for their professional and meticulous work.

Because of the limitation of the authors' experience and time, there are inevitably omissions and deficiencies in this book. Any comments and suggestions are welcomed. We have made every effort to provide a comprehensive list of references and viewpoints mentioned in this book. If there are any omissions or if it affects the rights of the authors, we apologize and please feel free to contact us at any time. We apologize for any omissions or if the rights of the authors are affected, and please feel free to contact us at your convenience.

Compiling Group of This Book

June 2023